Rationality and Religion

Rationality and Religion

Does Faith Need Reason?

Roger Trigg

First published 1998

2 4 6 8 10 9 7 5 3 1

Blackwell Publishers Ltd
108 Cowley Road
Oxford OX4 1JF
UK

Blackwell Publishers Inc.
Commerce Place
350 Main Street
Malden, Massachusetts 02148
USA

British Library Cataloguing in Publication Data

A CIP catalogue record for this book is available from the British Library.

Library of Congress Cataloging-in-Publication Data

Trigg, Roger.
Rationality and religion: does faith need reason? / Roger Trigg.
p.   cm.
Book is based on the Stanton lectures delivered at the University
of Cambridge, Lent term, 1997.
Includes bibliographical references and index.
ISBN 0-631-19747-8 (hardbound: alk. paper). – ISBN 0-631-19748-6
(pbk.: alk. paper)
1. Religion – Philosophy.   I. Title.
BL51.T65   1998   210 – dc21
97-38754   CIP

Typeset in 11 on 13 pt Baskervill
by Best-set Typesetter Ltd., Hong Kong
Printed in Great Britain by MPG Books, Bodmin Cornwall

This book is printed on acid-free paper

Contents

Introduction

This book is based on the Stanton Lectures in the Philosophy of Religion which were delivered at the University of Cambridge throughout the Lent Term, 1997. There were eight lectures in all, and each appears here in a considerably expanded and modified version. In addition, I have added two further chapters, and these appear as chapters 8 and 9.

The last book I wrote was on *Rationality and Science* (Blackwell 1993). It had the subtitle 'Can science explain everything?', and the argument of the book was intended to produce a resounding 'No' as an answer to that question. I suggested that physical science itself needed a rational basis. Its practice could not be self-justifying. In particular, it depended on assumptions about the character of the physical world, particularly its intrinsic order and regularity. Science needs to postulate the uniformity of nature, and that must be a metaphysical and not a scientific postulate. The work of science may itself be a supreme example of human rationality, but it cannot itself fully explain that rationality, without a gross begging of the question. This raises further questions about the grounding and scope of human reason.

In recent years, there has been a progressive disillusion with what may appear to be the inflated claims of physical science, and a breakdown of trust in the simple empiricism which many felt accompanied a scientific conception of the world. Not everyone shares this loss of faith in science, and some still wish to espouse a 'physicalist' or 'naturalist' view which sees reality strictly in the terms of contemporary science. Nevertheless, there has been a widespread reaction against the linking of rationality with the methods of science. The problem has been that many have gone to the other extreme. They are not content with denying that science can provide the only path to truth. Instead, they decry the very idea of one truth, or indeed a single reality. 'Postmodernism' has reacted against a previous confidence in human reason, and any view which claims to be able to provide a true account of the world. Instead it has stressed the historical situation of each of us, and the dependence of our understanding on our local context and particular presuppositions.

Science, particularly when championed by the logical positivism of philosophers such as A. J. Ayer, as set out in his famous *Language, Truth and Logic*, has often appeared to be the enemy of religion. It is, therefore, perhaps hardly surprising that some should willingly embrace postmodernism, as a way of rescuing religion from the overbearing claims of science. This is, however, a terrible mistake. 'Postmodernism' is itself a vague term, and some of its charm is that it can be defined in many ways. It is clearly reacting against something, and many may feel that it is a friend, because they are against the exaggerated claims of the sufficiency of human reason which accompanied the growth of science in the modern period. Yet postmodernism in its typical manifestations undoubtedly challenges the possibility of any universal rationality, or objective truth. It must, in fact, be relativist in its conclusions. All beliefs must be judged only as true relative to their background. A religion is true for its adherents, who may have their own reasons for belief. Such reasons could never, be regarded as having any possible validity for those from another historical or social context. There could be no question of there being a God as part of the objective constitution of things. Talk of God will only make sense in a particular context. To invoke a distinction to which I shall return in the book, this means that all that matters is the fact of belief, and not what the belief is about. Metaphysics becomes a forbidden subject, and the very idea of any freefloating rationality, free of social context, will be ruled out.

Part of the argument of this book is that, religion, like science, cannot dispense with metaphysics. The claims of religion purport to be about a world to which we all can have some access, even if it transcends the physical one. Religion and rationality cannot be separated, at least not without fatal consequences for religion. Once the latter retreats into its own ghetto, afraid of making claims that are subject to rational assessment, it can no longer claim to be of universal significance. It is no longer claiming truth.

In many ways, therefore, although the subject matter is different, this book is intended as a sequel to *Rationality and Science*. There is the same stress in it of the importance of the idea of rationality, and of its link with an objective reality. There is the same opposition to relativism in its many forms. Indeed, my first attempt to expose the dangers of different forms of relativism in both religion and science was published in my *Reason and Commitment* in 1973 (Cambridge University Press). I argued then, and still hold, that the simplest (and deepest) argument against any relativism is its self-refutation. The mere assertion of a relativist position (presumably as true) shows its falsity. Our mere ability to ascertain the (objective) fact of widespread disagreement both in the area of religion and elsewhere demonstrates our ability to see what is in fact the case. Unfortunately, however, these simple allegations, made against relativism from the time of Plato onwards, have not stopped the spread of the position. In many quarters it has attained a high degree of philosophical respectability. The result has been a catastrophic decline in any faith in the power of human reason, in a way that has seemed to sweep away the pretensions of all grand metaphysical schemes, including those of religion. One aim of this book is to argue how important the related notions of rationality and reality are for religion. I have previously argued for a full-blooded realism, particularly for the various sciences, in my book called *Reality at Risk* (Harvester Wheatsheaf, Simon and Schuster, 2nd edition, 1989). I have also in various books argued, against relativism, for a culture-transcendent view of human nature.

This book is intended to be a contribution to the philosophy of religion. As I have already indicated, many of the same philosophical arguments that occur in the philosophy of science also arise in parallel discussions in the philosophy of religion. The philosophy of science is concerned with the status of scientific claims, and their relation to truth (however that may be defined). It is concerned to see if a viable epistemology can be produced which could underwrite scientific progress. It questions the relation between sociological attempts to explain the development of science and such an epistemology. What it does not do is become involved in particular scientific controversies and adjudicate between them. The discipline is concerned with the status of science and of its claims to knowledge. In other words it is asking how far one can talk of truth in science, not trying to find out what is actually true.

The philosophy of religion has a similar function. Its purpose is not to try and decide on the truth of a particular religion, let alone become an advocate for it. The question is how far a viable epistemology can be produced in the sphere of religion which might help us to decide what is true. More fundamentally, the philosophy of religion is concerned with the challenge of relativism, and with whether it is legitimate to talk of truth in religion at all. Even if it is, is religious truth different from other kinds? Although anyone writing with a background in Anglo-American thought is bound to take Christianity as the obvious example of a religion, these issues are not confined to any one religion. Indeed, as chapter 3 makes clear, the mere existence of different religions raises further questions about the status of any religious claims to truth. Nevertheless it is impossible to deal with all religious claims at once. Even though the same issues undoubtedly occur in many different religions, I shall be forced to concentrate on issues raised, in particular, by Christianity. I shall also from time to time deal with the work of Christian theologians, when they seem to be relying on philosophical assumptions that need to be made explicit.

Nevertheless the philosophy of religion must be distinguished from philosophical theology. The philosophy of religion makes no presuppositions about religious truth. Just because it may argue about whether Christianity, say, can be making particular claims to truth, does not mean that it can say that Christianity is true. Even if the argument is about how the claims of the New Testament are to be understood, it is important to distinguish two positions. The first is the philosophical one of asking (as chapter 5 does) how far certain claims can be regarded as claims to actual historical truth. The second is that of the preacher, saying that these events did occur. It may be that the preacher is implicitly assuming the viability of a certain philosophical understanding of the texts. The point is, however, that it is only if real claims are being made that they can be disproved as well as proved. The rejection of Christianity will normally demand certain philosophical assumptions about the status of the claims that are being rejected. The making of space for the rational assessment of religious claims may enable truth to be proclaimed. It also allows falsehood to be exposed. That, of course, is precisely what some religious believers (and theologians) fear, and is one reason for a continued stress on the importance of faith as an alternative to reason.

One reason for taking many examples from within the tradition of Christian thought is that it is there that the influence of the European Enlightenment has had its greatest effect. This has shown itself particularly in a growing scepticism about the historical basis of traditional claims and in an increasing, and perhaps excessive, respect for modern scientific method. The temptation has been to reinterpret Christianity in a way which yields to contemporary notions of what it is rational to believe. Yet little attention is paid to the putative nature of reality, which, whether in science or religion, should govern our reasoning. This attitude owes much to the verificationism of logical positivism. The latter held that any reference to a reality beyond our reach was totally meaningless, and it had a devastating effect on the philosophy of religion. I was very conscious, when, a generation ago, I was studying philosophy in New College, Oxford, and being taught by A. J. Ayer, that any attempt to discuss the status of religion would be liable to be met with derision. The result was that for many years, in England at least, the study of the philosophy of religion was not considered to be a serious part of philosophy. That has changed over the years and the subject is thriving at many different levels. Perhaps there is a renewed and confused tolerance of all views, simply because nothing, not even science, is considered capable of claiming truth. I hope, however, that it is now realized that instant dismissal of the beliefs on which our Western civilization was founded is neither very sensible nor very scholarly. It may be that in the last resort religion in general, and Christianity in particular, are making claims that cannot be rationally sustained. This book will argue that at least a rational space can be made, in which it must be understood that religion is still making substantial claims. Moreover those claims deserve prolonged rational assessment. They cannot either become part of a conservation area, preserved but never criticized, or be thrown on a rubbish heap as relics of past age. Moreover, it must be recognized that many of the contemporary attacks on the rationality of religion are also made against science. In a defence of the possibility of human rationality, both science and religion should recognize that they are allies and not opponents. The chill winds of nihilism can sweep both away.

No writer in the area of religion can fail nowadays to be aware of the concern felt in some quarters about the way in which masculine language, particularly in reference to God, may reflect a deep patriarchy in society. Yet clearly a transcendent God could be neither male nor female. I shall be discussing some forms of feminism, but there is a problem as to how far so-called 'inclusive' language can be used consistently to refer to God. Since one of my arguments is that theism has to be understood as referring to an active, personal God, I have found that it is difficult to avoid the use of personal pronouns. Once one finds it difficult to talk naturally of God as a person, a very fundamental change has been made in religious thinking. Unless one resorts to the clumsy reiteration of references to 'God' or to ugly neologisms such as 'Godself', such pronouns become inevitable. The only alternative is to write about God in an impersonal way as 'the divine reality' or some such phrase. Some writers, as we shall see, have philosophical reasons for preferring reference to a possibly impersonal 'Real', but as I am explicitly opposed to such views I can hardly emulate their language. I have, therefore, decided, with some misgivings, to revert to the traditional way of referring to God as 'He' or 'Himself'. I hope the somewhat old-fashioned use of the capital letter will signal that the pronoun is of a unique sort, and signifies personhood, but not masculinity. The resources of the English language do not allow reference to a person without the apparent specification of gender.

I have discussed the topics of this book with many people over a considerable time. I am particularly grateful to my friends and colleagues in two groups, one national and the other international, which have been meeting for many years. The former, after meeting regularly in Oxford, has now become the British Society for the Philosophy of Religion. The latter assembles in different places in Europe, and is now the European Society for the Philosophy of Religion. The views of many of the members of these groups are both directly and indirectly discussed in these pages. I am most grateful to them for the stimulus which I have received from them. One philosopher to whom I must express particular thanks for discussing some aspects of my work with me is Professor William Alston. He came over to England in autumn 1996 especially to deliver a lecture in London to the British Society for the Philosophy of Religion, of which I was then President. Another American philosopher of religion to whom I owe a debt of gratitude is Professor Charles Taliaferro who has been a continuing source of help and advice.

I much enjoyed my weekly visits in the Lent Term 1997 to Cambridge to deliver the Stanton Lectures in the Philosophy of Religion, and must express my warm thanks for their kind hospitality to the Cambridge Faculty of Divinity, and to Trinity College. In addition, I visited the Princeton Theological Seminary, in New Jersey, in April 1997, to conduct seminars and deliver a public lecture (derived from chapter 10). I am very grateful to Professor Wentzel van Huyssteen for making that visit possible, and for being such a welcoming host. My own university, the University of Warwick, had given me two terms of study leave in the summer and autumn terms of 1996 to enable me to write this book. During that time, I was lucky enough to be able to have a congenial base in the University of Oxford. I am very grateful to the Principal (Dr Ralph Waller) and Fellows of Harris Manchester College who elected me to a Visiting Fellowship for the two terms. I was pleased to be there for the celebrations marking the grant of its charter as a full College of the University. Yet its own history stretches back to the early impact of the Enlightenment on English religion in the eighteenth century. As such, it embodies in its history as an institution many of the strains and stresses in the relationship between rationality and religious faith which I shall be examining in the pages of this book.

1

Should Religion be Publicly Recognized?

1 The Pluralist Society

No modern discussion of the nature of rationality, particularly in relation to religion, can ignore the fact that the place of religion in public
life is controversial. While some may concede that religion can be a
private affair for the individual, it is often claimed that a parade of
religious convictions in public and political life is inappropriate. In a
sense, religion has been 'privatized'. Even politicians with a deep religious faith feel that somehow they should not refer to it in the pro-
nouncement of public policy, let alone suggest that it provides a reason
for their position. Yet in the end, this is to hold that religion and
rationality have little do with one another, at least if it is assumed that
rationality is a public matter.

This is, however, a very recent development. It has often been
thought that religion binds a society together, and that an official
religion was essential. Anyone challenging the religion of the state was
thereby challenging the authority and indeed the very existence of the
state. Very often the state apparatus has found objectionable the mere
challenge to consensus and the breakdown of uniformity. Truth may
have been at stake but governments usually prize compliance if not
actual agreement. The problems with dissent and nonconformity pose
for any settled society can be considerable, and disputes often centre on
religion. The very fact that terms like 'dissenter' and 'nonconformist'
can immediately be seen to apply to people who have taken up particular positions in religious disputes in England is significant. The fight for
religious toleration has caused divisions in England for centuries that
run very deep and still have their effects. These same divisions were
exported to America in the seventeenth century and account for much

of the traditional American distrust of too close a relationship between Church and state.

As the United States attracted more immigrants and became less obviously Protestant, and in its turn England has received a substantial number of non-Christian immigrants, the question of the place of religion in society has become more urgent. In addition, of course religion in general, and Christianity in particular, has been challenged more and more. Political disputes are no longer between different brands of Christians determined that one group will not get unfair privileges. The issue now is whether Christianity as such should have any public role. Yet the question has become much wider than a merely political one. It may often seem to be merely an issue of how different groups of people, with different beliefs and practices, can learn to live with one another. It can also appear to be a moral question. We should not, we may feel, impose our will on others, any more than we should wish to be dominated by them. The issue of toleration is certainly an important one. In the end, however, because religions typically claim truth, there is an even more profound question at stake. How far can anyone claim to be right or to believe what is true and yet claim no privileges over those who might appear to be deeply mistaken? This does not surface so much in simple intolerance of others' beliefs. It becomes much more of an issue in decisions about the organization of society. A particularly sensitive problem would be how children should be taught. Should schools, a parent might ask, teach the beliefs of the parent, someone else's or no beliefs at all? Should the law encourage the teaching of a particular religion, religion in general or no religion at all? The more I, or anyone else, believe something to be true, the more it will seem important that society should recognize that truth. Conversely, if it appears undesirable for something to achieve public recognition, it would seem, at least in a democracy, that that must be because it is not true, or at least cannot be shown to be. Truth and public recognition seem closely connected. Physics is presumably taught in schools because it is generally recognized as comprising a body of truth. Astrology is not, because it cannot be demonstrated to provide such knowledge. Yet if a body of purported truth which someone considers false, still receives public recognition, this is bound to provoke resentment.

The move to increasing toleration in a diverse and even fragmenting society is clearly laudable. Liberalism is in the very air we breathe in a modern democratic state. There is an understandable fear of authoritarian regimes, and totalitarian philosophies. Appeals to truth can seem themselves totalitarian as they point to one right viewpoint against which others should be judged. The problem, therefore, arises in acute form as to how in a modern state, which includes many conflicting beliefs, truth can be claimed in a way that does not provoke civil conflict. One solution is to make a distinction between the beliefs of individual citizens to which they are entitled in a free society, and their willingness not to impose them on others. There must be found, it will be said, a way in which people can live together in a common society, even though they are profoundly divided on some issues. John Rawls has stated the problem of political liberalism succinctly by asking: 'How is it possible that there may exist over time a stable and just society of free and equal citizens profoundly divided by reasonable though incompatible religious, philosophical and moral doctrines?'[1] Rawls himself hopes to provide a conception of politics which will allow people with what he calls 'deeply opposed though reasonable comprehensive doctrines' to live together under the same constitution.

Rawls writes against the background of what he believes is a permanent pluralism. In other words, it is not just an unfortunate fact that people disagree profoundly at the present time. He believes that the diversity of religious and other doctrines is not an aberration but 'a permanent feature of the public culture of democracy.' He continues: 'Under the political and social conditions secured by the basic rights and liberties of free institutions, a diversity of conflicting and irreconcilable – and what is more reasonable – comprehensive doctrines will come about and persist if such diversity does not already obtain.'[2] He amplifies this later by asserting that 'reasonable pluralism – as opposed to pluralism as such – is the long-run outcome of the work of human reason under enduring free institutions'.[3] Clearly Rawls places much stress on the notion of the reasonable, which he distinguishes sharply from that of truth. There can be only one true comprehensive doctrine, he claims,[4] but many reasonable ones. It is the job of a free society to champion what is reasonable, while remaining neutral about the question of truth. The notion of the reasonable allows room for diversity. On the other hand, holding a particular conception of the political as true, and 'for that reason alone the one suitable basis of public reason' is, says Rawls, exclusive, even sectarian, and as such likely to foster political divisions.

This political approach to reason takes diversity to be a positive feature of society, and not a symptom of defective reasoning. It is very easy to assume that where there is disagreement, one side at least to the dispute must be mistaken, and that if enough effort could be put into the matter, we may together all be able to arrive at truth. This has certainly been the model for reasoning in science. Yet because Rawls is dealing with politics and not with epistemology, is concern is how, given the persisting fact of diversity, there can be public procedures of justification and acceptable reasoning which do not beg the question in favour of one of the parties to the dispute. He says: 'In recognising others' comprehensive views as reasonable, citizens also recognise that in the absence of a public basis of establishing the truth of their beliefs, to insist on their comprehensive view must be seen by others as their insisting on their own beliefs.'[5]

Rawls is building a large edifice on the contingent fact of diversity in contemporary society. It is perhaps significant that he slides so easily from noting the fact of disagreement to asserting the absence of a 'public basis of establishing the truth of their beliefs'. The idea of a public basis, like that of public reasoning or public justification, is firmly rooted in what can as a matter of fact be publicly accepted. It is in other words a sociological and not an epistemological concept. Rawls refers to 'publicly shared methods of inquiry and forms of reasoning', assuming, he says, 'those methods to be familiar from common sense and to include the procedures and conclusions of science and social thought, when these are well-established and not controversial'.[6] These general beliefs, he thinks, reflect 'the current public views in a well-ordered society'. This notion of a 'well-ordered' society is itself a technical term for Rawls, delineating an ideal state of affairs. By it he means a society in which 'the publicly recognised conception of justice establishes a shared point of view from which citizens' claims on society can be adjudicated'.[7] Everything in fact depends on citizens being reasonable enough to put aside their particular beliefs in order to come to procedural agreements, with those they differ from, about what could count as a public justification.

The notion of the reasonable thus goes with the idea of the public and is indissolubly linked with the fact of pluralism. Political liberalism for Rawls accepts not just that there are many differences, religious and non-religious in society. The idea of pluralism is much stronger than that. As we have already seen, he believes that it is built into the nature of our society. He denies that it is a disaster and asserts that it 'is the natural outcome of the activities of human reason under enduring free institutions'. He continues: 'To see reasonable pluralism as a disaster is to see the exercise of reason under the conditions of freedom itself as a disaster.'[8]

We come thus to the nub of the question. In areas such as science there seems to be a sufficient lack of controversy for Rawls to talk of the procedures of science as 'well-established.' We might wonder, however, how far scientific institutions with their stringent standards of what constitutes correct scientific procedure really allow much freedom. However that may be, in religious matters Rawls believes that because of the great divergences in society, it ought to be recognized that the exercise of reason, combined with freedom, will never produce a consensus. There will always be a gap between what can be accepted by everyone and particular religious views. Yet why is this supposed to be both inevitable and desirable? A particular facet of a modern liberal approach is perhaps revealed here. There are those who yearn for a settled society where people agree on fundamentals, and there are those who welcome the fact of diversity and difference. Liberals are generally included among the latter. Yet the problem remains how an encouragement of diversity can be properly reconciled with a passion for truth. We have already noted how scientists will place limits in what can be counted as proper science.

Rawls tries to meet this kind of problem with his distinction between the reasonable and the rational. The core of the notion of being reasonable is not so much the exercise of reason as a willingness to cooperate with those who differ. The issue can be clearly stated in terms of what must be expected of the members of a constitutional convention. There the members have to agree on the rules to be adopted within a state. It is vital therefore that each is willing to consider the interests of everyone. Terrorists who refuse to renounce violence as a way of achieving their ends are a perfect example of being unreasonable in Rawls's specific sense of the term. Their sole object is to reach a particular destination by whatever tactics necessary. Rawls and other liberals do, however, see that the single-minded claim to truth and unwillingness to compromise which is the mark of many religious people is also an example of being unreasonable. For Rawls the idea of the reasonable is clearly linked with that of fair, social cooperation.[9] Rational agents, on the other hand, says Rawls, pursue their ends both individually and collectively without due regard to the projects of those with who they disagree. According to liberals, people have to be both rational and reasonable. They cannot cooperate without ends of their own which they wish to advance. They have, however, to recognize that they live in a pluralist society, in which other people are equally entitled under the law to pursue their own different ends.

2   Public Reason

The distinction between the rational and the reasonable links with another, that between the public and the non-public. For the liberal, the public world, in which terms of cooperation are agreed, is not one in which particular controversial doctrines, such as those of religion, can find a place. Rawls says that 'one must distinguish between a public basis of justification generally acceptable to citizens on fundamental political questions and the many nonpublic bases of justification belonging to the many comprehensive doctrines and acceptable only to those who affirm them'.[10]

Religion is the obvious example of a so-called 'rational' comprehensive doctrine that should not, because of its apparent essential contestability, be allowed into the public arena. Toleration should allow citizens to pursue any or no religion, but not to impose it on others or expect recognition in the public sphere. It is important, though, to see that the distinction between the public and the non-public, with Churches regarded in this context as 'non-public' institutions, should not be identified with the similar distinction between the secular and the religious. It is easy to slide from one to the other. The point is that religion is to be excluded from the public sphere because of its essentially controversial nature. Atheism as a doctrine would be equally excluded, as would other socially controversial views. The ideal is a form of rationality which does not exclude the possibility that a particular religion may be true. Given the fact of pluralism, however, this religion could not be accepted into the public arena.

Such a position seems to follow from the fact of religious diversity and the fact that many reject religion altogether. In other words, the liberal project often seems to be founded on the contingent matter of what people will or will not happen to accept at a given time. Does that mean that given enough agreement, religion could be accorded public recognition in a given society? It is at this point that doubts creep in as to whether liberalism can be as neutral as it claims to be from the standpoint of epistemology. Rawls's previous acceptance of the un-controversial nature of science as compared with religion should sound a warning. The doctrine of pluralism sits well with that of fallibilism. Mutual toleration may seem advisable if we cannot claim knowledge anyway but have to admit that there is a significant possibility that we are mistaken. Because, too, science can lay claim to 'publicly shared' methods in a way that religion cannot, there may seem more room for doubt in the case of the latter. Similarly, religions typically wish to make statements about the transcendent, about what on some accounts may seem by definition beyond our reach. That gives rise to more room for doubt, which gives added point to Rawls' contention about limitations on our ability to arrive at truth. He says: 'Many of our most important judgments are made under conditions where it is not to be expected that conscientious persons with full powers of reason, even after full discus-sion, will all arrive at the same conclusion.'[11]

Thus Rawls's version of liberalism appears to be based on something more than the current fact of disagreement in Western societies. He recognizes limitations on our ability to reach unanimity. People not only happen to have different perspectives, but, given freedom, always will. This is itself a large claim, in that in assumes a permanent inability to reach a settled agreement about what is true. Thus what is at stake is something more than a simple disagreement about what is true. A philosophical doctrine is also being enunciated about the limits of our powers of reasoning, given free democratic institutions. The implication is that agreement has been the result in the past of the exercise of power and the restriction of freedom. Pluralism is the inevitable concomitant of democracy. Yet this, given the acceptance of science as publicly respectable, is not just a judgement on human reason and its ability to grapple with the multifaceted character of reality. It implies a particular judgement on certain forms of so-called comprehensive doctrine. Rawls never suggests that particular scientific theories, or the pursuit of science as such, are to be banished outside the public domain. There is no suggestion that science should be the preserve of private societies in the way that Churches are to be relegated to the position of non-public associations. The suspicion must be that this is not so much that science happens at the moment to be less controversial than religion as that the standards of proof adopted by the latter are regarded as defective in comparison with the former.

This tendency is exacerbated by other writers who make no secret of their view that the secular world should be privileged over and above the religious. This is not necessarily because of any prejudice against religion, but usually stems from a belief in religious liberty. For instance, Robert Audi has put forward what he calls the principle of secular rationale. He thinks that in the name of liberty people 'should not argue for or advocate laws or policies that restrict human conduct unless they offer (or at least have) adequate secular (non-religious) reasons to support the law or policy in question'.[12] Thus he will not allow into the public domain arguments which depend on religious assumptions. For instance, opponents of abortion on religious grounds (because, say, they believe human life is God-given) would be discouraged from bringing their opposition to abortion into public life, unless they could provide arguments which would be acceptable to those who rejected their religious position. Questions about the health of the mother could be discussed, but references to God's will would be ruled out. In all this, Audi himself would claim that his main concern lies with the standards desirable in public advocacy. He does not wish to restrain the free expression of views, but is questioning the wisdom of using religious arguments in a pluralistic society.[13]

An even stronger argument produced by Audi is not just that one can produce reasons that are generally acceptable but that one should oneself be motivated by adequate secular reasons. In other words it is not enough that I can provide convincing arguments. I must actually believe them myself and have them as my grounds. Yet a requirement based on appeal to motivation seems impossibly strong. How far, indeed, can I ever be sure what my own true motives are? If I am unconsciously motivated by religious faith when I put forward what I consider to be independently good reasons, does that invalidate my reasoning? In an argument put forward in the public domain, when there are several grounds supporting it, who is to say which is the operative one? All this poses problems in the law of the United States. One writer declares: 'In light of existing Supreme Court precedent, it is doubtful that a law motivated in fact by religious considerations could withstand Establishment Clause scrutiny simply because it arguably furthers an ostensible secular public purpose.'[14] His point is that the

Supreme Court has struck down an Arkansas law prohibiting the teaching of evolution on the ground that its passage was motivated by religious opposition to evolutionary theory. Yet that state could well have merely wanted to maintain civil peace in the classroom over an issue that had raised high emotions. Who is to say what was really motivating the legislators?

Certainly the case of public officials my be special. We expect them to administer the law impartially even if it does not coincide with their private beliefs. A judge may grant a divorce while privately disapproving of divorce. A licence to sell alcohol may be granted by magistrates who privately disapprove of the role alcohol plays in parts of society. There is nothing hypocritical about administering a system one finds defective in some way. These cases, however, typically arise when a society has agreed on its policy and expects it to be carried out. What is at issue when the role of public reason is discussed is how far so-called 'private' reason may be invoked in a debate about what that policy should be.

The tendency all the time is to move religion into the private sphere. Religion, it seems, is a matter for individual decision and should not be invoked in deciding public policy. Yet even Rawls did not explicitly pick out religion in this way. He was more concerned about insoluble controversy than religion as such. For both Audi and Rawls, the effect is the sundering of religion and public reasoning in the name of liberal values.

The question must be asked whether all this is as fair as it appears. It may seem tolerant to take up a neutral position on religion, but excluding any agreement involving religion is far from neutral. Many religious believers will be excluded from public debate as their beliefs are ruled a private matter. This does not necessarily solve vexed matters of debate, and does not allow different parties to a dispute to come to any mutually satisfactory arrangement. It might be argued that the requirement for freedom of worship, for example, does produce this result. No one is forced to go against his or her conscience. When, however, an issue like abortion is fought over, the exclusion of religious grounds will only leave religious believers disgruntled and feeling that their voice has not been heard. They have not even been overruled. They have not been listened to, if one follows Audi. It is not clear why someone who believes on religious grounds that a human foetus is a person should be excluded from the debate while a non-believer is under no such restraint and is free to argue that the foetus is not a person. It might be thought, according to Rawls's view, that both substantive positions belong to comprehensive doctrines that have to be excluded because of their controversial nature. This would mean that the resources of public reason would not be able to get to grips with a major political debate. Rawls himself comes down in favour of a duly qualified right for a woman to decide whether or not to end her pregnancy in the first three months. He says: 'Any comprehensive doctrine that leads to a balance of political values excluding that duly qualified right in the first trimester is to that extent unreasonable.'[15] This is significant, not so much as a point about abortion, as indicating a willingness to take on comprehensive doctrines and condemn them as unreasonable. Neutrality apparently can only go so far for a liberal.

This is of importance when questions arise about the teaching of religions in a public context. Of course, a liberal approach might exclude all religion rigorously from schools and hold that religious education is a matter for the home or Church. If this is done, one must once again inquire on what grounds. If it is because of the controversial nature of religion, as opposed to, say physics, it is unclear whether this is because of the contingent state of opinion in a given society or because of some perceived epistemological difference. It is now received opinion in the field of religious education in Britain that state schools should not propagate a religion but should be willing to teach children about religion in general. Yet recent law has also insisted that there be daily acts of worship of a predominantly Christian character in schools. In this as in other matters there is a significant difference of tradition between Britain and the United States. This is symbolized above all perhaps by the fact that whereas the rigorous separation of Church and state is built into the American constitution, there are still established Churches in England and in Scotland. In Britain, therefore, there is an oscillation between political liberalism of the American kind and a traditional stress that it is a Christian country. Establishment has in recent years come to mean less the domination by one Christian denomination over others. The resentment of that led to the disestablishment of the Anglican Church in Wales in the early years of the twentieth century. Now what is at issue is whether privileges, in the form of special recognition, should be accorded the Christian religion over other religions (or no religion at all). In practice, the forces of liberalism and secularism have often been ranged on the same side in this debate and there is more than a suspicion in some quarters that liberalism is 'the religion of secularism'. Indeed one writer who uses this phrase asserts: 'Both liberalism and anti-liberal religious views inhabit the same realm and make conflicting claims within it.'[16] Certainly Rawls's attempt to separate politics from metaphysics can seem very artificial when one approaches actual disputes.

3 Politics and Metaphysics

The fact of disagreement is a powerful factor in inclining liberals to tolerance. When one is confronted with parties to a disagreement who each claim that they are right, it is easy to see how the argument can move to assertions that no one can finally know what is right, and then to the position that there is no distinction between being right and being mistaken. There is, it will be said, only the fact of divergent belief. Rawls hoped to circumvent these difficulties, with his claim that liberalism is a political and not a metaphysical theory. People could then agree to cooperate in the public arena without settling basic issues of truth. They could concentrate on procedure and not substance. Yet the more the fact of belief and the fact of pluralism are emphasized, the more we have to traverse the shifting ground of what is accepted in a given society at a given time. Traditionalists themselves can base their argument on this as well as their opponents. The claim that England is a Christian country becomes dubious precisely because it is an appeal to what happens to be believed in a given place at a given time. The argument can then become the factual one of how many today regard themselves as Christians. Liberals, on the other hand, are perhaps inclined to concentrate on the fact of diversity and are then vulnerable to suggestions that opinion may not be as diverse as they think it is or would like it to be. Attempts to fit multicultural education on the settled environment of a traditional English village can sometimes seem as bizarre as attempts to ignore the cultural diversity of a major English city.

Why, though, do such arguments become factual disputes about the extent of particular beliefs? As was evident in Rawls's views, liberalism typically takes its stand on the fact of reasonable disagreement. In other words, it accepts that such disagreement cannot be rationally resolved. Rationality, as such, cannot be a feature of the public world and is excluded from it. The reasonable plays its part precisely because its aim is the limited one of obtaining political cooperation between opposing positions, and not the resolution of the conflict. The notion of rationality has been privatized and turned over if not to the individual, then at least to different associations of individuals. It is sundered from the public world and hence by implication from the world which is objectively real, independent of human judgements. There can be no thought of such an objective state of affairs to which we all in principle have equal access from our different vantage points. What is objective is not differentiated in this context from people's judgements of what is objectively true. We thus immediately slide from the idea of reality to the mere fact of differing judgements about it. Without the possibility of a rational access to reality that is publicly recognized, we are helpless in the face of conflicting claims to truth. The issue has to be seen as political since there is no other one left. Politics has replaced metaphysics. In the absence of any rational means of arriving at truth that can be accepted universally, we have just to find some way of enabling people to live together even when they cannot agree. Liberalism is, in their words, an heir to the apparent failure of metaphysics.

This becomes explicit in the work of Thomas Nagel, the American philosopher, who stresses that an appeal to truth as opposed to belief is bound to be empty when there is no public standard of justification. It will then appear that referring to truth in a context of disagreement will only involve a reiteration of my commitment to my own beliefs about what is true. He writes:

> A disagreement which falls on objective common ground must be open-ended in the possibility of its investigation and pursuit, and not come down finally to a bare confrontation between incompatible points of view. I suggest that conflicts of religious faith fail this test, and most empirical and many moral disagreements do not.[17]

His discussion is about political argument, where coercion by the state would only be justified by procedures and argument that could be accepted by everyone. His idea is that it should be possible to share with others the basis of one's own beliefs, so that as he says, 'once you have done so, they have what you have, and can arrive at a judgment on the same basis'.[18] He says: 'This is not possible if part of the source of your conviction is personal faith or revelation – because to report your faith to someone else is not to give him what you have, as you do when you show him your evidence or give him your arguments.' It is clear that a sharp divide is here being made between faith and reason. Faith, it is assumed, is something one can report but not justify. Religion thus can never be brought into the public domain and given a justification that it is open to everyone to accept. This is a much stronger epistemological position than one that merely starts from the fact of disagreement.

It is being claimed here that the reason for religious disagreement lies in the nature of religion itself. Yet Nagel does not want to say that religion cannot claim truth. He both wants to allow that people may be justified in their beliefs and to refuse to conclude that those who do share them are irrational or unreasonable. I can have my reasons but others may not share them. His position may be summed up when he says: 'Belief is reasonable when grounded on inconclusive evidence plus judgment.'[19] In other words, there is in some cases a gap between what can be shown to be true and what people accept as true. This may seem uncontroversial in that faith, of its nature, goes beyond evidence and cannot be deduced from it. Yet in recent years, it has become accepted that this as true of the development of science as of any other area. Judgement always enters in under the guise of theory. Nagel, however, is basing his views on what reasons and beliefs can be admitted to the public stage on a stringent distinction between religious and other kinds of commitments. He admits that it is not altogether easy to say what distinguishes stances taken on matters of fundamental importance as a result of faith, and cases where those who are not convinced can be dismissed as unreasonable. Nevertheless, he continues: 'It seems to me clear that as things now are, those who do not accept the truth of a particular religion (or of atheism) ought not to be judged unreasonable by those who do, and that anyone who today is unconvinced by the germ theory of disease must be judged irrational.'[20]

Nagel is explicitly using the terms 'unreasonable' and 'irrational' as synonyms, and is not making the kind of distinction which Rawls has made. He means quite simply that religion must be treated differently from other beliefs in the public arena, because there is scope for a reasonable divergence of view about religion. In contrast, beliefs about germs and hygiene can be publicly established. The fact that he can so easily run together the notion of the unreasonable and the rational shows the dangers of making either of them technical terms. Rawls's association of the reasonable and the public easily lends itself to a view which holds, as Nagel seems to do, that objectivity and 'common reason' belong to a public world with public standards to which private beliefs cannot always live up. However much we may think we are justified, and however much we may believe that we have attained truth, the evidence is somehow lacking because it cannot be sustained in public. It cannot be given an impersonal justification, but is somehow irretrievably tied to particular perspectives.

Nagel is concentrating on the role of political argument and has no intention of challenging the truth of religious beliefs. Nevertheless his position may well have that effect. 'Evidence' and 'justification' and 'claims to truth' are concepts that are not just related to the contingent fact of belief. Evidence is not what I judge to be evidence. If something is good evidence it should be so for everyone. Nagel accepts this in so far as he recognizes the need for interpersonal standards of argument which can sustain political discussion about what can and cannot be enforced. Religious orthodoxy, he thinks (along with sexual and cultural orthodoxy), should not be enforced. No doubt he would accept that public standards of cleanliness can be. Yet the point is that it is difficult to imagine that someone has a good reason for religious belief which makes that belief rational, without also assuming that it must also be a good reason for someone else. There may be good grounds for religious toleration, but an intrinsic doubtfulness of religious beliefs when compared with science would not seem to be one, Nagel's problem is that he wishes, in true liberal fashion, to avoid making judgements about truth or falsity concerning religion, while keeping it out of public life. There may be an implicit positivist faith in the preeminence of science lurking behind this, or simply a judgement about what can or cannot command assent in contemporary society. What, however, is intrinsically unstable is a view which accepts that an individual can be reasonable in a belief, while not allowing that it rests on grounds that can be shared. I can, it seems, have a true belief, but not one which can be defended publicly. I can be justified, but cannot rely on my beliefs in supporting public policies. Objectivity becomes bound up with a fuzzy notion of publicity, and both are then contrasted with the internal reasons provided by commitment to a religion.

It follows that religious views cannot in principle be defended on a wider stage. Further, if they only hold for those who already believe them, the idea of rationality in that area must collapse. A reason that is only valid for those who already accept that it is valid, is no reason at all. A belief that rests on grounds generated by that belief is in the last resort subjective and arbitrary. If the grounds are only what I think of as good grounds, any will be as good as any other. It will not be their validity but my thinking them which is operative. If I believe in the truth of a certain religion because of evidence which relies on a belief in the truth of that religion, I am involved in a destructive circle. It means not only that I cannot provide a justification for those who do share my belief. It means that I have no justification for myself.

Nagel relies heavily on the assumption that if I have good grounds for a belief, others who do not share the belief must recognize the grounds as good themselves. He does not quite put it like that since his distinction is between what can be made public, appealing to standards to which an impersonal appeal can be made, and what in the end is a matter of personal faith. This, though, inevitably leads him to consider that truth depends on public justification rather than private belief. He even contrasts 'the appeal to truth as opposed to belief'.[21] Yet this must always be an unreal distinction in any area. What I believe is what I believe to be true. The concept of belief can never be prised apart from that of truth. Truth is its target. I cannot believe something if I consider that truth is not at stake. A belief that certain things are so cannot be detached from the question whether they really are so. If someone believes that it is raining, it will seem curious if they fail to see the lack of connection between their belief and the sun shining brightly outside. It will, though, be immediately claimed that religious belief is not propositional in this simple way. That, however, is precisely the point. Beliefs about the world cannot be impervious to evidence arising from the world. If it is suggested that religious belief or faith is not like that, and is not based on evidence, it will immediately be clear why no public justification can be given for it. It does not involve the kind of attitude that can be justifiable or unjustifiable.

4   Liberalism and Religion

The connecting of truth to appeals to impersonal standards, and the linking of faith to personal perspective, is not so much a way of dealing with a knotty political problem. It is a philosophical move, which implicitly takes away the right of any religion to claim truth for itself. The connection of objectivity with the public world may seem at first sight sensible, as a contrast to the individual insights of particular believers. The public world, however, is the world of people and of their judgements. What is acceptable is what is not controversial. What is publicly established depends on the mood and preconceptions of the so-called 'public' at a given time and place. There is always the danger that the demand for a public justification becomes a demand to meet the fashions of the time. The place of religion in society then becomes questionable, not because of is failure to meet certain standards of justification, but because it runs foul of current prejudices. For some thinkers, of course, that is enough, because the problem they raise is explicitly a political one. For some, politics is substituted for metaphysics, and the recourse of those who find metaphysics powerless to settle the major disagreements current in modern society. Yet this is often not so much a pragmatic move as a principled revision of the idea of objectivity. One writer deliberately wishes to substitute the idea of public justification for any grander ideas of reality or the objective world. He suggests that claims are only objective if they can be publicly justified.[22] He continues;

> This analysis of objectivity enables us to overcome, or at least avoid, metaphysical and epistemological difficulties that we will encounter if we embrace an account of objectivity based on the notion of 'access' to some independent realm of objects that our claims are held to be 'about'.

In other words, the notion of public justification is an explicit replacement for any form of metaphysical realism.

This form of liberalism is therefore far from neutral when it comes to questions of truth. It is dealing with them by actually denying that metaphysical truth is possible. The switch from what is true to what is believed to be true involves the repudiation of any such truth as a goal so that all we are left with is the fact of conflicting belief. D'Agostino himself wishes to deal with this by drawing on Richard Rorty's idea of 'conversation'.[23] He wishes to contrast two competing conceptions of objectivity, one as 'transcendence' and the other as 'conversation'. The idea of transcendence, of reality independent of any particular perspective, is, he considers, a theistic one even when it appears after the Enlightenment in non-theistic concepts. For D'Agostino the objectivity of the world on this model depends on some view of its intrinsic nature, perhaps as it was created by God.[24] For D'Agostino and for Rorty, such theistic understandings have to be repudiated, and in their place the political conceptions of solidarity and of conversation, of public justifiability, have to be invoked. Liberalism then becomes a replacement for realism, rather than an attempt to deal at a different level with a purely political problem. The metaphysics and the politics merge into one another, or rather politics comes to replace ontology.

Yet the very idea of public justification is itself far from clear cut. There will be arguments about what counts as a justification, and similar differences about what counts as an adequate public justification. We will always be forced to acknowledge the mere fact of different beliefs and the holding of varying values. An emphasis on 'conversation' means that we will never arrive at a sound rational basis for resolving disputes. Even public justifiability, it seems, must always in the end be brought down to the concrete level of actual people discussing their differences. D'Agostino meets this problem by proposing that a community of delegates would be an institutional means for settling disputes, even those 'about the idea of public justification'.[25] He points out that such disputes may not be settled once and for all, but that as circumstances change, the previous consensus may again disappear. Nothing could make it clearer that the goal has become mere agreement rather than justification, and that agreement is a shifting, unstable affair depending on the contingencies of time and place. Perhaps for a pragmatist, there could be nothing else, but there has certainly been a loss of any conception that agreement is about anything. Indeed, in a pluralist society, it is not even clear that agreement itself needs to be prized. The true liberal will surely rejoice in diversity as much as or even more than the achievement of uniformity in belief. This attitude will itself be encouraged by the awareness of the inevitability of divergent belief if there is no rational method of resolving differences.

Does the liberal then simply accept differences? Why should even the importance of 'conversation' be extolled? Yet even if the liberal may be detached about other people' beliefs, it is always impossible to be totally detached about one's own. It has been remarked that liberals are people who cannot take their own side in an argument. Yet one of the paradoxes of liberalism is that it seems impossible for a liberal to be tolerant of the opponents of liberalism. In the end, each person with a belief has to believe that that belief is true. A liberal view about the importance of so-called 'conversation' cannot be combined with indifference as to whether such conversation takes place. A liberal conviction that beliefs should not be imposed merely because they claim truth (or even are true) cannot be held along with apathy towards the coercion of one group by another. The paradox of liberalism lies in a dilemma. Should liberalism as a doctrine be imposed, in whatever context, even though liberals believe that beliefs should not be imposed? Should anti-liberal views even be encouraged given the view that pluralism, of a religious or other kind, should not only be tolerated but even positively encouraged? The problem is that the adoption of pluralism as an aim might suggest that those who decry a pluralist society cannot be allowed to trade on its freedom to try and subvert it. This is an issue that appears within the Church in connection with arguments about doctrine and in the wider society over more general issues. Many professed liberals become uneasy at this point, since they can easily find themselves as members of just one more faction in the midst of warring factions. It is for this reason that they may with to differentiate their position from those who champion particular points of view. Thus liberalism is presented as a procedural and not a substantive theory.

When truth is not at stake, the only problem can be how divergent groups can live with each other. The settling of arguments either within an institution such as the Church, or between institutions, thus becomes a purely political matter. The world 'settle' is, indeed, always ambiguous in that it can seem to involve the achievement of truth, or alternatively of mere agreement or compromise. The liberal concentration on the latter can be, as in the case of Rorty, because the idea of objective truth has been repudiated. Yet as always, the repudiation of truth, even as an ideal, leaves the status of that repudiation unclear. Must liberals who are uncommitted to the idea of truth also in the last resort be uncommitted to their own beliefs? Liberalism cannot in the end be a totally neutral position. It must have a substantive notion of the good society, namely as one in which the toleration of diverse views is positively encouraged. Either criticism of this conception will be tolerated or it will not. If there is no way in which one perspective can claim priority over another, it would seem dubious to suppose that liberalism is any more than one view among others. If, on the other hand, perspectives can claim truth, why should not the opponents of liberalism be allowed to do so as well? In particular, it could in consistency be claimed, whether rightly or not, that a society founded on a particular religion is preferable to one founded on nothing more than an allegiance to a set of procedures.

Much of the argument about liberalism and religion has proceeded through attempts to put the claims of the one in a different category from those of the other. Thus liberalism claims to be political rather than metaphysical, or procedural rather than substantive. This stratagem too often proceeds because metaphysics is discarded or the possibility of making substantive claims about the world undermined. This makes liberalism's claim on anyone's attention very insecure, because it seems to reduce epistemological issues to questions about political arrangements. It removes from liberalism any right to assert its own validity. There cannot be created some epistemological distinction between liberalism and the sets of beliefs over which it claims 'neutrality'. Yet an attempt to distance itself from other beliefs has been particularly marked in liberalism's approach to religion. One writer says:

> The liberal's rejection of religious-based policies suggests some sort of epistemological divide or discontinuity between what we can claim justifiably to know secularly, so to speak, and what we can claim justifiably to know religiously, the latter being an inferior form of knowledge for purposes of public policy, though perhaps not for other purposes.[26]

We have seen how Nagel for one assumes that there is more room for individual judgement about religion than about science. In other words, unless he is appealing merely to current fashion, he is saying that religion should have a different place in society precisely because it is less well established. If we are content to follow fashion, liberalism is highly unpopular in some quarters and it is by no means impossible that the dominant view in society could become illiberal. Yet once liberals wish to move to firmer ground, they have to face the fact they must appeal to precisely the same kind of epistemological criteria, and to the same world, as anyone else. They must be willing to reason about what is true. Although toleration would be seen by many as a virtue, liberals have to face as much as anyone else the vexed problem of how far they should be willing to tolerate the views of those with whom they fundamentally disagree. The liberal's approach to the intolerant or illiberal is no different a question than that of how a religious believer should tolerate those who belong to different religions or to no religion at all. We may choose the exercise of reason to the use of coercion, the role of argument to the application of force. Freedom may be seen as the precondition of rationality. This itself may be a view derived from a religious view of the world, a reflection perhaps of an acknowledgement of the divine gift of freedom. Some forms of liberalism could be driven by a religious vision. This, however, only illustrates the tact that liberalism cuts itself off from religion at its own peril. A liberalism that floats free of all substantive views is by definition one that is ungrounded. In that case, instead of moulding public opinion, it will always follow it.

There is in the end no way of avoiding the complicated and messy arguments both about what constitutes truth and about which views are true. It might be politically convenient to come to some kind of social arrangement which ensures that we can live together without having any arguments about the things that matter. In the end, however, that is an illusion. Religion's place in society, or alternatively its banishment to the private worlds of individuals, depends on assessments of its truth. It may be tempting to imagine that we can have a sanitized form of reason for the public world while still making rational judgements within the cocoons of our private lives. That kind of schizophrenia is ultimately impossible without judgements being made to the detriment of our private beliefs. Objective truth and the public world cannot finally part company. If we want to claim truth for our beliefs, they must be able to pass scrutiny on the public stage. How far religious beliefs can and should do so will be the theme of subsequent chapters. One thing is clear. If religion cannot claim truth, it can have no genuine public role to play.

Notes

1   *Political Liberalism*, p. xviii.
2   *Ibid.*, p. 36.
3   *Ibid.*, p. 129.
4   *Ibid.*
5   *Ibid.*, p. 247
6   *Ibid.*, p. 67.
7   *Ibid.*, p. 35.
8   *Ibid.*, p. xxiv.
9   *Ibid.*, p. 51.
10 *Ibid.*, p. xix.
11 *Ibid.*, p. 58.
12 Audi, 'The separation of Church and State', p. 228.
13 For a further discussion about religion in public life by Robert Audi see Robert Audi and Nicholas Wolterstorff: *Religion in the Public Square*.

14   Levison, 'Religious language and the public square', p. 2071.
15   *Political Liberalism*, p. 243.
16   Alexander, 'Liberalism, religion and the unity of epistemology', p. 790.
17   Nagel, 'Moral conflict and political legitimacy', p. 232.
18   *Ibid.*, p. 232.
19   Nagel, *Equality and Partiality*, p. 162.
20   *Ibid.*, p. 161.
21   Nagel, 'Moral conflict and political legitimacy', p. 231.
22   D'Agostino, *Free Public Reason*, p. 5.
23   D'Agostino, 'Transcendence and creation', p. 87.
24   *Ibid.*, p. 90.
25   *Ibid.*, p. 180.
26   Alexander, 'Liberalism, religion and the unity of epistemology', p. 774.

2

Is Religion Merely a Social Fact?

1 Reasoning about Religion

The issue of what kind of truth a religion can lay claim to is hotly contested. There is, however, a prevalent temptation to avoid the question by changing the subject. This becomes particularly apparent when different religions are studied and compared. Religion, whatever else it may be, clearly embodies social practices and bodies of belief expressed in particular ways of life. Social scientists and those studying different religions are therefore going to be drawn into concentrating on these unquestioned social effects. They will quite rightly feel that consideration of religious claims to truth will involve them in matters that are more properly the preserve of philosophy or even theology. The fear of some hidden 'theological agenda' makes them very jealous of their status as independent scholars and 'scientists'. What people believe and the reasons they give for so doing will tend to be ignored. The mere fact that they have those beliefs and that they are encapsulated in public, social practices will be enough. Yet the problem that must be confronted is whether such an approach does violence to important features of religion. For one thing, it appears to ignore the claim that religious beliefs can themselves be held on rational grounds and hence have a right to claim truth.

The claim that it is rational to hold a religious belief must be sharply distinguished from a parallel argument. Can we study the nature of religion in a rational way? How far can we capture its nature if we view it simply as one among many kinds of social phenomena? Is it possible to talk of the scientific study of religion, and accept the possibility of a rational examination of religion in a dispassionate and objective manner? For those who doubt whether social science should be modelled on a science like chemistry, this will be one more example of a more general problem. There is a perpetual tug between those who wish to understand human behaviour and those who want to explain it. Some have the goal of interpretative understanding, stemming from a hermeneutical approach. Others wish to provide a causal explanation, integrating human social activity firmly in the natural world. Whatever difficulties arise from the standpoint of social science, religion brings additional complications. A social scientific approach to religion must treat religious beliefs and institutions as social facts. In other words, it is not dealing with the content of such belief, but its context. Religion, it may be held, promotes social solidarity and contributes to the stability of a society. Whether true or not, this is a thesis about the effects of religious belief and the function religion plays in a society. It has such effects and functions whether it is true or false. Social science has no need to assess the rationality of a belief to see the role it plays in society.

The sociology of religion becomes a species of the sociology of knowledge, so long as the latter is understood in a benign way. One classic statement of the phenomenological brand of the sociology of knowledge is that given by Berger and Luckmann. They say: 'It is our contention that the sociology of knowledge must concern itself with whatever passes for "knowledge" in a society, regardless of the ultimate validity or invalidity (by whatever criterion) of such "knowledge".'[1] This brand of the sociology of knowledge looks at how reality is constructed in a given society. Its role will, given its 'bracketing off' of questions of truth and falsity, be ultimately descriptive. It will show how systems of belief are held and unfold their nature. Such phenomenological analysis, according to Berger and Luckmann, 'refrains from any causal or genetic hypotheses, as well as from assertions about the ontological status of the phenomenon analysed'. Clearly if this method is applied to the study of religion, it can be both liberating and restricting. It enables students of religion to look at what religious belief means to the participants of a particular religious way of life, without getting involved in theological judgements about what is true. At the same time, however, many would find such an analysis too bland, since it aims at nothing deeper than description. It is certainly empirical in that 'fieldwork' of various kinds would be essential to find out how beliefs and purported knowledge appear to those who hold them. Yet if science aims to do more than show what happens, and if it aims at some deeper form of understanding and explanation, this kind of survey of religions may not seem to get very far. As one writer says: 'To restrict the study of religion to pure description precludes what seems to be of the essence of science, namely explanation and theory.'[2] This argument about the proper way to approach religion is, of course, one instance of a general dispute about the role of social science.

Endemic in such disputes is the question of the 'insider' and the 'outsider'. Accounts of social science derived from the views of the later Wittgenstein on meaning stress the fact that the only way to understand a concept is to learn how to use it. At first sight, this merely shows the importance of fieldwork in placing concepts in their proper contexts. Yet what is really at issue is whether someone coming to a society, whether that of a remote tribe, or merely a particular religious institution, can be in a better position to know what is going on than a participant. Again the problem of whether social science is more than elucidation and description arises. This is particularly important in the case of religion, since the issue of whether anyone else can explain religion in terms that would be rejected by the participants is a crucial one. Phenomenological analysis will, by its very nature, be in no danger of challenging the beliefs of the people it is investigating. By its procedure of 'bracketing off' questions of truth, it practises a methodological agnosticism about the substantive issues. Yet the question must remain how much it can achieve. It would certainly seem difficult for it to add anything to an understanding of religion which was not already implicit in the believer's own perspective.

For anyone schooled in the idea that we should be able to reason about anything, it may seem odd if religious beliefs together with the other elements of human culture, cannot themselves be an object of our reasoning. Why, it may be asked, should there not be a clear demarcation between being religious and studying religion? This becomes impossible, if religion can only be understood from the inside. One either understands and believes, or one fails to understand. In that case, atheism would be impossible, since no one could understand enough to deny the truth of what is understood. The assumption, however, in the case of those who would study religion is not that they are confronting internal questions of truth and falsity. Instead they wish to take up an external position and look at religion and its role purely as a cultural construction. The whole point of this approach is that the observer takes up a different stance from that of the participant. A certain distance is needed to look at the religion and its effects. The question, however, must be whether this distancing can allow us to do justice to the object of our study. Since the fact of belief becomes more important than what is believed, the inevitable tendency will be to look for explanations of the belief elsewhere in society and in the human mind. The very fact that we stand back from the beliefs, and refuse to examine their truth, will have the result that scientific explanations of such belief will have to dismiss any idea that a belief is held because it is true.

Many investigators into the nature of religion are quite sure of what is true and what is not, and they consider that scientific method is the sure path to the possession of knowledge. They can ignore or even deny religious claims to truth, because they are certain that by standing apart from religion and investigating it in a scientific manner they will gain important new knowledge. Many would feel that the studies would somehow be contaminated by the inclusion of theological categories. Thus for them an external stance would be a precondition for attempting to explain religion. Don Wiebe discusses the controversy between 'insider' and 'outsider',[3] between those who see the importance of the inclusion of religious categories into the study of religion and those who deny it. His sympathies are with the outsider and the resistance to any scientific study being dictated by ecclesiastical or theological considerations. Any methodological demand for reference to theological categories in understanding religion seems to him to threaten the integrity of science. He says that it puts 'in jeopardy the very existence of an academic study of religion because it opens to debates whether the agenda for that study is finally to be determined by the academy or the "church"'. There are echoes here of battles between theology and religious studies as academic disciplines. The issue should not be seen as a power struggle, whether between University and Church, or even between different groups of academics. The issue is the more subtle one of questioning the limits of any scientific enterprise, and the role of scientific explanation. The Church as an on-going institution is a social fact whether its beliefs are true or false, and questions about its social role will remain whatever the status of its claims to knowledge. Much more important is the underlying question of how far self-styled 'scientific' approaches can produce adequate theories about the nature and character of religious belief.

2 Explaining Religion

The sociology of science has often taken a strong explanatory line instead of a neutral descriptive one in its approach to the physical sciences. Yet it seems set on a self-defeating course if it holds that no scientist can ever hold a belief simply because it is true. There will always be some other explanation why it is thought true. The same mode of argument will then be used about the sociologist who has been conditioned to see things in one way rather than another. Does the study of religion fall into the same trap, holding that a religious person is somehow the product of social forces when the student of religion is miraculously not? The more this question is pursued, the clearer it becomes that an invocation of science is in fact promoting it above religion. What is being proclaimed is a scientistic attitude according to which knowledge is restricted to what can be produced by human scientific method. There is an echo here of the old positivist insistence on science being restricted to empirical data, which were public and could be shared, to experiments that could be repeated and to observations which were accessible to all. Positivism lives on in a naturalism that refuses to countenance specifically religious claims to truth, but restricts itself to what is within the province of science. 'Naturalists' of this kind will inevitably want explanations as to why anyone should have peculiar beliefs of the kind afforded by religion. For many such thinkers rationality demands evidence, but the evidence produced in favour of religious faith would be regarded as inadmissible. Appeals to revelation would be seen as private, idiosyncratic beliefs which cannot be validated in a manner which enables them to be shared with others. Even when such beliefs are held by a community, there still remains the question how they can be discussed with those outside the community. At the root of such an attitude is a view of reason which stems from the Enlightenment, with its opposition of reason to revelation and of the natural to the supernatural. The consequence is to assume that religions are cultural constructions. All that can be known about a religion will, it is said, be known scientifically. Science can have no access to whatever transcendent reality is proclaimed by religion, and there will be no difference to the scholar whether it exists or not. It can only be understood within the ideological context of the religious life.

The problem is that it is always easier to accept such an approach to a religion that appears primitive and superstitious than to the 'higher' religions. Even a Christian theologian might be willing to accept a naturalistic explanation (in terms, say, of social function) for an African tribal religion, while indignantly refusing to accept that similar explanations can exhaust what can be said about Christianity. The field of comparative religion has produced those who want to give a naturalistic account of all religion. Anyone wanting a scientific theory of religion would want a general account which could be genuinely transcultural. Accounts on the other hand which insist on appealing to the conceptual scheme of the participants could never get beyond the bounds of the culture they were investigating. Yet once the student occupies a vantage point beyond religion, the pressure will undoubtedly exist to give reductionist theories of religion which deliberately ignore the particular claims of particular religions. Social scientists have often been drawn to functionalist accounts which focus on the functions a religion may serve in society. They stress its role in promoting social solidarity, although it is also rather obviously a source of division and dispute in many societies. They also stress its contribution to the maintenance of social order. The point of such explanations is that they can be applied to any religion regardless of the content of its beliefs. Sacrificing to the Roman emperor could serve the same function as a great state occasion organized by the Church of England. Both serve to uphold the established order, and yet may be motivated by different beliefs. Some participants may be taking part in a ritual for its own sake, but in the latter case a belief in the truth of Christian doctrine would surely be motivating some of the participants. The function may not be the purpose, and even unacknowledged or latent functions may not provide a full explanation of what is occurring. Applause at a central meeting of the old Soviet Communist Party may have fulfilled a similar function to the singing of the Gloria in church. Yet the systems of belief being upheld are markedly different. Even if the fulfilment of function might serve to perpetuate the holding of the belief, it fails to explain its origins. Why should people hold one set of beliefs rather than another? The danger of accounts given by social scientists (and scientists of other kinds) is that they tend to flatten out differences in belief as being of little account. Since what matters to them are the social effects of religion what is believed is subordinated to the fact of belief.

A naturalistic approach certainly encourages this process. Religion has to be explained in ways that take no account of the object of belief, if it is assumed that there is no such thing as the supernatural (however defined), or that if there is such a thing, it cannot be in contact with us. This approach is summed up by Drees when he says: 'I do not see religiously relevant gaps in the natural and human world, where the divine could somehow interfere with natural reality.'[4] He concludes that as a result of this 'the origins and functions of religions may be intelligible'. Without the possibility of divine intervention, the origins of religious belief clearly lie wholly in this world. On the other hand, if there is a God who is revealed to some in a special way, we may feel that we need look no further for an explanation for the sparking of religious faith. In other words, it may seem as if the question of the scope of the scientific explanation for religion comes down to whether religious claims are true or not. If they are, that is their justification. If not, we then need some further reason as to why people should produce and hold to such beliefs. A similar pattern of reasoning has marked the development of the sociology of science. It was tacitly assumed at first that truth was its own explanation while the occurrence of scientific error seemed to demand a special explanation. The so-called 'strong programme' in the sociology of knowledge[5] undertook to provide a causal account of all scientific beliefs. The weight of explanation was moved from truth to what is considered true, and that was thought to be wholly within the scope of sociological investigation. Truth, it was thought, could not be abstracted from what is held true. All emphasis was put on the social environment and the agreements negotiated, not on the internal character of the beliefs themselves.

This way of looking at things must become profoundly anti-realist in that no distinction is drawn between what is the case and what is believed to be the case. Reality drops out in favour of understandings of reality. The latter seem to be firmly within the province of the social scientists. Yet in the end it has to be realized that a distinction has to be drawn between the object, of whatever kind, under study and the beliefs of the sociologist or anthropologist conducting the study. At that point, the very same distinction between the subject and the object of belief is bound to re-emerge. Social scientists cannot claim validity for their discipline without allowing that it is motivated by the very same search for truth that they wish to suggest in others is merely the expression of social or psychological conditions.

Dangers of self-reference arise when truth is reduced to issues about the causes of belief. There is a further difficulty which arises when a stark contrast is made between the insider and the outsider. It can look as if a choice is being forced between service of the interests of an ideology or a critical stance. We must either be prepared to accept without question the claims of a religion or stand outside and unmask it as a rationalization of deeper social pressures. It is either absolute knowledge of the divine or a sham. Yet, it will be pointed out, a subservient commitment to an authoritarian structure or received dogma is the antithesis of the questioning of the scientific spirit. We are brought back once again to the values of the Enlightenment. A sleight of hand has made reason the enemy of religion. Even though criticisms of religion are being made in the name of rationality, little credence in all this is in fact being given to the powers of human rationality.

Much of the motivation for the sociology of science and for the study of religion comes from the assumption that most scientific and religious belief has proved to be mistaken. Such a conclusion would seem inevitable given the plurality of such belief. If the earth is round, those who believed it flat were in error. If there is one God, polytheists have always been wrong. If there is no God at all, most of humanity has been mistaken. Error is widespread. Once it appears to be wrong to talk of simple error in such contexts, that position can easily degenerate into relativism. The study of religion, however, has undoubtedly gained impetus from the fact of the multiplicity of religions and the ensuing conclusion that they are all held on grounds far removed from issues concerning truth. Yet it is unwise to assume that the possession of rationality can be identified with the acquisition of truth. People can stumble on the truth by accident, and it is also possible that they can be perfectly rational but be constrained by the imperfect information available to them. Given what they do know, their beliefs may be not only intelligible, but even rational. This ground alone should make us hesitate in assuming that all religious beliefs must lie beyond the bounds of rationality.

3   The Autonomy of Religion

Many students of religion find it convenient not so much to hold that every religion is fundamentally in error, but to conclude that in fact a religious attitude to the world can have no cognitive basis. Wiebe makes this assumption explicit in his quest for a naturalistic explanation for

religion. He asserts: 'Religious thinking is mythopoeic in nature –
that is, it is a mode of thought that is not rational or cognitive in the
sense that modern western science is rational and cognitive.'[6] This
noncognitivist approach to religion is a familiar move in the philosophy
of religion, particularly in the face of positivist attacks on religion based
on the supremacy of science. When the methods of physical science are
made the epitome of rationality, religion can appear to constitute a non-
rational, if not irrational, set of attitudes, merely because it purports to
deal with realities beyond the reach of human science. Yet much depends on what is meant by science. Even theology has at times been
characterized as a science with a reality to investigate and its own
systematic body of theory. The study of religion, similarly, might be seen
as 'scientific'. 'Science' can be understood in a wide sense to mean
something like 'knowledge' (as the Latin *scientia* did). The German
Wissenschaft can include disciplines such as history. Wiebe and others,
however, would be much more restrictive in their views of what would
constitute a 'scientific' attitude. In their pursuit of a naturalistic account
of religion, they would rule out the transcendent and the supernatural,
because they wish to give priority to the physical world and its workings.
The criterion is what is acceptable to physics. Thus science on this
understanding will only countenance whatever can be reduced to physical terms.

This is itself a controversial and problematic way of dealing with any
social science. A reductionist programme reducing social reality to
individual conceptions, to psychology, to neurophysiology and so down
through biochemistry to physics, will encounter opposition at every
stage of the attempted reduction. Many will contend that there are
different levels, each with their own emergent properties. The point at
issue, however, is that a naturalistic attempt to study religion will tend
to treat social science itself as an enterprise that can be reduced to
physical terms. It will no longer be able to be seen as an autonomous
discipline or set of disciplines, with its own object of study. Instead its
terms will have to be reduced to those acceptable at a lower level.

Wiebe may not be too anxious for his own academic study of religion
to go the way of all social science and be turned into something else. He
is, however, only too pleased to attack the 'autonomy of religion'. He
says: 'To assume that the academic study of religion is exhausted in an
empirical/historical analysis of a particular religious tradition or traditions only makes sense if one assumes "the autonomy of religion".'[7] Yet,

he believes, once one accepts the fact that religion is a phenomenon, which can only be understood in its own terms, one is accepting an 'implicit although perhaps unconscious theological agenda in the academic study of religion'.[8] Problems arise, however with the adoption of a naturalistic agenda, since this also militates against the autonomy of social science. Wiebe wants to import explanation and theory into studying religion. Yet these will only be important in the academic study of religion if they are somehow distinctive at that level. If they are dissolved in a reductionist drive down to the physical level, the study of religion will itself be left without any distinctive subject matter. This is not an idle worry since sociobiologists, for example, have been ready to give explanations in terms of human genes and differential reproductive success to explain the survival of religion, and genes themselves are purely physical segments of DNA. Without a clear differentiation of levels of reality keeping social reality distinct from physical reality, sociology will be dissolved and so will the study of religion as a specialized branch of social science. The very same need to insist that religion is a proper object of academic study will lead to the dismissal of reductionist aspirations. If religion does not form a distinctive level of human activity, practice and belief, there can be nothing distinctive to study. Yet if religion is distinctive enough to form a special object of study, it must be understood to have a certain autonomy.

Questions can be raised about what constitutes such autonomy. Apart from general difficulties in defining religion, the crucial issue remains the status of claims to truth in this area. Phenomenologists often refuse to face the problem, but many social scientists who do, merely discount them. They do not wish the scope for social scientific explanation to be limited, as it would be if it were accepted that religion might be making claims to truth which were rationally grounded. Instead they assume that religious belief is a symptom of such irrationality that it needs causal explanation. In addition they are taking it for granted that the only kind of genuine explanation is causal. Some writers on religious studies implicitly echo the stance of phenomenology when they advocate 'methodological agnosticism'. For instance we are told that 'methodological agnosticism involves taking seriously the reasons believers give for their beliefs and taking seriously (though not endorsing) the concepts they use to describe the object of their beliefs'.[9] This would be contradicted by most anthropological work on religion, the relevance of which is difficult to see unless all religion is assumed to be in need of some further explanation beyond the terms it sets itself. The whole point of anthropological explanation is to link religion to features of human life which might explain why humans might feel the need to believe in superhuman beings.

In other words, as Feuerbach stressed, religious belief is not to be understood as a reflection of some transcendent reality but a projection of human needs and aspirations. It might, for instance, reflect human feelings of vulnerability and dependence in the face of a natural world that can be capricious in its effects. One anthropologist is quite explicit about this. He says: 'Few anthropologists appear to subscribe to the theory that humanity has religion because it was originally given or established by God. Rather, most account religion to be a variable cultural creation.'[10]

What is claimed within a religion is only relevant in so far as a theory can be produced as to why such things are ever claimed. The content becomes the mere projection of some feature of the human condition. Anthropologists seem quite ready to start off by believing that religious claims are false. No doubt the multifarious and conflicting character of the claims appear to support this presupposition. Instead, anthropologists look for a theory from within anthropology which can provide an independent explanation. The result is that religious beliefs are in the end not so much viewed as false but as the expression of something else. They are not genuine claims but have a role in human life that must be explained on other grounds. Yet there seems something odd about this reasoning. If it starts from an assessment of certain beliefs as false, the conclusion cannot be that they are not genuine beliefs after all, but symbols of something else. The initial refusal to accept the truth of the claims might suggest that the claims could be detached from their context and evaluated in precisely the manner which most anthropologists would seem to deny.

One problem any attempted comparison of religions must encounter is that of ethnocentrism. Saler defines this as 'understanding, and perhaps judging, the professed convictions and other behaviours and cultural products of persons in other societies in terms of the categories and standards of one's own'.[11] Even the term 'religion' could be said to carry with it particular assumptions about what a religion is and the part it plays in society. The very act of identifying religious belief in an alien society may be as much a reflection of the presuppositions of our own society as a discovery of features of the society being studied. Saler recognizes this and admits that as a western analytical category, 'religion' is an abstraction, and is certainly not neutral. He says: 'In extending the category religion and applying the category label to certain phenomena amongst non-Western peoples, we are claiming some similarity to what we deem an important aspect of human life in the West.'[12] In other words, our concepts are always going to be rooted in our own way of life, and the notion of a scientific 'neutrality' or 'objectivity' is a myth. We can never stand outside our own conceptual system to see things as they are.

This view brings us back to the issue of realism which must reoccur at every level of study. How far does what we are investigating exist in its own right or merely as a construction out of our own presuppositions? The temptation for any investigator is to treat the object of study as a product of construction, while assuming that the investigation itself is in the business of discovery. The question of levels is important. If I am investigating an independent reality, namely the beliefs and practices of a people, why should I be reluctant to accept that their beliefs in turn at least purport to be about an independent reality? Conversely, if I am convinced that the content of their beliefs is the projection of a conceptual scheme, how confident ought I to be that my own anthropological or other theories are not similarly involved in projection? It is received wisdom nowadays that all categories are rooted in some conceptual scheme, and are never just read off the world. Theory imbues them at every level. Religion will itself, it will be said, be an example of this. Yet if such a view is pushed too far, we can never discover anything, but in every context merely inhabit a world of our own construction.

Anthropology reduces content to context whereas if truth is ever to be an issue, what is asserted at any level must be detachable from the circumstances in which it is asserted. This is as important for the history of science as the study of religion. Unless the same content can be passed on through different generations and in different contexts, one cannot refer to the development of a particular scientific theory rather than a succession of different ones. In the same way, one would be unable to distinguish between differing forms of the same religion rather than a succession of different religions. The very notion of Christianity, for example, would become problematic, as would the idea of religion itself. The concept of a social fact, existing independently of the investigator, and perhaps detachable from its surroundings would be dissolved.

4   Scholarship as Cultural Construction

Attacks on the possibility of a content beyond context have proliferated. Yet the possibility of comparison between religions presupposes an ability to describe religions as they are independently of the external observer. Like any intellectual discipline, comparative religion demands a certain distance between the scholar investigating and the object being investigated. The increasing emphasis on the role of theory in the philosophy of science in marshalling and selecting data has begun a process of reaction against any idea that we see the world as it is.[13] Instead, many, such as postmodernists, choose to stress the active role of researchers and the manner in which their perspective shapes the material. This follows a Kantian epistemology according to which the human mind with its categorial framework moulds reality as it appears to us. Today, however, many are unduly impressed by the differences in beliefs and perspectives that they encounter. They assume that the plurality of conceptual schemes they see ensures an incommensurable plurality of interpretations. The object being interpreted, whether a religious belief or anything else, recedes into the background.

In contrast to the views of Kant, who thought that humans share a set of concepts, the sheer contingency and accidental character of the various conceptual schemes seems their most important feature. There is a refusal to accept that what we are interpreting can in any way be separated from the apparent fact of our interpretation. We must not therefore deal with religion as a simple cultural construction. We must realise that we are constructing a picture of religion for ourselves which depends as much on us and our situation as on anything we are attempting to describe. Following Nietzsche, the distinction between subject and object is abolished, in a way that renders the scholarly examination of religion impossible. The same reluctance to admit that religious belief can even purport to be about anything, rather than be an expression of a particular cultural context, can engender the same conclusions at a higher level. Scholars cannot, it seems, abstract themselves from their own circumstances sufficiently to reason about other people's beliefs. The latter cannot be understood as they are, but at best through a distorting lens of the assumptions of a particular place and time, namely that of the student of religion. At worst they themselves are mere cultural constructions reflecting the context of the scholar.

Jonathan Z. Smith, for example, applies this kind of thinking in comparative religion, in his case starting from a comparison between religions of antiquity, including early Christianity. His whole message is that comparison is a product of the scholar's mind for the scholar's own intellectual reasons. It is the scholar who sees similarities, where others might only see differences. The allegation is that there are no 'natural' affinities. As he says, 'There is nothing "natural" about the enterprise of comparison.'[14] Indeed, the very idea that comparison could tell us how things are is repudiated. Smith draws attention to the fact that any genealogical account of religion, drawing out its origins, is relying implicitly on the notion of 'real' historical connections. For Smith, it is an illusion to think that the process of comparison somehow latches on to any form of reality. Rather, he says, 'comparison tells us how things might be conceived, how they might be 'redescribed'.[15] He sums up by saying that 'comparison provides the means by which we "re-vision" phenomena as our data in order to share our theoretical problems'.

According to such views, any exercise in comparing religions is bound to be a profoundly self-indulgent process. We do not see them as they are but only as they might fit into our preconceptions. We pick out which 'data' we regard as significant, and than work out the relation between them and our theoretical interests. The latter, needless to say, gave shape to the process from its beginning. In fact, if its conclusion is predetermined by our prejudices, there may seem little difference between scholarly study and writing fiction. The latter, too, is the product of the author's mind, and is the outcome of a selection and shaping of material. It is fiction because it is not about anything that actually happened. Postmodernist emphases on the role of imagination and the creativity of the author in all contexts can only serve to blur any distinction between scholarship and research on the one hand and the writing of novels on the other. Postmodernist scepticism will refuse to accept any idea of the 'real' world but questions why any one view of that should be privileged over any other.

The demolition of the distinction between subject and object makes it impossible to conceive of different levels of understanding. We cannot distinguish between the understanding of a participant in some religion and that of the external scholar. We cannot refer to the 'myths' of a religion and reflect on their origin and significance, perhaps comparing them with apparently similar myths elsewhere. That would be to assume an ahistorical context for them. Smith says: 'The claimed ahistorical character of myth is a product of the scholar's gaze and not of course of some native world-view.'[15] We are all, it seems, the product of social context and history, and everything we accept in whatever circumstance is the outcome of our perspective. There is no possibility for an ahistorical content of belief that can be abstracted from its surroundings and tested in isolation, whether we are looking at religious beliefs themselves or the beliefs of those studying them. In other words, we can never break free of our assumptions in a self-critical, rational manner. The very possibility of rationality is being denied. It is a favourite ploy of postmodernists to link the idea of reason with that of the Enlightenment, so that a conception of rationality is made to appear a historical accident. The assumption is that the idea of Reason popularized in the seventeenth and eighteenth centuries and linked with the rise of physical science, was a historical product which we, living in a different age, have now outgrown.

Such accusations always contain a grain of truth. Ideals of reason have been historically influenced by the conditions of a particular time. Historians can no doubt show how, say, a reaction against the power of the Church played a role in the development of modern views. Yet the conduct of history as an intellectual discipline itself presupposes an ability to reason and not just to voice the prejudices of the current age. Our thinking may be rooted in history, but as rational thinkers we can also stand apart even from our own intellectual inheritance and to reflect on it. The categorizing of the Enlightenment as itself an historical episode which may now have been superseded does not destroy the ideal of rationality. It provides an example of rationality by showing that we are able to criticize even our own assumptions concerning how we reason about the world.

5 Religion and Rational Detachment

A powerful argument supporting the human ability to stand back from an object of study, whether our own belief or someone else's, and even to criticize it, comes from the fact that it is not a transient phenomenon of the Enlightenment. This is noticeable even in the case of criticism of religion. The pre-Socratic thinker Xenophanes noted that 'the Ethiopians say that their gods are snub-nosed and black, the Thracians that theirs have light blue eyes and red hair'.[17] His conclusion is that everyone credits the gods with their own characteristics, and that 'if cattle and horses or lions had hands or were able to draw with their hands and do the works that men can do, horses would draw the forms of the gods like horses, and cattle like cattle'. This ability to stand back from religious beliefs, note their plurality and even to theorize about their origins, marks the beginning of a rationality that underlies all intellectual questioning. W. K. C. Guthrie called Xenophanes' foray into the study of religion 'the foundation of social anthropology'.[18]

A movement like postmodernism which stresses the plurality of perspectives, undoubtedly must take as an assumption the fact of difference between beliefs and customs among different peoples. It makes little sense if the plurality is simply a projection from the perspective of the investigator. It is because of such plurality that it seems difficult to set one interpretation and one vision above another. Yet the admission of the reality of plurality is already an admission of something that is the case independently of the scholar. Even the ability to quote historical precedents and parallels with the Enlightenment itself presupposes the operation of rationality. The postmodernist must hold that comparison involves creating those similarities rather than discovering them.

Another example of a rational critique of religion that owes nothing to the European Enlightenment comes from the writing of Tominaga Nakamoto, who wrote in the context of the merchant society of eighteenth-century Japan. Although he was a contemporary of Europeans who were developing a critical historical perspective on the monotheistic religions of Christianity, Judaism and Islam, he was insulated from such developments. He wrote in the midst of a different culture about very different religions, such as Shinto, Confucianism and Buddhism. He brought a historical perspective to bear upon them, being apparently the first to question how far the Mahayaman sutras and others were transmitted from the Buddha himself. He claims that 'the scholars of later generations vainly say that all the teachings come directly from the golden mouth of the Buddha and were immediately translated by those who heard him frequently'.[19] He thus took a critical distance between himself and the beliefs current around him, and reasoned about them, their origins and nature. He saw that the teachings were the result of a continuous process of development and should not be taken at face value. Clearly such remarks had the same kind of impact as a critical approach to the texts of the New Testament which refused to take their historicity for granted.

This process of critical reasoning about religion would seem the very essence of an intellectual discipline such as anthropology. The fact that it can occur in different epochs would suggest that it is no accidental creation of a particular culture. The exercise of rationality, the ability to abstract ourselves from our particular situation and to question our presuppositions, lies at the root of any intellectual endeavour. All this, as we have seen, involves the ability to distinguish between, say, religious belief and theories about it. There is a distinction between the practices of a society and a sociological analysis of those practices. Just as beliefs within a society typically involve an appeal to truth, so theories about those beliefs at a different level also involve an appeal to questions of truth. In each case the believer is distinct from the object of belief. As a result there is always the possibility of error. Religious belief may be mistaken, as may theories about it. To put the matter the opposite way, some religious beliefs may be true and so may anthropological theories about them. This, though, brings back the question of the relation between the two levels. If anthropology is not some form of fiction, merely reflecting the perspective and creativity of the theorist, does not this mean that it is likely to undermine religion? Rational accounts of the origin and nature of religion whether from Xenophanes or the European Enlightenment have been seen as attacks on religion. In writing about Tominaga and his similarity to European developments, Michael Pye notes the emergence of a rational, historical critique of religion and says: 'We may observe the same freely ranging critique of received traditions, the same searching historical investigation of their origins, the same attempt to perceive general laws of religious development.'[20]

The last phrase may give pause for thought in that the very idea of 'general laws' of religious development suggests a positivist view of social science, in which social trends can be subsumed under general laws, in much the same way as chemistry, it may be said, tries to deduce physical laws from the observed behaviour of gases. This rests on large assumptions about the role of social science and about the similarity of social systems and physical systems. The notion of general laws may be difficult to sustain in every part of the physical realm. There is also the danger of assuming without argument that a rational examination of religion will always have the effect of questioning received traditions rather than upholding them.

The dangers of equating a respect for reason with a particular view of reason are illustrated here. Reason has too often be equated with that expressed in scientific method. The Enlightenment did not have a monopoly of reason, but it was characterized by a particular view of it, one which was notably unsympathetic to any idea of the supernatural. Yet we should not allow ourselves to be boxed in with a choice merely between a crudely 'scientistic' view on the one hand, or a collapse into the chaos and nihilism of postmodernism on the other. The issue is not that either science can have the last word or we cannot appeal to reason. Those involved in religious studies who look to science as their model fail to understand how much of a threat it can become if it becomes avowedly reductionist and physicalist. If everything is reducible to terms that can be explicable in terms of physics, how can they be sure that their own discipline can count as science? The study of religion may certainly appeal to a rational basis, but if its practioners wish to pursue their own level of analysis and claim truth for it, they are accepting the limitations of all scientific explanation. They must always be faithful to the level of reality they are investigating. An explanation that dissolves that reality or changes it into something else cannot be a proper explanation. Just as the study of religion is entitled to claim a certain intellectual autonomy, so it must recognize that entitlement in the religions it is investigating. The naturalist denial of the autonomy of religion implicitly involves denying human reason any proper scope at all in the search for truth. Yet it is the same human reason which is being employed in the study of religion.

We can distance ourselves from all religion and reason about it. The assumption, however, that anthropological and other explanations will not only be forthcoming but will be wholly adequate to explain the origins and persistence of religion not only assumes the falsity of religious claims but also relies on the truth of anthropological ones. Yet why is religion untrustworthy and social science trustworthy? Allegations of a 'theological agenda' made against those who are not willing to assume the falsity of religious claims from the outset rather invite the rejoinder that there seems to be an anti-theological agenda in place. Why should it be taken for granted that claims to truth can be rejected at one level and yet be accepted at the next? When postmodernists query anyone's right to occupy a 'God's-eye view' and enunciate the truth, this is not an idle debating point. The very distinction between levels of belief, between religious belief and the study of it, indicates that truth cannot be arbitrarily claimed for one level and denied at the other. Once truth is denied at one level, the same form of argumentation may be repeated at the next.

If we acknowledge that humans are capable of reasoning about what is true, one explanation for a belief may be that is held because it is true. The blanket assumption that all religious beliefs are mistaken and stand in further need of explanation itself stands in need of further justification. It does not follow from the mere fact of human rationality that there is no transcendent reality of the kind sought after in the religions of the world. That assumption was the product of the Enlightenment. However that may be, we can still reason about religious beliefs in a critical way. Such reasoning does not, however, have to conclude that their content is irrelevant to the fact of their being held. Social scientists may not like that, because it may put limits on the scope of their investigations. They may not be able to explain everything about religion. Yet even if a particular religious belief were true, there would still be matters that social science could tell us about. True or not, the belief would still have a function in society.

We must always be reluctant to make the easy assumption that religion is inevitably purely human in origin. The danger is that in some quarters this will be shown, merely because it is assumed from the outset. If one accepts with Drees that 'no phenomenon in the world falls outside the domain of the natural sciences',[21] claims to the contrary will be bound to be given a 'scientific' explanation. The problem is that the status of such disciplines as sociology or anthropology, let alone history, is very suspect from the standpoint of 'hard' science. Once religion has been 'explained', no doubt other subjects will be next in line for the same treatment. Without a prior respect for truth at each level of inquiry, the situation is bound to degenerate into destructive attempts by one intellectual discipline to dominate the others. Everything will be reduced to physics, or alternatively the sociology of knowledge will attempt to demonstrate the social basis of our understanding. Each discipline must learn to accept that while at its level it is investigating part of the world, it can never tell us the whole truth. A respect for truth should also engender a certain humility. We can learn much about religion in many societies by standing back from it, seeing its role in society, and noting the differences and similarities between religions. That does no mean that we can understand everything about a religion. By this method we may not be getting to grips with the most important feature of any religion, its belief in some form of divine reality.

Notes

1 *The Social Construction of Reality*, p. 15.
2 Wiebe, *Beyond Legitimation*, p. 121.
3 Wiebe, *The Irony of Theology and the Nature of Religious Thought*, p. xi.
4 Drees, *Religion, Science and Naturalism*, p. xi.
5 See D. Bloor *Knowledge and Social Imagery* and my *Understanding Social Science*, pp. 27ff.
6 *The Irony of Theology*, p. 40.
7 *Beyond Legitimation*, p. 121.
8 *Ibid.*, p. 122.
9 Clarke and Byrne, *Religion Defined and Explained*, p. 68.
10 Saler, *Conceptualising Religion*, p. 7.
11 *Ibid.*, p. 8.
12 *Ibid.*, p. 259.
13 See my *Rationality and Science*.
14 Smith, *Drudgery Divine*.
15 *Ibid.*, p. 52.
16 *Ibid.*, p. 109.
17 Xenophanes, Fragment 16, p. 119 in Burnet, *Early Greek Philosophy*.
18 Guthrie, *History of Greek Philosophy*, p. 373.
19 *Emerging from Meditation*, p. 81.
20 *Ibid.*, p. 47.
21 Drees, *Religion, Science and Naturalism*, p. 50.

3

Can All Religions be True?

1 The Problem of Many Religions

In the last chapter the relevance of the concept of truth for the study of religion was stressed. No form of study can become important unless some claim to truth can be made as a result. What emerged was also the deeper point that religion as an object of study has to be recognized as itself a possible claimant of truth. Religions are typically making claims about the nature of reality, and pretending that they are something quite different is to misrepresent their nature. A study of religions which becomes a mere description of the celebration of festivals is sheer trivialization. In the Christian context, for example, this would be to suggest that the meaning of Christmas, including the truth claimed by Christians of the Incarnation, was somehow to be equated with the custom of decorating Christmas trees and exchanging presents. Yet the more that it is insisted that any religion is more than the sum of its social practices, the more the issue of competing claims to truth must be faced. It is then not so much a matter of saying that religion concerns truth. The issue is which truth, among the many purported truths on offer.

Only those who have lived in isolated and homogeneous societies could have been unaware that humans hold to very different religions. This has seemed to matter more at some times than others, and particularly when there has been increasing contact between those with different beliefs. This was true at the time of Plato, and led to his championing of the idea of objective truth in the face of relativists and sceptics. It is certainly true now, when global travel and communications, not to mention large-scale emigration and immigration, have made everyone aware that not everyone worships the same God. That at least is the first reaction, but many are impelled to look for a common core in all religion.

This is not just the social problem of how people with different outlooks and customs can live together. We have seen how political liberalism has tried to meet this problem. It is also a fundamental issue for any religion. If one religion is true, does that mean that the others are false? If God is revealed in one religion, does that mean that He does not have any concern for those who sincerely believe that divine reality has been revealed in a different fashion? In fact the mere existence of other religions can become an obstacle to belief. If there is a God, it can seem as worrying that He does not make it easier to believe in Him as, say, that there is suffering and evil in the world. It is pointed out that the conception of a deity that we are called on to accept or reject seems to be rooted in social conditions. If I am born in Baghdad I am more likely to be a Muslim than if I am born in Canterbury. What I have the opportunity to respond to depends on the beliefs held around me, and they are the product of particular religions. No conception of God is neutral between religions.

At this point a form of pluralism which can make room for different religions while not undermining them all becomes tempting. The easy conclusion may be that God has somehow been revealed in different ways and that they are all equally valid. This would allow us to respect all religions while still holding that they are each expressing truth. Yet in many ways this begs the whole question. Which God has revealed Himself (or herself or itself)? The idea that God is glimpsed in every religion can be a surreptitious way of asserting the priority of a particular conception of God as the one that sets the standard. If, for example, we have already decided the Christian God truly exists, we may wish to say that other religions provide paths to Him. Other believers are 'anonymous Christians'. When, however, the whole nature of 'ultimate reality' is in question, there seems no way of determining whether all religions go in the same direction, since we cannot even decide what direction they should be going in. Even the notion that there is an ultimate destination has still to be established.

The dogmatic attitude that sweeps other religions aside as of little account, while upholding one as true, is difficult to put forward consistently. It appears obvious that adherents of other religions can do the same, and there is then no rational way of resolving the ensuing disputes. To say that a religion is true because it is the one we happen to hold is not very helpful. My concepts are my concepts, but that does little to settle the question of whether they are the appropriate ones to have. It is hardly surprising that many are attracted by a pluralist position which accords an equal place to different religions. The problem is what basis it needs to be able to do this. The existence of human freedom, which is often proclaimed as a theological necessity, is given due respect by pluralism. We are, it seems, free to choose what we are to regard as true in religion. Such an assertion of freedom might explain the existence of different religions but in many societies the choice between religions is hardly a real one. We are born into one tradition or another. It may be possible for those in advanced Western societies to pick and choose between religion but that has not been the normal human experience, and is still not so in many areas.

The freedom referred to may, of course, be supposed to be more than individual free will. If so, the issue of truth becomes pressing. Is it being suggested not just that we are each free what to believe, but that we are free even to decide what shall be true? In other words, pluralism may hold not just that there are many paths to truth, but that there are many truths. This immediately involves us in claiming that it is true that there is no truth or that there is no reality because reality consists of many realities. The contradictory nature of such relativism is always obvious. That does not stop the view seeming attractive because for many it appears to encourage toleration. *Contradiction*

The assertion of objective truth, coupled with a claim to know it, can undoubtedly lead to totalitarian excess. If I claim to know what is in your interests and insist on imposing it in you, paternalism can soon become oppression. Yet the existence of objective reality, my knowledge of it and my imposition of my will on you are all distinct. Many wish to impose their will without any claim to knowledge at all. Plato made such people his target in *The Republic* when he tried to harness power to knowledge. Similarly I can know what is true and still allow that others should make their mistakes. I could even know that it is wrong to impose my beliefs on others. Further, to take the issue further back, it does not follow from the fact there is a world to know that my beliefs about it are correct. I must hold them true, but I am not infallible and can realize that, even in the case of religious beliefs, one can believe something, and be sufficiently committed to base one's life on it, and yet still be wrong.

This may seem paradoxical. How could one be willing even to die for what could be an illusion? The logical point about the possibility of error may seem inappropriate in the sphere of religious faith. Yet when we are confronted by those with a deep allegiance to faiths we do not share, they surely claim our attention because they are claiming truth. That does not guarantee truth in their case, and nor does it in our own. We may even be able to learn from them just as they might from us. This insight encourages talk about dialogue between religions, and that is important for mutual understanding. Too much may be expected from it, since differences cannot always be reconciled. Reality cannot be assumed to be an amalgam of beliefs any more than it can be automatically thought the private property of one religion.

For this reason some pluralists are tempted to object to the idea of an objective reality confronting us all. If their only goal is toleration, the logical possibility that one side in a dispute may be right and the other wrong is itself not to be tolerated. They wish to challenge the ideas of reality and truth, in order to undermine the basis for making any claim to knowledge. Respect for freedom then means not only toleration of mistakes but the full-blooded freedom to decide what should count as true. They thus embrace with enthusiasm opposition to realism. Claims to truth and knowledge cannot then be allowed to have the universal implications which a realist would insist on. Our truth may not be your truth, and pluralism can become a synonym for relativism.

Another motive for various forms of pluralism is provided by the fact which has already been referred to, namely human fallibility. This holds true of all human reasoning in science and elsewhere, and is why certainty has to be a psychological rather than a logical category. Even greater problems loom, however, when humans confront what is transcendent. The notion is a complicated one (and will be examined in chapter 10) but one aspect of it is conceptual. Particularly in the case of religion, it is claimed that we confront a reality that outstrips our understanding. We are bounded by the limits placed on all humans. We have finite minds and are trying to grasp what appears to be infinite. The problem then becomes not why everyone cannot agree, but rather why anyone should imagine that any knowledge of the utterly transcendent is even possible.

From positing a view of the world where it might seem understandable that there are many religions, it suddenly becomes difficult on this line of reasoning to see how there could be any religions at all. Our limited perspective might suggest that alternative views of the same reality are possible. The old story of different blind people feeling different parts of an elephant and coming to different conclusions about its nature illustrates this. It might seem as if bringing all religions together might help to provide a fuller picture of the nature of the transcendent. Yet none of us is in a position to know the nature of the transcendent apart from the insights of the different religions. There seems to be no one able to say what the religious counterpoint of the elephant is. We cannot stand outside ourselves and see ourselves and everyone else trying to understand something, the nature of which is already clear. We cannot even say that all religions grasp aspects of the same reality. Given their deep disagreements, it must be optimistic to imagine that they are really complementary.

2 Religious Pluralism

Whether or not a respect for freedom or a recognition of our finitude in face of transcendence leads to some form of pluralism, there is still the underlying issue about the desirability of pluralism. This would suggest that pluralism means something more than the mere fact of different religions. Pluralism is not just the acknowledgement of plurality. That could hardly have been controversial and the impetus to evangelism and mission assumed it. The recipients of such endeavours have not usually been sophisticated atheists, but the adherents of religions deemed to be inferior. Pluralism must be precisely the view that questions the easy assumption of the inferiority of other religions. It can even rejoice in diversity and see the value of having alternative insights. Yet this is to assume that one religion does not have the monopoly of truth. The very fact of Christian missions through the centuries suggests that this is not a position which has appealed to Christians, any more than it has to a religion such as Islam.

The problem is how one can be a pluralist rejoicing in diversity, while holding an allegiance to the insights of one religion. It is difficult to be indifferent to the fact that others differ if one holds views which one takes to be true. Anyone who believes that we all confront the same reality must accept that in the end those who disagree cannot all be right. Some at least must be mistaken. However much the existence of alternative scientific theories may be of use in the development of science, that does not mean that a scientist can view a colleague's disagreement as positively to be welcomed. The progress of science demands that the matter be resolved. If continued disagreement is tolerated, it follows that it does not matter which theory is held. Any view is as good as any other. Similarly in the sphere of religion, too much toleration and even the welcoming of difference can lead to the view that it does not matter which religion one holds, and that can soon be taken to mean that it does not matter whether any religious belief is held at all. Toleration can lead to indifference and that can then lead to contempt. If there are so many religious options on offer, and it does not matter which is adopted, then why, it may be asked, should one believe any of them at all. Truth has slipped totally out of our grasp.

Those who delight in cultural diversity believe that in the end it would be arbitrary to favour one view rather than another. Pluralism is regarded as the opposite of uniformity. Some are conscious of an analogy with the development of science and see the interaction of religions as a means to progress in religion. They would perhaps look for a developing convergence between all religions in the long term. Hans Kung argues 'that the boundary between true and false today, even as Christians see it, no longer runs simply between Christianity and the other religions, but at least in part within each of the religions'.[1] He advocates the principle that nothing of value in the other religions is to be denied, but nor is anything of no value to be uncritically accepted. His hope is that on this basis 'a consensus should be possible among representatives of the various religions'. He considers that we are all on the way to an 'ever-greater' truth.

This approach might answer those who see pluralism not as the simple opposite of uniformity, but as the contrary of unity. If there is one reality, truth should have a universal appeal. What is true should be shared, and a lack of unity of belief necessarily implies error or ignorance on the part of some or all. A plurality of religions is not of itself to be welcomed but might be accepted as a necessary preliminary to something greater. Scientists may yearn for a Theory of Everything and not be content with a diversity of theories even though they seem hard to integrate. Similarly even those who are eager for dialogue with other religions may still recognize that the existence of alternative religions shows a woeful deficiency in human understanding. Unity is still regarded as more desirable than plurality.

It seems as if the nature of ultimate reality has to be answered from the perspective of religious views in isolation or combination. Yet even this assumption and reference to 'transcendent reality' will beg the question against the atheist and the materialist. Why, after all, should reality be anything different from what we with our finite minds encounter daily? The dualist notion of two worlds will be immediately disputed. Religions may on the whole agree with each other that the physical world is a mere part of a wider whole. Yet even that cannot be too easily assumed since it depends on some agreement on what can count as a religion. It would be too easy to argue in a circular fashion that all religions talk of God and possibly life beyond death, merely because it is being tacitly assumed that any body of belief that does not cannot be a genuine religion. Buddhism is sometimes, for example, held to be a philosophy rather than a religion. There can be an assumption that all religions possess a common core, or at least points of contact. Yet this all too often is made possible by the exclusion of many religions from consideration. Hans Kung looks at what he terms 'world religions', such as Islam, Hinduism and Buddhism. Should neo-paganism equally be considered a religion? Is African tribal religion somehow to be considered inferior? The notion of a 'world religion' suggests that the number and spread of adherents is somehow relevant, but from an epistemological point of view it is hard to see why this is relevant to questions of truth.

One temptation in this area is to take the example of movements towards Christian unity and assume that these can be extended. The so-called 'ecumenical movement' looked, perhaps optimistically, to the 'coming great Church'. It wanted to emphasize what Christians held in common, and to suggest that their differences were not sufficient to hold them apart. Such a process is fraught with difficulty in that the prejudices and injustices of centuries have to be overcome. Yet arguments about Church order, for example, can often seem to be minor in comparison with the doctrines that are agreed. They can seem important precisely because they are sometimes wrongly presented as differences of doctrine. It would, for instance, be hard to argue that Protestants and Catholics do not worship the same God. It has been one of the purposes of the ecumenical movement to show that whatever may sometimes be carelessly implied, they are each adherents of the same religion.

Hans Kung says that 'ecumenism should not be limited to the community of the Christian churches: it must include the community of great religions if ecumenism – in accordance with the original meaning

What?

of oikoumene – is to refer to the whole "inhabited world".[2] Kung therefore sees the development of dialogue and mutual understanding as continuing beyond the bounds of the Christian faith, to encompass other faiths. Yet he only wants to deal with the 'great religions' and does not even envisage contact with devil worship or witchcraft. He is already operating with some principle of exclusion. The reference to the inhabited world should mean that he is willing to deal with all religious belief contained within it and not just the most widespread. Such a method sounds like a political exercise rather than a search for truth. On the other hand, it may be because he is operating still with certain preconceptions about the kind of thing that could be true that he does not think some religions worthy of attention. They are not the 'higher' religions. Yet it is all too apparent that the source of such a judgement is in fact a Christian outlook, however attenuated it may have become.

The genuine pluralist has a problem. The multiplicity of religions may be welcomed, but does that mean that every religion, however defined, is to be welcomed on a par with the others? It can seem very open minded to want dialogue with the 'great' or the 'world' religions. Most typically, apart from Christianity and Judaism, these would be Buddhism, Hinduism and Islam. Yet these do not exhaust the religious options taken up by humans even at the present day and even in so-called advanced societies. Those religions that make high moral demands (again judged from a Christian perspective) may seem admirable. Unless, though, some view about what is true is being smuggled in at an early stage, it is hard to see from a pluralist standpoint just why they are the only ones to concentrate on. Pagan, pre-Christian, religion has never totally died out in Western Europe in folk culture, and there are signs of its revival. Should that be taken seriously? Perhaps many pluralists would do so, but what of the many cults through human history that have practised human sacrifice? If they are encountered as exotic survivals in remote regions or are even revived in Western society, must the pluralist take them seriously because they exist as bodies of belief and practice? Even toleration has to have its limits, and pluralism usually advocates an attitude to other religions that goes far beyond mere toleration. The reference to the ecumenical movement suggests that a Christian's approach to another religion should be as positive as that to another Christian denomination. To approach all other cults and beliefs, not just with an open and uncritical mind, but even with a willingness to enter into dialogue would in some circumstances be to abrogate our basic moral responsibility as human beings.

[Once we start making judgements about which religions we are going to take seriously, or even about what we shall count as a proper religion, we are inevitably doing so from a particular perspective and making judgements about truth. The issue then is not so much whether we are truly neutral but how much of a tradition we are prepared to jettison in our search for common ground.]The pluralist is typically prepared to make fewer judgements about the truth of a particular religion than are others. The point is, however, that some judgements are inevitably still being made. The pluralist then has to defend this selective attitude to claims to truth. Why are some religious attitudes defensible and others not? Indeed, the real pluralist should not be confined to religion anyway. In a sense the worry about what should count as a religion is superfluous. Other forms of belief should be taken seriously, including those that oppose all religion. Why should not a pluralist wish to encompass atheist beliefs and enter into dialogue with them as much as with theist beliefs? There could be no reason for exclusion unless there was a prior conviction that religion was somehow correct in wishing to invoke the transcendent. Yet once this step has been taken it is not clear why the tenets of one religion could not be upheld as true. It is no longer the general categories of truth and falsity that are in question, but rather how much of a religion can be accepted. Some may no doubt wish to see a confluence of the main religions as a way of reducing sources of conflict. That, however, is a political and not a philosophical judgement (and one that perhaps makes a rather simplistic analysis about the role of religion in human conflict). It is not a substitute for meeting philosophical questions about truth. This is particularly so since such an attitude itself obviously depends on a judgement that claims truth, namely that the overriding priority in human life is the reduction of the causes of conflict.

The pluralist can never escape making judgements of truth. It is just a question of which judgements are to be made. Pluralism is as much a substantive position claiming truth and excluding certain positions, as any religion. One writer, Gavin D'Costa, indeed claims there is no such thing as pluralism because all pluralists are committed to holding some form of truth criteria.[3] By virtue of this, anything that falls foul of such criteria is excluded from counting as truth. If one follows a widely used typology, one can distinguish between 'exclusivism', 'inclusivism' and 'pluralism'. 'Exclusivism' holds that only one religion or revelation is true and that salvation can only be achieved by the one path. Inclusivists try to claim that only one religion provides definitive truth but that other religions provide opportunities for truth and therefore salvation in a less complete way. Pluralism tries to avoid both positions and, as we have seen, attempts to be more open minded to alternative religions and their claims. Yet it initially has to exclude some views as false, or at least as unworthy of consideration. It is unlikely to want to take seriously Nazi views, or those of the kind of extreme cult that encourages mass suicide. Even if this is because they are not regarded as religious, it is clear that pluralism is already working with a substantive view of what a religion should be. More likely, it is because they have an implicit view of what could count as truth. D'Costa says:

> If any pluralist were to claim that they did not operate with any such exclusive criteria, they would be unable to distinguish between any two claims to revelation or truth such as the claims of the confessing Church and those of the German Christians following Hitler. Such a pluralism would therefore be entirely unable to distinguish between true and false claims to revelation. It is very difficult to find a pluralist who would go to this extreme.[4]

In fact, the logical outcome of a pluralism that refused to make any exclusivist claims would be a position that accepted all claims to revelation, however contradictory or morally repugnant. That in the end must surely be tantamount to denying the validity of any revelation. If anything can be accepted as revelation, nothing can. There could in that case be no such thing as revelation. Pluralism cannot avoid being tinged with exclusivism unless it is to collapse into meaninglessness. If it is claiming anything at all, it must in logic be no different from the exclusivist position. If it wishes to include anything and leave nothing out, it becomes an empty view. No distinction is then made between a clear religious doctrine and empty babble. In fact what is usually the case is that pluralists are merely using different criteria for truth from that of the proponent of a particular religion.

This not the view of John Hick, who explicitly criticizes D'Costa's position. Hick holds that religious exclusivism and religious pluralism are, as he puts it, 'of different logical kinds, the one being a self-committing affirmation of faith and the other a philosophical hypothesis'.[5] Yet if the exclusivist position is seen as a claim to truth and not as a mere expression of personal commitment, it can be on a collision course with pluralism. The latter, Hick believes, explains the data from the history of religions better, at least 'from a religious, as distinguished from a naturalistic, point of view'. It is thus itself already making definite assumptions about the kind of world we live in. It is itself a substantive metaphysical position, which must then operate in the same logical space as exclusivism. It considers that the world is such that religious attitudes in general are warranted, but not such as to underwrite any particular one. The very reference to commitment and faith makes it clear that, according to Hick, pluralism prevents the exclusivist claiming truth for a particular religion at the expense of others.

3   The Nature of the 'Real'

No one has been more forceful in arguing the case in Britain and America for a pluralist vision in the realm of religion than John Hick. His views present a sophisticated neo-Kantian analysis of the epistemological status of different religions, making a firm distinction between the 'Real' as it is in itself and the way it is conceived within different cultures. Influenced by his experience of religious life in contemporary British cities (and Birmingham in particular), where immigration has brought a colourful rainbow of different faiths, Hick makes much of the fact, as already mentioned, that our religion is likely to be the product of our upbringing. He says: 'It is evident that in some ninety-nine per cent of cases, the religion which an individual professes and to which he or she adheres depends on the accidents of birth.'[6] This is no doubt so, but the question is what conclusion is to be drawn. No doubt even today someone born in the middle of England is more likely to accept quantum mechanics as true than someone born in the middle of New Guinea. What bearing does that have on what is true? To push the issue back a stage, it is easier to be a pluralist in contemporary England or America than in, say, Iran, and certainly easier at the end of the twentieth century than in the Middle Ages. Does that say anything about the acceptability or otherwise of pluralism? Relativizing belief to a context never answers the question of whether the belief is true. It either dodges it or ends with denying any idea of truth, apart from what as a matter of fact is believed.

[Hick's views are important since he has tried explicitly to hold pluralism together with a thorough-going realism.] This involves taking very different views seriously while acknowledging that there is one ultimate reality. His aim is to encourage each religion to modify its characteristic claims to truth through a reinterpretation of its outlook.] He says: 'Insofar as each of the world religions comes, in today's global city, to see itself as one among many, it will . . . deemphasise its own absolute and exclusive claim, allowing this to fall into the background and eventually to become absorbed into its own past history.'[7] As the reference to 'world religions' might indicate, Hick is one of those who surreptitiously makes the task of a pluralist easier by excluding atheism, and some of what might be regarded as the less savoury religions. This means that he is able to draw parallels between the different religions in enabling our human condition to be transformed. He is able to talk of 'salvation' in connection with all of them. He is also able to make the tremendous assumption that ultimate reality is benign, a Christian view that can certainly be found in some other religions. Not all religions, however, have seen reality in that way.

[A basic approach, adopted by Hick, is to consign all contentious issues to the realm of 'myth'. He says: 'We can identify the various systems of religious thought as complex myths whose truth or untruth consists in the appropriateness or inappropriateness of the practical dispositions which they tend to evoke.'[8] The Christian doctrine of the Incarnation would be a good example of a 'myth'. It is of particular concern to Hick since clearly the doctrine that God became incarnate in Jesus is the major source of Christian claims to truth at the expense of other religions. However much tolerance and respect there may be for them, the doctrine suggests that in the end Christians have had a revelation of the nature of God which is unique and according to which other religions have to be judged. This is precisely what pluralism opposes. Hick, however, wishes to retain a notion of objective and transcendent reality while ruling out such exclusive claims. The only way this can be done is by making ultimate reality so far removed from us and our understanding that religions fail in effect to get a grip on it. They are highly fallible. [The more that religions are shown to be constituted by humanly constructed concepts, the more God recedes beyond the horizon of even a limited understanding. The same noumenal reality evokes different forms of awareness in different religions, together with what Hick terms 'parallel salvific transformation' of

human life.[9] He argues 'that the great post-axial faiths constitute different ways of experiencing, conceiving and living in relation to an ultimate divine Reality which transcends all our varied views of it'.[10]

[The Real can recede beyond our comprehension. Just how radical
Hick's position is can be seen when he says of the Real in itself that 'it
cannot be said to be one or many, person or thing, substance or process,
good or evil, purposive or non-purposive'.[11] None of our normal
descriptions can apply literally to, as he puts it, 'the unexperiencable
ground of that realm'. His point is that the phenomenal world, the
world as humans experience it, is structured by our conceptual frame-
works, but the noumenal ground is not. Nevertheless he still wants to
claim that in the case of Christianity, the love and justice of the heavenly Father is an authentic manifestation of the Real, just as the consciousness and bliss of Brahman is. The Real in its transcendence can
only be experienced in many inadequate, finite ways.

The advantage of this analysis from the point of view of pluralism is
that it grounds all religions (or at least the favoured, 'respectable' ones)
in Reality. It manages to suggest that however inadequate they may be
in the face of transcendence, they somehow all equally reflect something
of ultimate truth. They are all grounded in the same way. Yet the great
problem with Kantian views of reality is that they can easily appear to
make noumenal reality seem redundant. If all we can have are concepts
of reality, what is the sense of trying to envisage the nature of reality as
it is in itself? For Kant, this was not so much a problem, since he did not
suggest that there could be alternative views of reality. Human experience may be structured by the concepts we possess of space, time and
cause, to mention only a few. Once, however, the split between
noumenal and phenomenal reality, reality in itself, and reality for us, is
made, the possibility of alternative phenomenal realities can become a
threat to our whole way of talking of concepts and reality. We can then
merely be confronted with alternative conceptual schemes, such as
religions, and no possible criteria with we which we could choose
between them without begging the question. Hick's appeal to so-called
'salvific criteria' suggests that what is common to all religions (again of
the pre-selected kind) is 'the transformation of human existence from
self-centredness to Reality-centredness'.[12] [Yet he is assuming that it is
possible somehow to stand outside all religions and apply a common
criterion, even though the pluralistic hypothesis suggests that that will
always be impossible.]

Although Hick wishes to be a realist, his pluralism inevitably leads to a downgrading of the role of Reality in our thinking. If Reality is beyond our comprehension and our concepts inadequate, how can we go on being committed to the truth of any religion? Hick expects Christians to acknowledge that Christian understanding is misleading. God is not really a Father, or even a person, or indeed personal at all. God is not really good or just, as we conceive these qualities. The notion that Jesus was in any sense Son of God is a myth. God in fact is not God but 'the Real'. Yet the Real is not really singular rather than plural, impersonal rather than personal. It has receded into a realm about which nothing can be said with confidence. In what sense, though, can religion be grounded in something which though infinite and transcendent, can give rise to apparently contradictory insights?

Even the notion of transcendence can be empty. It is a theoretical term which provides a space in which we can compare different understandings of what grounds reality. To reify the Transcendent and regard it as a Ground beyond all grounds is to try to find a commonality between different religions which is simply a stipulation. Notions of divinity, of God, of gods, of the Absolute, and so on can all be subsumed under the concept of the transcendent and thus compared. They are all attempts to deal with the same problem. Yet to assume that because the problem is the same, there is one solution, and that all these attempts are really concerned with the same entity is very optimistic. Because all religions talk of the transcendent, that does not mean there is one thing called the Transcendent (or the Real) which all religions are about. The fallacy involved in such reasoning should be clear. Basic disagreements will remain even if pluralists illegitimately narrow the scope of what is to count as a relevant religion.

Ideas about the nature of the self and of God can differ to the extent that Buddhism does not have room for the notion of a continuing self, or of a Creator who is an explanation for the existence of the world and is in relationship with it. As one writer puts it: 'Buddhism has no room for a God who desires justice, forgives sins and enters into a relation with people as a "partner" in history.'[13] If we are then told that the Real transcends all such issues, so that there is neither a Creator nor not a Creator, we are left with the impression that the ground of religions is a ground in such a remote way that it becomes unclear even what is meant by a ground. The connection between the nature of the Real and the claims of, for instance, Christianity itself becomes something that transcends our understanding. How can we even be sure that Christianity is grounded in the Real? Hick seems very certain that religious manifestations like devil worship could not possibly be so grounded but one wonders how, given his presuppositions, he could possibly know. Even if he claims that he is merely putting forward a hypothesis to account for the facts about religions, he is being very selective about which data he chooses to count as relevant. Without some clear characterization of the nature of the Real, it would be impossible to draw any firm conclusions.

4 Forms of Realism in Religion

Hick is emphatic in his belief in the goodness of reality. He writes: 'In thus affirming the good, or to-be-rejoiced-in nature of the Real, the great world faiths are forms of cosmic optimism.'[14] He amplifies this by saying that 'a non-realist interpretation of religion inevitably entails a profound pessimism'. His reasoning is that all the world faiths see our present life as part of a wider whole. They do not look for the realizing of our potential in this life alone. Religion is not just about the lucky few who find fulfilment in this life but about the limitless better possibilities that await everyone. Hick writes:

> It is only if this universe is the creation or expression of an ultimate overarching benign reality, and is such that the spiritual project of our existence continues in some form beyond this present life, that it is possible to expect a fulfilment that can justify the immense pain and travail of the journey.

The reality of a life beyond this one is thus crucial, as is the nature of the Reality in which all things are grounded. 'Non-realists' can never reinterpret these beliefs in away that retains their inherent optimism. We cannot hope for something that we recognize is an illusion, a picture or a myth. Religion ultimately has to be grounded not in human understanding but in the very nature of things. Yet the problem is that while Hick wishes to proclaim just this, he has all but made such claims impossible. He adopts a so-called 'critical realism' which is opposed on the one hand to 'naive realism' and on the other to non-realism. It might appear, then, to comprise a sensible middle course. Things are, however not so simple. For Hick, a 'naive religious realist' is analogous with a naive realist in the field of perception. The latter believes that things are as they appear to be and that common sense is right. Similarly in the field of religion some assume 'that what is spoken about in the religious language that one has learned is just as described in this language, understood literally'.[16] Such naive realists might also be termed fundamentalists in that they would be attracted to a literal understanding of what the Bible, or comparable sacred text, says, rather than understanding the whole or parts of it as metaphor, or myth.

Hick is concerned, however, with more than the meaning of texts. He broadens his use of the term 'naive realism', to include assumptions that 'the divine reality is just as spoken about in the language of some tradition'.[17] Any Christian who believes in the truth of Christianity, in a way that excludes other religions, can then be classified as a naive realist, who should in fact be more 'critical'. Anyone who says that Christianity is true can thus by sleight of hand be aligned with the most extreme forms of fundamentalism. If someone claims that the Christian God, the Creator of the world, actually exists, the immediate response can be that this is to put one's faith illegitimately in the assertions of one tradition. Somehow we are expected to abstract ourselves from one tradition and see the character of the Real which grounds the tradition but which also grounds others. Yet Hick would be the first to acknowledge the impossibility of this.

Hick is also vigorously opposed to what he terms 'the religious non- or anti-realism which rejects the idea of transcendent divine reality'.[18] His claim is that this is indistinguishable from naturalism, which views humans wholly in the context of the physical world. In other words non-realism would not seem very different from atheism, particularly in the denial by both of any eternal destiny for human beings. From the point of view of the believer in some form of transcendent, spiritual reality, the two are indistinguishable. Yet although non-realism and atheism have arrived at a similar destination, they have reached it by different routes. The true atheist denies the reality of God, but in so doing tacitly accepts that the idea of God's existence is no more problematic than the existence of anything else. It is just a matter of fact that there is no God. Anti-realists, however, are trying to reinterpret religion and are typically reluctant to take the notion of the existence of God at face value. Instead they question what belief in God amounts to. When it is unclear what is meant by God, a simple denial of any divine reality becomes as problematic as a simple assertion that God exists. It may then be held that even traditional believers do not in fact refer to a transcendent God but mean something different by the 'reality' of God. The fact that they would vehemently deny this may be a problem for this approach, but it is distinctive from a denial of God's reality.

Atheism is an assertion about the real character of the world as it is independent of anyone's conceptions of it. As such, it would appear to be itself a typical realist position. A denial of something's existence, like an assertion of existence, is surely an attempt to refer to the nature of an objective world. It does not necessarily constitute a non-realist position but rather the opposite. William Alston makes a point that is often made. He says: 'Surely, if one is committed to the proposition that there are no such things as Xs, that counts as being nonrealist about X, in the strongest possible way.'[19] Yet it depends on the grounds on which the assertion is made. The position can merge into anti-realism about Xs, if it is suggested that all talk about Xs is really to be reinterpreted as being about something else. Reductionist positions can be seen as anti-realist. If, however, what is at stake is a simple denial of something's existence, even though it may be conceded that it could have existed, the position would seem quintessentially realist. If you claim that there is a Loch Ness monster, and cite alleged evidence, such as photographs, and I deny its existence, I am not being non-realist about the monster and its ilk. I am merely trying to talk about what is in fact the case independently of people's conceptions of it. I am not treating reality as a human construction but as something to be discovered. Metaphysical realism, as a general position, is concerned with the objective character of reality, independent of judgements, beliefs, concepts, language and so on.[20] An anti-realist would on the other hand always change the subject from what a belief is about to the general character of the belief. The belief in a Loch Ness monster would have to be reinterpreted as, say, an expression of some deep human need, rather than a claim about something in the loch.

When, therefore, John Hick talks in the same breath about non-realism and anti-realism, he must be careful not to run together two distinct positions. So-called non-realism can be seen as a species of realism, if it is a simple denial of the reality of something. Naturalist views themselves can be realist in that they are making claims about the character of reality. In so far as non-realism implies a claim to truth independent of anyone's conceptions, it is in fact realism. Yet it might entail a cosmic pessimism as great as that of anti-realism. It is not, therefore, realism that brings optimism, but particular realist beliefs. Hick must therefore find himself having to argue for the truth of some view as against others. In other words, we see once again that he is in the same logical position as any exclusivist. The difference merely lies in which beliefs are being advocated. Hick chooses not to defend any belief in the unique divine nature of Christ, but would see it as culturally conditioned. He does on the other hand believe that in the end all will be well, and that there is a life beyond death. Somehow, such beliefs are not culturally conditioned. He may argue that they are common to a wider range of religious believers than an allegiance to Christ. He cannot, however, claim that they are common to all religions, any more than he can claim that all people accept religion. At some point even Hick has to accept confrontation and contradiction since he is making claims about the nature of reality that others are denying.

Hick's contempt for 'naive realism' in the end removes the right of Christianity or of any other religion to claim truth. Once particular religious outlooks are seen as culturally conditioned, in part or whole, the 'Real' recedes beyond our grasp. A 'Real' that is revealed in many conflicting ways would seem as useless and impossible to grasp as no Real at all. The running together of the literalist approach of the fundamentalist with the Christian claim that Christ is a unique revelation of the nature of God puts a big question mark over the right of Christianity to claim any truth. If we can never in principle determine how much belief is culturally and socially conditioned we must face the real prospect that perhaps all of it is. The same argument applies to any religion. Hick's position will not so much raise the status of the great world faiths as reduce them all to impotence. He maintains that his 'critical realism' holds that religious experience and belief is not wholly projection or illusion.[21] Instead it constitutes what he terms 'a range of cognitive responses, varying from culture to culture, to the presence of a transcendent reality or realities'. A realism that cannot even be clear as to whether it is confronting one reality or many, and which only succeeds in casting doubt on whatever conception of reality we do have, would seem indistinguishable from a general scepticism.

How then can we understand the fact of different religions? We must think that the disagreement matters, unless we give up the concept of truth. If disagreement in religion is of little account (as long as we learn to live with each other), it seems an inescapable conclusion that what is believed in the sphere of religion does not matter at all. The inevitable conclusion is that it is equally of little account if we reject all religion. The problem is not just that we are faced with people who differ from us. Even if all religions are somehow reconciled, there will still be disagreement with atheists, or those who just do not wish to be religious. Hick might achieve agreement between one set of people but he would still find many who would still disagree. The problem, then is not disagreement but how we can seek to establish truth, and how we treat those who still repudiate what we say. The desire for mutual respect and tolerance meets the second concern. It should not influence us in our attempts to discover what is true.

A realist stress on the distinction between beliefs and what they are about should serve to remind us not just that others may be mistaken or have partial knowledge, but that that is our own predicament too. If we care about truth we cannot give up some of our most important beliefs just to accommodate others. Equally, we should not fail to take seriously their respect for truth as they see it. We cannot all be right, but it would also be fallacious to conclude, as Hick seems to, that none of us could be. Yet religions are not monolithic bodies of belief which are either completely right or completely wrong. It is possible to see overlaps between religions and for one religion to learn from another without being compromised. Even if it is believed that God has been revealed in a special way to one set of people, it does not follow that the others know nothing about God. It does not follow, either, that all revelation becomes so contaminated with a cultural overlay that no one can gain knowledge of God. Neo-Kantian views of that sort in fact make all knowledge in every field impossible, since by definition all reality is put beyond our grasp (even that of the physical world).

The giving up of claims to knowledge of God, perhaps on the grounds that it is not universally shared, is fraught with danger for religion. Hick wants the adherents of the various religions to retain their systems of belief. Yet how can one retain the view that 'the gods are different authentic personae of the Real',[22] while recognizing how far they are from sharing its character? The more distant the 'Real' is from the apparent object of worship, the less easy it will be to continue to worship. A proper relationship with a loving heavenly Father, for example, would seem impossible if that idea is simultaneously recognized as a cultural construction. The problem with critical realism is the distance it can create between reality and us. In another context (talking about the concept of pain) Wittgenstein said: 'A nothing would serve just as well as a something about which nothing could be said.'[23] A 'Real' that somehow floats free of all religions will soon find itself in a similar position. Unless it can be shown how we obtain any knowledge of whatever divine reality there may be, a corollary of the neo-Kantian approach to religion would seem to be that there can be no direct contact with God. At the very least, we can never distinguish between, say, God's action and what appears to us to be God's action. The whole reduction of revelation to a predominantly cultural category underlines this.] - *Trigg says we can draw line. He also says this is impossible*

Once the distinctive claims of any religion are compromised in this way, the religion itself is weakened. Belief cannot be separated from a conception of truth, as we have seen. Yet once it is suggested that such truth is unobtainable, it must logically be impossible to go on believing. A 'pluralist' view of the fact of different religions must in the end question their separate rights to claim truth. It will do this not by piecemeal rational criticism of separate claims, but by a generalized suspicion that no religion can gain a grasp on reality. That must be to suggest that the believers of each religion have no right to believe it.

Notes

1   *Christianity and the World Religions*, p. xviii.
2   *Ibid.*, p. xiv.
3   D'Costa, 'The impossibility of a pluralist view of religions', p. 225.
4   *Ibid.*, p. 226.
5   Hick, '"Religious pluralism": a reply to Gavin D'Costa', p. 163.
6   *An Interpretation of Religion*, p. 2.
7   *Ibid.*, p. 2.
8   *Ibid.*, p. 353.
9   *Ibid.*, p. 15.
10 *Ibid.*, p. 235.
11 *Ibid.*, p. 246.
12 *Ibid.*, p. 36.
13 Vroom, *No Other Gods*, p. 38.
14 *Disputed Questions*, p. 12.
15 *Ibid.*
16 *Ibid.*, p. 6.
17 *Ibid.*, p. 7.

18 *Ibid.*
19 *A Realist Conception of Truth*, p. 65.
20 See my *Reality at Risk*.
21 *An Interpretation of Religion*, p. 175.
22 *Ibid.*, p. 275.
23 *Philosophical Investigations*, #304.

4

Are Science and Religion
Equally Rational?

1 The Relationship between Science and Religion

In chapter 2 we have already encountered the view that 'science' is to be regarded as the epitome of human rationality. It gives us knowledge through its distinctive empirical method, and anything else has no right to claim objective truth in the scientific sense. Such views implicitly appeal to a very narrow view of science, in which physics is regarded as the model. They restrict what can be regarded as 'literal' truth to the knowledge produced by the scientific laboratory, or at least to what can be accepted as consistent with it. It is perhaps hardly surprising that such an arbitrary limitation of what can count as human knowledge and the proper realm of human rationality has led to a 'postmodern' reaction against the possibility of any global rationality.

In comparison with the glorification of science, religion has seemed so different that it has often appeared to be the product of anything but reason. A strong contrast has been drawn between faith and reason, and the implication has often been that once scientific method was applied to an examination of the claims of any religion, they would soon wither away. 'Facts' were the province of science. They were what humans could agree about and could be verified through the procedures of the physical sciences. As a result, religion, the area of so much controversy and apparently insoluble disagreement, was unable to claim truth. If, then, it had any function, it was merely to express attitudes to the world, rather than to say what the world was like. It was consigned to the sphere of 'values'. Religion may reveal what we think important, but in so doing it would be saying something about us and not the world. It could not claim anything distinctive about reality, since such a claim would immediately be subject to judgement by the processes of science.

References to anything transcendent or supernatural were then ruled out. What was inaccessible to science could not exist.

Many contemporary theologians appear reluctant to allow religious claims much cognitive content. The reason, perhaps, is that if factual claims are firmly within the province of science, it may seem easier for them not to make any. Religion will then not be in the position of possibly being proved mistaken. It will avoid a collision course with science, if it is seen as primarily a symbolic enterprise. Anyone could then express a 'truth' (in the sense that Aesop's fables express truths) while not actually making assertions about what is true in the world. It is tempting for some to accept the olive branch offered by scientists who sometimes suggest that religion and science are each concerned with totally different aspects of life. The views of the later Wittgenstein have also had their effect on the debate about science and religion. If meaning is to be identified with use, and language is seen as being used in a different way to express faith or make scientific claims, then each can be understood as operating in different spheres. They are parts of different 'forms of life' and associated with different practices. Statements cannot be torn from the context which gives them their meaning and then compared with each other. Yet the emphasis on local practice suggests that in the end any idea of reasoning with a universal applicability will have to be challenged.

Both science and religion become impoverished if they lose hold on claims which ought to be accepted universally. Yet if they are both asserting truth, the question of the relation between them inevitably arises. One advantage of stressing their different logical character is that they then need never find themselves in a position of mutual confrontation. There need be no conflict if each is regarded as 'true' only within the confines of a particular language-game, any more than there can be a conflict between the rules of cricket and those of football. They are just different. A similar view has been taken up, in a less sophisticated philosophical manner, by those who say that religion and science are complementary because they answer different questions. Science may tell us 'how' and religion 'why'. This may seem plausible since they do each have a different focus of interest. The issue is, however, whether the two can be kept entirely separate. Telling how something has evolved may explain why it is as it is. This is often true in the study of the natural selection and development of organisms. There are, it is true, 'limit-questions' such as why there is anything rather than nothing.[1] Even though such questions are beyond the scope of science to answer, it by no means follows that they are irrelevant to science. Showing why the universe exists could go some way to explaining how it has to operate. To take the example of the so-called 'anthropic principle' in physics, which links the constitution of the universe to the existence of humans,[2] one conclusion that could be drawn is that if the purpose of the universe is to produce human beings, it has to be of a certain size and age. A younger, smaller universe could not have produced the conditions necessary for life. No doubt the idea that the universe's only purpose is to produce us is too strong an interpretation of the principle, but the example does show that how things have developed can never be totally distinct from questions of purpose.

The blurring of the questions 'how?' and 'why?' would be challenged by those scientists who believe that science must be purified of all teleology. Modern science has certainly been concerned with mechanisms rather than purposes. It will of necessity see chance events where theology can see divine intervention. This lies behind the idea that religion is concerned with values and science with facts. That view, however, treats values as whatever humans happen to take seriously. As a result, purposes and values have to be given a human origin, and the view is avowedly atheistic. The ascription of purpose to the processes of reality, rather than to our attitudes to them, could be a rational recognition of the way things are. This, however, would be vehemently denied by those who see no possible reason for any collaboration between religion and science. Richard Dawkins, for example, says flatly: 'Scientific beliefs are supported by evidence, and they get results. Myths and faiths are not and do not.'[3] He later on refuses to accept the relevance of questions about 'why' rather than just 'how'.[4] He complains about the 'unspoken but never justified implication that since science is unable to answer "why" questions, there must be some other discipline that is qualified to answer them'. The suggestion is that this implication is 'quite illogical'.

While it is right to point out that not all questions have to have an answer, it does not follow that because science cannot answer a question, there is no answer. Dawkins is clearly defining what counts as evidence and what counts as getting results, in such a way that it is only science that can rest on such evidence and get that kind of result. This is to fall back on the narrow scientific view of rationality that appeals to prejudice about the power of science rather than to issues about the nature of reality. His position is that 'the universe we observe "*Open Brief*" has precisely those properties we should expect if there is no design, no purpose, no evil and no good, nothing but blind pitiless indifference'.[5] However controversial such a bleak view may be, at least it is making assertions about the nature of reality, about how the universe is actually constituted. Dawkins is not talking about his own subjective reactions to it, or the way in which things are conceived in one form of life. His statement is intended to be about the character of the world, and it is one which, if true, would remove any real justification for religion.

2   The God of the Gaps

Questions about the rationality of religious belief are forced back to issues about what there is. Such issues must at least partly be within the province of science. Yet how far science can adjudicate on disputes between itself and other disciplines is a vexed point. The problem of the scope and purpose of science can only be encountered from the standpoint of the philosophy of science. Arguments about the general relationship of science and religion will be quintessentially philosophical arguments. Advocates of naturalism, for instance, are upholding a philosophical, even a metaphysical position about the status of science which has profound implications for the position of religion. For example, Drees, referring to the domain of the natural sciences as 'the natural world',[6] insists that 'the natural world is the whole of reality that we know of and interact with'. A corollary of this that he draws is that 'no supernatural or spiritual realm distinct from the natural world shows up within our natural world, not even in the mental life of humans'. This dismisses any form of dualism between mind and body, and resolutely denies the possibility of any gaps in physical processes which might provide space for divine intervention. Any idea of a 'God of the gaps' has long been thought unsatisfactory, not least because the gaps concerned may be epistemological rather than metaphysical. They may indicate a failure of understanding which scientific progress might be expected to redress. As the Oxford physicist, C. A. Coulson, wrote in the 1950s: 'There is no God of the gaps to take over those strategic places where science fails: and the reason is that gaps of this sort have the unpreventable habit of shrinking.'[7] His view was that God had to be in the whole of Nature, not just parts of it.[8] 'God' he said, 'must be found within the known and not the unknown.'

More recently, when chaos theory seems to acknowledge intrinsic limits on our ability to predict, the problem has arisen whether unpredictability indicates a real openness in reality or just ignorance on our part.[9] John Polkinghorne, a physicist turned theologian, has pointed out that, in quantum mechanics, physicists like Heisenberg moved from epistemology to ontology. From the fact that limits were placed on our ability to measure both the momentum and position of an electron, we could assume something about the character of reality.[10] He suggests that we do the same with chaos theory. For Polkinghorne, ontology mirrors epistemology. He writes of chaos theory: 'Aligning epistemology and ontology as closely as possible to each other favours an open rather than a deterministic interpretation of the unpredicabilities all acknowledge to be present.'[11]

This is an appealing move, since it may be that if we cannot know something, the reason is that there is nothing to know. Not all gaps can be closed. Nevertheless chaos theory is itself normally considered deterministic. Just because a minute alteration in initial conditions can be undetectable, even though it may be amplified to have major effects, there may be a causal process at work. Many would hold that chaos theory tends to show how finely tuned mechanisms can be, not that they are not mechanisms. Polkinghorne acknowledges that his own position is controversial, but bases his claim on a firmly realist position, saying that because scientists are realists 'they believe that what we can or cannot know is a reliable guide to what is actually the case'.[13] As a result, he believes that unpredictability is an indication of 'ontological openness'. This is, however, a questionable interpretation of realism. The independence of reality from our conceptions might, on the contrary, lead us to conclude that there can be no link at all between human limitations and the character of reality. Why should our apparent shortcomings reflect ontological gaps, rather than merely our own ignorance?

Polkinghorne is not afraid to draw large theological conclusions from his linkage of epistemology and ontology. Because he can see an open system, where others may only see our ignorance, he can claim that 'There is much cloudy unpredictable process throughout the whole of the physical world. It is a coherent possibility that God interacts with the history of his creation by means of "information input" into its open physical process . . . Mere mechanism is dead and a more subtle and supple universe is accessible to the providential interaction of the Creator.'[14]

Polkinghorne thus draws radically different conclusions from Dawkins out of contemporary science. The latter sees scientific method as ruling religion out. The former sees ontological gaps opening up in our current physical understanding of the world, and sees in them an opportunity for the providential action of God. How far, though, could reference to God ever be allowable within a scientific world-view? The view that there are gaps in physical processes for divine action certainly challenges views about the integrity of science. The obvious difficulty is the danger of relying on gaps in our knowledge. As Coulson indicated, a perennial difficulty in seizing on a current physical theory to support a particular theological position is that science can move on, and subsequent theories may not be so hospitable to theology. Polkinghorne claims, of course, that he is talking about reality and not our knowledge of it. Any view, however, which relies on contemporary scientific theory is by definition relying on a state of human knowledge that may be transient. It is certainly highly fallible.

Arguments about the relevance of the so-called Big Bang to Creation also illustrate the problems about using scientific theories which happen to be held at the moment to bolster theological conceptions. The idea of God as Creator is fundamental for any monotheistic religion, and a refusal to accept that theology can offer any kind of explanation for the existence and nature of the physical world must be to give up the notion of Creation, even in the most symbolic and attenuated sense. Theologians have often talked of creation from nothing (*ex nihilo*) and it may seem as if the physical theory of the Big Bang describes the mechanism of how this occurred. Yet theology should not hope to weight the scales of a debate within physics. Certainly such a move provides hostages to fortune. Stephen Hawking, for example, can even imagine that he has dispensed with the need for God when he puts forward a theory about the beginning of the Universe which rejects the notion of a singularity or an absolute beginning. Hawking says:

> There would be no singularities at which the laws of science broke down and no edge of space-time at which one would have to appeal to God or some new law to set the boundary conditions for space-time . . . The universe would be completely self-contained and not affected by any-

thing outside itself. It would neither be created or destroyed. It would just BE.[15]

This kind of scientific theory would still be unable to say why there is anything at all, but it does offer an alternative, albeit a contentious one, to the idea of a definite beginning, which would need God as a cause. In fact, such an invocation of God seems a classic example from the scientific standpoint of appealing to the God of the gaps. God is in fact being appealed to as one scientific cause among many possible ones, rather than as the ultimate explanation of everything.[Theology is being resorted to merely for want of an adequate scientific explanation. There must be something incongruous about an argument between theologians and physicists about the role of a quantum vacuum.] It is often emphasized in theology that God is just not one more cause among many, any more than He is just one object among many.

It might seem, therefore, as if theology and science ought to resist the temptation of trespassing on each other's territory. That would mean that Hawking was as wrong to draw an anti-theological conclusion from science as any theologian might be in 'proving' the existence of God from science. There are certainly dangers for theology in getting involved in scientific debates. In the same way, scientists can often look ridiculous in drawing large conclusions about the non-existence of God, purely as a result of the current stage of scientific debate. Yet even so, it is dangerous to decide that there are just different kinds of explanation so that science and theology have no mutual relevance. That is the first step to conceding that religion, and theology, as rational reflection about religion, are not dealing with reality, at least in the sense that science does. If, however, religious claims are intended to be about the nature of the world (holding not least that it is God's world), there must be the possibility that scientific and religious claims may clash or even serve to support each other.

3   Methodology and Metaphysics

Arguing from the nature of the world to the existence and character of God has always been a controversial exercise, as we shall see when we discuss natural theology in chapter 9. Yet in recent years the issue of the relationship of science and theology has been put in sharper focus, because the relation of science itself to reality has been more and more questioned.[16] While science retains considerable intellectual authority, its own philosophical basis has become more problematic. Some have seen in this an opportunity for religion to re-establish its credentials. When modernity was linked to the assumptions of the Enlightenment with its stress on the role of human reason, and hence of science as its expression, it seemed that any 'postmodern' reaction could only help the cause of religion. Thus Diogenes Allen is able to assert that 'in a post modern world Christianity is intellectually relevant'.[17] It might seem that anything that reduced the domination of science might inevitably to strengthen the position of religion. Yet the currents of postmodernity run much deeper. They not only begin to sweep away our trust in science. They make our grasp on any conception of a real world very tenuous. Postmodernists make an assault on 'meta-narratives' and distrust any detached reason that can raise itself above its immediate social setting. The very notion of science being able to give a true account of the world is challenged. One writer on the philosophy of science and postmodernism says: 'The idea that there is a "natural world" for natural science to be about, entirely distinct from the ways human beings as knowers and agents interact with it, must be . . . abandoned.'[18] His advice is that we should not 'think of knowers as featureless and abstract reasoners, but rather as situated agents with an inescapably partial position'.

There was a time when physical science was thought to be able to offer something like a 'God's-eye' view of reality, in a way that implicitly replaced the human need for God. At first sight, the humbling of science may appear welcome to religion. Yet the conclusion to be drawn is that if there is no God's eye view to be had, all global claims to truth must be rejected. The very idea of God is clearly going to be the first casualty. Certainly the possibility of religion claiming any objective truth for itself seems far away.

Science itself needs a metaphysical underpinning. It cannot be taken for granted that scientists are indulging in anything more than the local practices of a particular group of people. For science to matter, we must assume that it is dealing with a world that is independent of our conceptions of it. Different scientific theories do not point to different worlds, but are in varying ways trying to account for the same world. If there is one, objective world, religious conceptions themselves presumably are dealing with the nature of the same reality. 'Naturalists' would restrict what could count as part of reality. Yet if they merely try to relate reality to what is accessible to human science, they are ultimately defining the nature of reality in terms of human capabilities. Science may not be as contextually restricted as postmodernists would have us believe, but it is the product of human reason. It could never provide a satisfactory basis for a global conception of reality, since it all too easily reflects the intrinsic limitations of the human predicament.

If science and religion each make claims about the same world, at what level could we expect them to interact? Religious claims cannot confront scientific claims directly in the scientific arena, without becoming something else. So-called 'creation science' is presumably doing just that. Religion is not science and even if they relate to the same world, that does not mean that their methods or presuppositions have to be identical. The authority of the Church has too often been invoked in matters that should have been left to the judgement of scientists, in the same way that Marxist-Leninist philosophy was allowed at times to determine which scientific theories were acceptable. Yet there is a difference between a proper concern about external interference in the conduct of science, and the much stronger assumption that somehow science holds the key to the nature of reality. Resistance to ecclesiastical control has historically led to the view that the domain of science was the concern of science alone. This, however, could easily slide into a principle of methodological positivism, which may have underpinned the growth of modern science. It does not permit the scientist to refer to forces beyond the physical world to explain its internal processes. This may seem an essential part of science, since too easy an assumption that something was the work of fairies (or even of divine action) would make a mockery of any scientific search for the underlying mechanisms at work in physical processes.

The problem is that such a methodology can be easily transmuted into a metaphysical principle. It is one thing to say that what scientists do not look for they will not find. It is another to hold that there can in principle be no part of reality outside the reach of science (and contemporary science at that). This can be crucial in the relationship between science and religion, because it can be made to appear as if science is unremittingly hostile to non-physical influences in general and divine intervention in the affairs of this world in particular. When the physical world was seen by science as one large closed mechanism, like a clock, it seemed as if a scientific vision could leave no room for God. Deists in the eighteenth century thought that perhaps a Being set the mechanism going, but the Christian view of a God in relationship with us here and

Deism

now seemed impossible. Contemporary physics certainly does not drive one to that conclusion, since the emphasis is much more on open, unpredictable systems. Many, though, feel instinctively that the notion of God interfering in the processes of this world in an intermittent manner still goes against the most basic assumptions of science. Limitations on our knowledge, they will say, should not be taken as an indication of real gaps in reality. This may seem a similar point to the warning against theology seizing on epistemological gaps. The argument, however, is at this point not just that theology runs risks when it gambles on the future progress (or lack of progress) of science. It is the full-blooded metaphysical question of whether science could in any circumstances accept the intervention of God. Is science of its very nature anti-theistic? It might seem so if it will never accept the justification for an appeal to entities beyond the scope of physical laws. Since metaphysics and epistemology are so often confused, it is crucial to stress the difference. Paradoxically, Drees uses precisely this distinction to express his refusal to pass from an inability to discover physical mechanisms to issues about God. He says:

> Claims about openness in complex processes rely, in my view, in many cases from an unwarranted move from epistemological considerations to ontological ones: unpredictability does not imply indeterminacy or openness to non-natural influences, either from humans or God. Such an influence hidden in unpredictable or unobserved but deterministic processes would be at odds with the integrity of science.[19]

Reliance on ignorance as a basis for claims about the nature of reality is a precarious, if not contradictory, way of achieving knowledge. As Drees says about religious apologists seizing on apparent limitations on our knowledge, 'the absence of evidence does not count as evidence of absence'. Scientists who say that there is no evidence for, say, a disease having a particular cause, should not be understood as denying that the disease has that cause. What they should be taken to mean is that we do not as yet know. Only a very naive positivist could confuse present evidence about what is so with what is actually the case. Yet Drees is not counselling caution. He is himself making claims about what can and cannot be counted as part of reality. Non-physical forces are ruled out, not just methodologically, but metaphysically. Drees is quite honest about this. He says 'My naturalism is a metaphysical position. It goes beyond the details of insights offered by the various sciences as an attempt to present a general view of the reality in which we live and of which we are a part.[20]

His strategy is to stay close to the outlook offered by the sciences, rather than to impose *a priori* metaphysical categories on them. In this he champions a common philosophical position, although it is one that is not always admitted to be metaphysical. One minor curiosity of Drees's position is that he accepts the possibility of asking so-called limit questions about the whole naturalistic framework, and allows that appeal could be made to a transcendent God as an ultimate explanation as to why there is anything. This is certainly not within the spirit of naturalism, as usually conceived. It poses the question why so great a breach in the 'integrity of science' should be allowed as to allow reference to anything transcendent.

There are also problems from a theological point of view. As Drees says, 'Even if one were to accept the mystery of existence as a ground of belief in a transcendent non-temporal God, such a philosophical concept of God is fairly empty.'[21] The perennial problem with a deism which admits God as creator but refuses to allow any further divine role in the conduct of the universe is that such a God seems all too easily expendable because totally irrelevant to human life. The position of such a God would be not unlike that of a constitutional monarch whose role has become more and more attenuated. He is Head of State but not allowed even a nominal role in the conduct of affairs, and is certainly not allowed, say, to appoint or dismiss a Prime Minister. Once other mechanisms are introduced and the Speaker of the Parliament or some such dignitary is given constitutional powers formally held by the Sovereign, the declaration of a republic would seem a small step. In the same way, a God denied any part even in the sustaining of physical processes can be dispensed with and no one would notice the difference. Dress's naturalism in fact makes the appeal to God pointless. By definition, what can be explained, can be explained by science.

4 Science and Theism

Yet science itself still stands in need of legitimation. By admitting that his position is metaphysical, Drees draws attention to the fact that we can only do science within a metaphysical framework which already incorporates a view about the nature of reality. Modern science has to assume a great deal before it gets to work, not least that there is a reality to investigate. Drees admits that in his naturalistic account, 'reality is assumed rather than explained'.[22] The very emphasis on the provisional character of scientific understanding draws attention to the gap between it and the world we are attempting to describe. The realist assumptions of science undergird its claim to our attention. The assumption that there is one world with a single set of characteristics, rather than many alternative worlds, is also important. The whole of science works on the presupposition that results can be replicated, that what holds good in Washington from a physical point of view applies in Moscow too. That is why science can be genuinely international. It assumes that its results can be generalized so that laws apparently in force in our minute part of the universe also hold elsewhere.

We can go from the known to the unknown, from what we have experienced to what lies beyond experience. This encapsulates the problem of induction which empiricist philosophers, like Hume, have always found insuperable. This is because it cannot be solved from within science. The very existence of science as a viable enterprise demands that we form a view of the reality that is its object of study. It has to be taken for granted that the world as investigated by science is ordered and structured. This is not a fact that can be discovered through science, since we need a philosophical assumption about the similarity of the unknown to the known. Otherwise, we could never generalize our scientific findings and assume that all segments of reality were equally uniform and comprehensible even if unobservable. Apparent order may in the last resort be illusory. We still need a basis for our confidence that the discoveries of science can be applied in different times and places with confidence. The applicability of mathematics to the physical world itself illustrates how an underlying rationale appears to be built in to the fabric of the world. It should, after all, seem extraordinary that symbols produced by the human mind could serve to unlock some of the deepest mysteries of physical nature and grant us a tremendous power over it, even to the point of being able to engineer complete devastation. There can, of course, be anti-realist interpretations of mathematics but they seem powerless to explain why through mathematics we are actually able to control the physical world. There appears to be an order inherent in things which, moreover, can be understood by the human mind. Science would be impossible without this human ability to grasp the way in which physical reality is structured.

There does seem to be a recognizable rationality about scientific method, with its willingness to be corrected by new evidence and fresh discoveries. Yet this is surely because scientists are being ultimately constrained, whatever role their own judgements play, by an independent reality that is not the product of anyone's imagination nor wholly subject to our will. Their rationality in the last resort depends on a more basic metaphysical rationality displayed by the inherent ordered structure of the universe. This is a particular example of the fact that rationality has to be constrained by how things are. A rationality that becomes detached from the world would be kept in check by nothing. There would be definition be nothing beyond it which could vindicate it or show it to be in error. Yet a rationality that was its own master would be worthless, since when there are competing theories, any would be as good as any other, as long as each was internally coherent. That is why it is so easy for anti-realist conceptions of science to collapse into sheer relativism.

Science does not just assume the existence of an ordered world, but also presupposes that it does not have to be as it is but is contingent. Otherwise it would have been sufficient for scientists to reason about what is necessary without needing to resort to observation and experiment. Experimental science would have no role. Why, though, should the world be contingent, and why should a contingent world be ordered? Why should a world that does not have to be as it is still exemplify a rationality that can be grasped by the human mind? Idealist accounts that suggest that the order is a product of the categories produced by the human mind and not a constituent element in reality merely serve to undermine science. It becomes a mere exercise in human psychology rather than a process of discovery.

One answer to the question of why reality has an inherent order is that that is just the way things are. Yet this is scarcely a weighty argument to warrant any confidence in the universal claims of science. A more substantial one is provided by the view that reality is like that because God made it like that. This is to move on from a metaphysical realism, stressing the independence of reality from our conceptions of it, to theism. The move to realism can, however, serve to explain the ordered nature of the physical universe and give us confidence that our small part of it may not be an area of order in a sea of disorder. The rationality which mathematics appears to capture may itself be an expression of the rationality of the mind of the Creator. This is a traditional view and recalls the notion of 'logos', or reason, which was so important in Greek philosophy and which came to be identified with the Christian God. Yet, as we have seen, the rational order found in the world is contingent, and theism can explain this through reference to the free creative activity of God. He was not bound by iron laws of necessity but was able to choose one kind of ordered creation rather than another. [The idea of creation from nothing leads one to expect that the world thus created would be regulated and yet contingent. It becomes reasonable to look for order, but not to anticipate the kind of order that we might find. If, though, it is the product of a Creator, rather than the chance occurrence some scientists assume, that would suggest that the natural order we appear to encounter through science is not an illusion.]

The crude view of a mechanism set in motion and then left alone could never do justice to the theistic vision of a world that is dependent on a God who may in part be seen through the natural order of things which reflects His rationality. We shall investigate in chapter 9 the problems of arguing from the world to God. At this point, the reasoning in question is not from the fact of order to a Creator, but the other way round. It may be that the idea of a Creator can give confidence to those undertaking a scientific investigation into physical processes. Indeed, science, it might be claimed, cannot gain proper legitimation in any other context. So far, then, from science being hostile to a religious view of the world, it could be said that the practice of science positively demands presumptions that can only be derived from theism. Certainly the history of the development of modern science tends to bear this out.[23]

5 Critical Realism

Could theism not only suggest that there is an order to be discovered but that human minds have a particular aptitude for understanding it? In other words can we be given any confidence that our science is reliable? Einstein's famous remark that the most incomprehensible feature of the world is its comprehensibility draws attention to the fact that the intelligibility of the world for us humans should not be taken for granted. The realist splitting of the subject and object of knowledge can appear to introduce an unbridgeable gap between us and reality. The very fact that we have to take the possibility of being mistaken seriously makes it seem more unlikely that we could be right.

If we look at the history of science, it is clear that theories can change radically. It almost seems part of the nature of science that this should be so. There can be no guarantee that any apparently rational belief is true. We are never infallible. Arthur Peacocke, for this reason, applies the same distinction between 'naive realism' and 'critical realism' to science as we have already seen employed by John Hick. Peacocke defines the former[24] as a view which 'regards scientific concepts, theories and mechanisms as literal descriptions of the natural world'. Yet anyone seeing the difference between, say, the physics of the end of the nineteenth century with that of the last years of the twentieth would find it difficult to accept that science is likely to have achieved such infallibility. How much could it change again in the next hundred years? Some, though, would find it inconceivable that we could ever discover that water was not composed of hydrogen and oxygen, and no doubt there is a gradual accumulation of reliable knowledge. It still remains true, however, that many theories may have to be revised in ways that we cannot at the moment conceive.

For this reason Peacocke prefers to talk of a 'critical realism' which 'accepts that 'the language of science . . . is fundamentally metaphorical and revisable, while nevertheless referring'.[25] He says: 'Critical realism recognises that it is still only the aim of science to depict reality and that this allows gradations in acceptance of the "truth" of scientific theories.' Such a notion is a somewhat slippery one, because there is an undeniable tension between the alleged successful reference of scientific terms and their revisability. There have been occasions in the history of science when words such as 'phlogiston' apparently referred to some substance and were later discovered not to. One aim of users of the term 'critical realism' is to apply it equally to developments in science and theology. Peacocke himself holds that a 'critical realism in theology would maintain that theological concepts and models should be regarded as partial and inadequate, but necessary and, indeed, the only ways of referring to the reality that is named as "God"'.[26] Yet just how ambiguous the notion of critical realism can be is demonstrated by Ian Barbour's use of the term. Writing about the relation of science and religion in a manner comparable to Peacocke, he says: 'As in the scientific case, I defined a critical realism that takes religious models seriously but not literally. They are neither literal descriptions of reality nor useful fictions, but human constructs that help us to interpret experience by imagining what cannot be observed.'[27]

This should be contrasted with Polkinghorne's view that there is an established link between reality and our experience: 'The rooting of knowledge in interpreted experience treated as a reliable guide to the nature of reality is an intellectual commitment that we may call "realism".'[28] Barbour seems more concerned to emphasise the provisional and non-literal character of both scientific and religious beliefs. His use of the term 'construct' serves to stress this. The issue seems to be how reliable our conceptions of the real world are likely to be, and how critical of them we should be.

It is an advance that both science and religion are seen as posing the same problems instead of one simply providing obstacles for the other. We cannot, for example, be confident that science has obtained complete truth, and then use its methods as a standard against which to judge the supposed deficiencies of religion. The provisional and hypothetical character of scientific theory, particularly emphasized in the work of Karl Popper, means that we cannot contrast the rationally grounded certainty of science with religious dogmatism. Writers such as Peacocke would wish eventually to stress the tentative character of religious knowledge. Yet just as people need a faith to live by and hence cannot be too agnostic about the truth of their religious views without in effect giving them up, so scientists have to work within some theory or other. They cannot afford to be so detached that they are unwilling even to assume for the moment the superiority of one theory. If they are, there lies the route to utter paralysis.

The notion of critical realism encapsulates important insights, namely that there is an objective reality, and that we can know it, even though we are not infallible. Even so, it inevitably runs ontology and epistemology together in a dangerous manner. As a result it can place considerable emphasis on the way that reality is approached through our current conceptions while at the same time stressing the revisability of those conceptions. It thus becomes very unclear just how reliable our present scientific or religious 'knowledge' can be. Might the search for a Theory of Everything in physics result in the overturning of all our current physical concepts? Might, on the other hand, present religious beliefs have to be revised perhaps in an effort to find common ground between religions? Keith Ward refers to the gifts of the Enlightenment in this context and says that 'what the Enlightenment does for religion is to liberate it from the dead hand of the past, of unquestioned authority and unrevisable truth'.[29] Yet once this process is started, it is hard to be sure of what knowledge there can be left to claim. If everything were revisable, it might seem as if nothing were knowable. This is as much a danger in science as in religion. Surely, it might be thought, the scientific advances of the last century could not all be overturned. They might be put in a new context, but as with the change from classical to quantum mechanics, previous knowledge was not repudiated. It was just seen to be far from the whole story.

In fact, although the label 'critical realism' can be used by those set on changing basic beliefs, it can equally be used by those of a more conservative theological position. Everything depends on how distanced from reality we are thought to be. If reality is virtually inaccessible, our beliefs are likely to be perpetually revisable. If it is knowable by us, an emphasis on fallibility and revisability will merely aid us in acquiring a more precise knowledge. The problem is how critical we are supposed to be of our conceptions of reality. Critical realism itself runs the danger, in its eagerness not to be 'naive', of becoming sceptical. It then puts all our different understandings into question, while retaining no firm grasp on the idea of reality. Everything becomes a model, or a metaphor. Nothing is to be understood as being literally true. Whatever the epistemological difficulties that we may have to face, however, it is vital that we keep hold of a full-blooded idea of reality. It is only within a metaphysical realist position that we have grounds for recognizing our own fallibility, and thus a reason for being critical about whatever theories we hold. Critical realism has to be parasitic on the view that our beliefs do not create reality, and that it has an independent character which can be discovered. Outside such a view, the idea of fallibility does not have much sense, other than as a vague willingness to revise views for no apparent reason.

Critical realism is too ready to start with what we believe rather than with what our beliefs are about. It then faces the problem of whether to accept many of our beliefs at face value or not. As a result it becomes a vague umbrella concept that can encompass Polkinghorne's belief that our experience in both scientific and religious contexts is broadly reliable, and Barbour's more sceptical position that we are actually in the business of constructing models. The result is that although Barbour accepts that our claims are intended to be about reality, whether they succeed in being becomes very problematic.

[The reason why it is important to keep metaphysical issues separate from questions about the reliability of our theories is that otherwise we can get lost in the varying and competing views with which we are surrounded. The positive feature of critical realism is its emphasis on reality as our target, whether in religion or science.]A corollary of this is that ultimately they must both be dealing with the same reality, and cannot be locked way in different compartments. If the idea of reality can be put at the heart of all our reasoning, and if it is understood as being the presupposition of all our thought and language,[30] we can then face the question of how far knowledge is possible. Starting the other way with the myriad claims to knowledge that confront us, without the assurance that there is something to be known, can merely generate epistemological despair.

The view that there is one world and that both science and religion are making claims about its nature, suggests that claims of monopoly rights for science in the field of knowledge take a lot for granted. Since science cannot even explain the existence of the conditions which make its existence as a discipline possible, a decision to keep within the limits it sets itself seems perverse. The minute it is admitted that naturalism is a metaphysical position, we are forced into a metaphysical discussion, and not a scientific one. It is possible to rule out the existence of the 'supernatural', however that may be defined, but one should have reasons. Mere concentration on science inevitably means a concentration on the means at our disposal here and now for building up certain kinds of knowledge. Our focus has implicitly changed from the nature of reality to the possibilities afforded by our own capabilities. We should, however, recognize the limitations of empirical science, and be reluctant to assume merely on the basis of the 'integrity of science' that anything beyond its reach should be ruled out. If the physical world is such that it has been created by a transcendent God able to intervene in its processes, besides sustaining its orderliness, then that is the nature of reality. Whether it is like that is a large issue, but the point is that we should not quickly form our conclusions merely on the basis of the current state of science, or of the nature of scientific method. Religion may also wish to advance its claims to understand reality, and they should not be dismissed merely because religion is not science, as it is currently understood. A bonus for seeing science and religion as attempts for different purposes to refer to the same world is that the latter may perhaps be in a position to answer the questions posed by the former about the existence and the inherent rationality of the universe.

Realism by itself cannot decide between theism and atheism. The point is that it poses questions about the nature of reality in such a way that there cannot be an automatic restriction on the kind of thing that can be real. As long as it is a coherent position, a theistic interpretation of the universe must be a live option, which cannot be dismissed by fiat. Just because, for instance, present-day science cannot countenance spiritual phenomena of any kind does not mean that they can be quickly ruled out if there is any reason to accept them (such as the testimony of honest witnesses). We must be open to what is the case and not just what we would like to be the case. Just as theists should not rush to create a 'God of the gaps', others should not assume at the outset that there could never be divine intervention.

Discussing the relation between science and religion Drees comments that 'if one is able to show how what initially seems to be for theology the most problematic results of science can be incorporated into a certain religious-metaphysical scheme, one can then claim real progress'.[31] He goes on to say 'Taking science where it hurts most offers the greatest profit with respect to credibility.' No doubt, what is credible can often be a sociological matter concerning the state of opinion at a particular time. There is, however, a problem about whether such a minimalistic approach to theology is in principle acceptable. Drees gives priority to science. If we recognize the independence of reality from any particular means of discovering it, why should this be so? If science itself were implicitly to depend on theistic assumptions about the grounding of rationality in God, there would seem little reason for letting science make the running in what should be a cooperative enterprise. The belief that what a science asserts, even tentatively, must be accepted without question by theology to the point of self-destruction betrays a lack of confidence in a religion and in theology's ability to reflect on its rational character.

If theology feels as confident in its claims to truth as do scientists in theirs, there should be no *a priori* reason for imagining that science must always be the dominant partner. Theology cannot afford to reject solid scientific knowledge. Many theories in science are by nature tentative, provisional and fallible. Error need not, then, be always one sided. If science appears to challenge a basic theological doctrine, involving appeal to divine intervention, on the basis that the things it claims just do not happen and would be inexplicable by science if they did, it is making a serious and important point. Theology, however, should recognize that this may easily be an expression of the limits of scientific capabilities, rather than a definite claim about what actually can happen. If it has reasoned grounds for its claims it should persist with them. [The limits of scientific understanding are not the limits of the world. Nevertheless the world which science investigates is the same one which, according to theologians, is created and sustained by God. Neither can afford to ignore the other.]

Notes

1　See my *Rationality and Science*, pp. 236ff.
2　*Ibid.*, pp. 131ff.
3　*River Out of Eden*, p. 37.
4　*Ibid.*, p. 97.
5　*Ibid.*, p. 133.
6　Drees, *Religion, Science and Naturalism*, p. 12.
7　Coulson, *Science and Christian Belief*, p. 20.
8　*Ibid.*, p. 22.
9　See *Rationality and Science*, pp. 189ff.
10　For a discussion of quantum mechanics see my *Reality at Risk*, chapter 6.
11　*Beyond Science*, p. 72.
12　*Ibid.*, p. 71.
13　*Beyond Science*, p. 71
14　*Quarks, Chaos and Christianity*, p. 71.
15　*A Brief History of Time*, p. 136.
16　See *Rationality and Science*.
17　*Christian Belief in a Post-Modern World*, p. 5.
18　J. Rouse, *Engaging Science*, p. 66.
19　Drees, *Religion, Science and Naturalism*, p. 247.
20　*Ibid.*, p. 11.
21　*Ibid.*, p. 274.
22　*Ibid.*, p. 268.
23　See Brooke, *Science and Religion: Some Historical Perspectives*.
24　*Theology for a Scientific Age*, p. 9.
25　*Ibid.*, p. 13.
26　*Ibid.*, p. 14.
27　*Religion in an Age of Science*, p. 45.

28   *Scientists as Theologians*, p. 14.
29   *A Vision to Pursue*, p. 215.
30   See my *Reason and Commitment*, and my *Reality at Risk*.
31   Drees, *Religion, Science and Naturalism*, p. 126.

5

Can a Religion Rest on Historical Claims?

1 Historical Proof

The modern preoccupation with the standards of proof and of evidence prevalent in the physical sciences has not just raised problems for religion. It also calls into question the standards of evidence used in academic disciplines which cannot resort to the normal procedures of empirical science, particularly involving the repeating of experiments. No academic discipline faces greater theoretical difficulties than history. It is not only faced with the major problem of interpreting and understanding the behaviour of those who lived in very different social contexts from those of the contemporary world. It has to do this in the knowledge that the events and people it is describing are long since gone and can never be recalled. What is left in the present are traces of various kinds. This may make the past appear inaccessible, and a simple-minded empiricism might wish to insist that we can never go beyond the memories of it that are left.

All this multiplies the difficulties of any religion which wishes to rest its claims on the importance of certain historical events. Several religions are in this position. Judaism, for instance, depends on claims that God has guided His chosen people through history. No religion, however, is as dependent on historical claims as Christianity. It is appropriate, therefore, to concentrate in this chapter on the particular claims of the Christian religion made in the New Testament. It is there above all that claims to historical truth are apparently being made for events that modern science would find it difficult to countenance. Can such claims lay any claim to rational examination?

The role of reason is to lay claim to truth, and such truth is universally valid. That has been the traditional picture of reason and one that has been put under threat by developments such as postmodernism which stress the dependence on any understanding on local perspectives. It also carries with it the implication that reason is only interested in a particular kind of truth, 'the truths of reason', which may somehow be distinguished from contingent truth – the kind of thing that happens to be true but need not be.

Yet the urge to separate reason and knowledge from the uncertain, changing world of history has remained strong. Rationality and universality have often seemed opposed to particular claims about fleeting events. Kant encapsulated this view when he declared: 'A church dispenses with the most important mark of truth, namely a rightful claim to universality, when it bases itself upon a revealed faith. For such a faith, being historical . . . can never be universally communicated so as to produce conviction.'[1]

The universality of truth and the universal claims of reason are thus opposed to the particularity of revelation. An historical event may have happened, but of its nature it did not have to happen. What is so and what must be are very different. Contingency is thus opposed to necessity, and empirical knowledge to the higher workings of reason. Kant says that 'recognition and respect must be accorded in Christian dogmatic to universal human reason as the supremely commanding principle in a natural religion'.[2] For Kant reference to revelation has to be subordinated to what we can know through reason alone. What he means is made clear when he says, 'The rationalist, by virtue of his very title, must of his own accord restrict himself within the limits of human insight.'[3] For Kant, morality is of supreme importance. Because what he refers to as 'the supernatural' lies beyond reason (or, at least, human reason) true religion has to be concerned with us and what we must do, not with what lies beyond our reach.

All historical claims are about contingent matters, and what is more they depend on the nature of the historical record. As Kant says, that immediately restricts such knowledge to those who have the requisite access to that record.[4] Thus their contingency is linked to having to be reported, and that means that they are not open to universal reason. Nothing could give a greater illustration of the faith of the Enlightenment in the power of unaided human reason than Kant's views here. There is a reaction in the name of the universality of reason against any doctrine based on particular historical events. The result is an explicit preference for 'natural' as opposed to 'revealed' religion, and a demand that reason sit in judgement on revealed doctrine. Kant firmly criticizes those who place the endeavour 'towards a good course of life' below the importance of the historical faith of Christianity. It is hardly surprising that, over the centuries, when confronted with the claims of rationality couched in such terms, some religious people feel that their faith is in jeopardy. The consequence has been that somehow reason and faith have appeared opposed to each other. The notion of God acting in history has, it seems, already been dismissed by the self-styled rationalist, on the grounds that such talk already exceeds the bounds of reason. Rationalism, in this sense, is firmly anthropocentric, concentrating on the capabilities of human reason and nothing beyond.

Such a ready dismissal of the importance of historical events to religion may seem astonishing. Christianity is a faith which appears to be based absolutely on the claim that certain things happened. If so, it is crucial to know whether they did happen. It is not just a question of deciding how to live our lives. Karl Barth was under no doubt that Christ's Resurrection, to take the most important example, was an actual historical event. He says, 'It has happened in the same sense as His crucifixion and His death, in the human sphere and human time, as an actual event within the world with an objective content.'[5] Nothing, it would seem could be firmer than that claim. Yet although Barth is ready to stress the objective and historic character of what appears to be a supernatural event, he is reluctant to talk in terms of 'proof' or 'evidence'. He says 'There is no proof, and there obviously cannot and ought not to be any proof, for the fact that this history did take place.'[6] He qualifies this remark by making it clear that he is using the word 'proof' according to the terminology of modern scholarship. Barth considers that no such proof is adduced or even intended in the New Testament. He expands this by making it clear that the kind of historical grounds he would regard as proof would involve the outline of an event 'independently of the stand-point of the onlooker'. He wants it to be established as 'having certainly taken place'. The New Testament itself often appeals to the testimony of eye witnesses, not least when St Paul gives a list (in 1 Corinthians 15) of those, including himself, to whom the risen Christ appeared. Does that not appear to be an attempt to provide evidence, and even proof? Barth's response, however, is as follows:[7]

The witnesses to whom Paul appears with such solemnity are not the outside impartial witnesses which such an attempt would demand. They are the tradition which underlies the community, which calls for a decision of faith, not for the acceptance of a well-attested historical report.

In his emphasis on the decision of faith and in his decrying of the possibility of historical proof, Barth is not so very distant from those who would view an account of the Resurrection as 'myth'. His protestation that it happened 'in the same sense' as the Crucifixion sits uneasily with his willingness to go along with, as he puts it, 'the thought forms of and terminology of modern scholarship'. He can accept descriptions of the Resurrection as 'saga' or 'legend'. He says, 'The death of Jesus Christ can certainly be thought of as history in the modern sense, but not the resurrection.'[8] The latter, it appears, is something 'which has actually happened' and yet 'cannot be grasped historically'. How can such a distinction be upheld? How can there be a divergence between historical knowledge and confident assertions about what actually happened in time and space? Barth is adamant that we do not do justice to the New Testament records if they try to explain away the history they recount. The Resurrection, he thinks, was not simply the result of a development of a conception of the disciples, but was an objective event underlying that development. Yet we seem to be denied any rational access to that event. It has to be a matter of faith.

In all this Barth appears to be setting an impossibly high standard for historical proof. He wants an impartial account, apparently independent of the standpoint of an onlooker. Only that, he believes would offer the kind of 'proof' that would satisfy a modern historian. Yet it seems to be an incoherent desire. An eye witness has to give an account of what he or she sees. It is not infallible, as anyone could attest who has listened to the conflicting evidence of supposedly independent witnesses in a court case concerning a traffic accident. Nevertheless such accounts may certainly be impartial in that they are given by people not connected with either side in the case. What they are not, and could never be, are accounts independent of their standpoint. Indeed, how could they be? The court does not wish to know what actually happened, regardless of what the witnesses saw and think happened. It has to base its decision on the evidence presented. What is likely to call into question such evidence is if witnesses claim to have seen something that they could not have seen from their standpoint, perhaps because of bad light or an obstruction.

Barth is not questioning the sincerity of the reports given of the Resurrection. His point is that the witnesses were not impartial, but were believers. There is, Barth holds,[9] 'no attempt at an external objective assurance that the history did take place'. The witnesses are, he says, 'those who have themselves made this decision of faith'. The implication is that the accounts are an expression of faith, or, in Barth's words, 'a recollection of the faith which constitutes the community'. Yet if this is so, how can he be so confident that the Resurrection was an 'actual event'? The Church may have the requisite faith that this is so, but the assertion of the objectivity of the occurrence would itself seem to be an expression of faith. Barth cannot allow that faith can be historically grounded in an objective event, because that would make faith dependent on reason, and reason, he thinks, is formed by secular society. We shall see in chapter 9 how he makes a similar objection to natural theology. Only through faith will it be possible to understand the work of God. Barth states that this is a sphere where it cannot be verified, 'but can be seen and grasped only imaginatively and represented in the form of poetry'.[10]

Even, therefore, what is claimed as real 'spatio-temporal history' slides away from the grasp of the historian, and indeed from the realm of rationality. We are placed instead in a realm of faith, imagination and poetry. Although these are categories much appealed to by modern theologians, they begin to look ominously subjective, although that was not Barth's intention. There is typically a withdrawal from claims about what happened and a concentration on responses to what happened, on the part, say, of the first disciples. The New Testament is, then, seen not so much as historic record as a testimony to faith, as if the two are inconsistent categories. It then follows that we only have access to particular events through those responses, and it is easy to begin to see the accounts as somehow deficient in objectivity. We can end up thinking that they tell us more about the assumptions of the writers of the New Testament than about the events they purport to be describing.

2 Historical Evidence and Faith

The distinction between historical verification and something else itself depends on presuppositions about the nature of verification and proof. The use of the term 'verification' is significant in that it raises parallels with positivist demands for verification in science. Such appeals to what can be publicly agreed, perhaps to neutral, uninterpreted sense-data, cannot be seen as the basis of science. Whether in physical science or in history, theory plays its part from the beginning. The urge to find a perspective that is somehow beyond all perspectives is incoherent. Barth was asking of historians a standard of proof which is unobtainable anywhere. Historians cannot transcend all perspectives any more than scientists can. They may hope for a true theory. They cannot leave theory behind. Barth's demand of impartiality appears to involve some hankering for a desire to allow as fact only what is agreed by everyone. There is nothing, however, so neutral that it must compel that kind of agreement. The wish to remove the presuppositions of faith suggests that those without faith are somehow more impartial than those with it, that secular history is more objective than any purported history of revelation. No doubt this is a similar attitude to the fanciful view that atheism is somehow more neutral about religious matters than theism. What has to be recognized is that everyone brings presuppositions to bear on every matter. The mark of the rational person is not to be without all such assumptions. That is logically impossible, since it would mean the end of rationality. What is necessary is to be willing to put one's presuppositions to the test and, if necessary, reject them in the light of new evidence.

The issue at this point becomes stark. Is it possible to talk of evidence at all, without begging the question? Is not one person's evidence of no account to another? The more the priority of theory is emphasized, the more it seems impossible to judge any theory by standards beyond itself. This is a perpetual problem in the philosophy of science, and the question presents itself as to the nature of rationality in historical judgement. Barth seemed to think that the presence of faith removed the possibility of rational standards. Yet in the wider sphere, all scientific theorizing depends on a degree of faith. Theory outstrips the evidence and governs even what is to count as evidence. 'Proof' in science is never proof to those who hold firmly to a conflicting theory.

The contemporary problem, indeed, is not that scientific standards of proof set a standard in secular history to which the New Testament accounts cannot aspire. It is that the universally acceptable standards, that appear to have been defended by conceptions of rationality, seem to be unobtainable anywhere. Rationality has often appeared to involve the idea that a rational argument is one which any rational person will accept. This may even seem self-evident, but it has the consequence that the rejection of such arguments convicts one of irrationality. It is perhaps not surprising that 'the rational' is sometimes restricted to the logically necessary. It can appear that the only sure way of appearing irrational is to be logically inconsistent. Reason can often be equated with deductive reasoning. Yet all this is far too restrictive and would preclude ordinary beliefs about contingent affairs from being a matter of rationality. History would be totally excluded from the bounds of rationality.

Standards of evidence and proof which render an historical event more or less probable, however, can and should be given. We return to the fact that the reports of eye witnesses are of the utmost importance in such a connection. We may still be told that in the case of the New Testament such reports must be discounted because they are the expression of faith. It is, of course, legitimate to question whether claims to be first-hand accounts can be accepted at face value. The issue, however, often seems to go deeper than normal historical questioning of the status of sources. The suspicion must be that the New Testament comes under particular scrutiny, because it is being tacitly accepted that apparently supernatural events such as the Resurrection could never be accepted on a rational basis. They could of their very nature never claim the kind of truth which could be upheld by historians. The notions of 'proof' and 'evidence' are then ruled out in this connection because they suggest the kind of universal acceptability which claims to supernatural occurrences do not have, at least in the modern world.

It is not just that some people find supernatural events hard to believe. Barth's refusal to accept that the Resurrection can be subject to ordinary historical verification suggests a deeper worry, which Bultmann made explicit. He said: 'Modern man acknowledges as reality only such phenomena or events as are comprehensible within the framework of the rational order of the universe. He does not acknowledge miracles because they do not fit into the lawful order.'[11]

We have here an explicit linkage between rationality and modern science. Bultmann affirms that 'modern man's' thinking has been shaped by science. His aim is to recover the deeper meaning which lies behind the 'mythological' conceptions of the New Testament, to prevent it being discarded as irrelevant to the modern age. This was Bultmann's famous programme of so-called 'demythologizing'. In other words, the interpretation of scriptural texts must be governed by the assumptions of modern science. We must, he believes, discover what the Bible 'has to say for our actual present'[12] rather than treating it simply as an historical document. What is important is not what the New Testament reports but how it speaks to us now. There is the same emphasis in Bultmann as in Barth on the role of faith, and the same contrast between what faith discerns and the ordering of historical events capable of proof. He says that 'the action of God is hidden from every eye except the eye of faith. Only the so-called natural, secular (worldly) events are visible to every man and capable of proof.'[13]

Historical evidence, it seems, cannot be used to provide rational grounds for a religious position. The eye of faith sees a different realm from one capable of proof. Yet why should there be such a radical break between faith and historical evidence? Christianity, after all, has often been thought to be grounded on claims about events in history. It seems as if faith is to be excluded altogether from the domain of proof, of evidence and hence of rationality. Instead it retreats to a position where what appears meaningful to myself or yourself seems to matter more than what is true or false. The world of truth, as so often, has been ceded to science and to what happens to be acceptable to contemporary science.

Barth and Bultmann cast a long shadow over parts of modern theology. Yet what they say has a resonance within philosophy. Wittgenstein did not accept that Christianity had any need to ground itself on historical evidence. He stressed that 'Christianity is not based on historical truth'.[14] Rather it confronts us with a narrative and tells us to believe it through thick and thin. He says of it: 'Don't take the same attitude to it as you take to other historical narratives! Make a quite different place in your life for it.' As always, Wittgenstein links the meaning of a statement with the difference it makes to action rather than simply with what it purports to be about. Words and practice cannot be separated. As he result he can observe that the Gospels might even, from the point of view of history, be 'demonstrably false', and yet religious belief would lose nothing. This is not, he adds, because he considers, in a Kantian way, that belief concerns universal truths of reason rather than particular historical events. His position is simply that 'historical proof (the historical proof-game) is irrelevant to belief'. The all-important point is the role that belief plays in people' lives. The fact of belief, and not its content, is given priority. We must seize on the Gospel message 'believingly', and it is significant that Wittgenstein adds in explanation 'lovingly'. It is our attitude to the Gospels, the place they are given in our lives, that will be crucial. Proof is so irrelevant that even definite proof that certain events did not take place is beside the point. The dichotomy between proof, evidence and reason on the one hand, and the life of faith on the other could not be made more stark. What (or who) we have faith in seems to drop out of account. The fact of faith and the stories we dwell on, and the 'pictures' that guide us, become enough. Much is sometimes made in other contexts of the notion of a narrative, but it is clear that the notion of a story is radically ambiguous. Many would tell 'the stories of Jesus' because they believed them to be true. Wittgenstein is saying that it does not matter if they are shown to be false. A narrative of apparent historic events comes to have the same status as a parable or fable or any powerful story with a moral.

3 'Gospel Truth'

A well-known distinction has often been drawn between the 'Jesus of history' and the 'Christ of faith'. The problem is that once we start separating the one from the other, there is no sure stopping place. It can be claimed with some plausibility that ordinary historical research about events two thousand years ago will not be sufficient to make me change my life. Yet a change that is unrelated to anything becomes a merely arbitrary commitment. I am giving allegiance to what Wittgenstein calls 'a system of reference',[15] but it has nothing to do with anything except perhaps my own subjective problems. This would mesh in with an approach to the Gospels encouraged in many different quarters. The postmodernist emphasis on the crucial role of interpretation when one is presented with any text, makes the latter seem inaccessible when unrelated to contemporary concerns. One writer who defines 'fiction' as 'a narrative whose purpose is less to describe the past than to affect the present' is thereby able to use the word freely in dealing with the Gospels.[16] He goes on to say: 'The Gospels . . . are largely fictional accounts concerning an historical figure, Jesus of Nazareth, intended to create a life-enhancing understanding of his nature.' Clearly their aim is held to be life-enhancing rather than accurate. One can wonder why it is even necessary to assume that religious proclamation has to be about a historical figure. Wittgenstein raises the question whether Christianity needs the historical figure of Jesus at all. Could it retain its significance in people's lives even without any attempt to be rooted in history? Existentialist interpretations, such as that of Bultmann, seem to suggest that it could.

Bultmann drew a distinction between the modern understanding given by science, and the world-picture current in the New Testament. This enabled him to view as 'myth' anything that was unacceptable to contemporary science. This very distinction has been in turn challenged by postmodernists who see no reason to keep the physical sciences on a pedestal. It is, however, intriguing that the seeds of a postmodern emphasis on the dominant role of interpretation can be found in Bultmann, with a consequent stress on historical context. Bultmann says of man that 'when he turns his attention to history, he must admit himself to be a part of history . . . In every word which he says about history he is saying at the same time something about himself.'[17] This is true, it is alleged, both at the general level and when we come to understand particular events. The report of the event cannot be prised apart from the circumstances of the reporter or of the reader. The meaning of the report does not exist in a vacuum. This approach allows Bultmann and his more recent followers to insist that the Gospel accounts cannot somehow be lifted out of the context of belief in which they were made, just as our understanding of such accounts cannot be abstracted from our own situation. It is paradoxical that Bultmann took it for granted that when man observes nature 'he perceives there something objective, which is not himself'.[18] A modernist faith in science seems to be dictating the agenda, rather than a more consistent stress on the all-pervasive role of context. The result of this is that it has in some circles become received knowledge that we can have no direct access to historical events independent of the way they are reported. The force of this usually comes from an implicit contrast with the direct knowledge we gain of the world through science. Schubert Ogden writes:

> Given the nature of the sources available to us, it is simply impossible to establish as an empirical-historical conclusion that anything they contain in the way of a saying or deed of Jesus himself as distinct from being associated with him in the experience and memory of those to whom we are in the earliest traditions redacted in our sources.[19]

We cannot, it is held, distinguish between Jesus as he was and Jesus as he was remembered in the earliest stratum of Christian witness. This position can relate exclusively to the peculiar conditions of early Christian witness. The contrast can be drawn between impartial, neutral witnesses, and those in the New Testament who have a message to preach. Yet it is a view that can and has been generalized, so that in the end nothing is recognized as being true in itself but only as holding from the point of view of whoever is giving a report. That is why any distinction between history and science becomes unstable. Science is practised by scientists with particular viewpoints. It could be said that we never learn about reality as it actually is, but only as it is described by the contemporary researchers of Western science. Even conceptions of physical reality are thus embedded in the theories and assumptions of an ongoing scientific tradition.

The idea that the Jesus of history cannot be separated from the experiences and memories of the earliest witnesses slides into the notion that all reports about him are somehow contaminated with additional presuppositions and overlaiden with layers of interpretation. Yet the idea that we can never see things as they are is itself clearly the product of post-Kantian philosophy. There may be a sense in which the furniture of the room I am sitting in cannot be properly separated from my perceptual experience of the furniture. Yet, if we are not careful, this will result in changing the subject from that of the nature of the contents of the room to questions of my own context and perspective. This is the path to solipsism or, at the least, idealism. The refusal to allow references to anything without alluding to the person experiencing it is in the end to give up the idea of one common, objective world to which we all can have access. Instead the 'world' splits into a myriad pieces.

We may try to distinguish between ordinary perceptual experience and the 'meaning' something has for someone. This is presumably the basis of an attempt to split so-called 'empirical-historical' judgements and religious affirmations. That, however, depends on a simplistic view of the supposed neutrality of science. Unless we simply wish to advocate a blind, unquestioning faith in the pronouncements of scientists at a particular time, we have to accept that scientific judgements, historical judgements and even religious ones are all human judgements subject to the same problems. A clear distinction between religious and other views will only be upheld because of a positivist understanding of the priority of science. Dismissing 'miracles' merely on the sweeping grounds that they could not be accepted in a scientific age, depends explicitly on a trust in science as the sole source of truth. Yet that stance itself cries out for philosophical legitimation. The issue quickly has to become whether anyone is ever in a position to claim truth, rather than simply what our attitude should be to the Gospel records.

There is, however, still much controversy about which issues can and which cannot be settled by historical investigation. One example is provided by arguments about the dating of three papyrus fragments of Matthew's Gospel, held in Magdalen College, Oxford. A German scholar, Dr Carsten Thiede, has claimed that they date to within twenty years or so of the life of Jesus, considerably earlier than most scholars believe. The claim is that the Gospels comprise a more or less contemporary eye witness record, rather than being the later expression of the developing beliefs of the early church. Whether or not this could be true, the more basic question is whether it would matter much if it were. If Wittgenstein is right, whatever the intrinsic interest of the argument, it is irrelevant to genuine religious faith. How, it might be pointedly asked, could this kind of scholarly argument about minute scraps of ancient papyrus have any possible relevance to the way I live my life? Others might be less scornful but feel there is only a slight relevance. The message of Jesus, it might be claimed, has its own validity whether or not it can be traced directly to his own lips. There may, it would be conceded, be a basis in history, but it must be seen as part of an ongoing tradition.

In his discussion of the Magdalen papyrus, Graham Stanton makes a distinction between what he terms 'Gospel truth' and historical evidence. The former, he believes, refers to the evangelists' theological convictions about the significance of Jesus of Nazareth. He writes that:

> No amount of historical evidence ever proves 'Gospel truth'. After all some who saw and heard Jesus for themselves drew the conclusion that he was a magician and a false prophet. Proof cannot reside either in any new papyrus fragment (however early its date), or in any artefact uncovered by archaeologists.[20]

Stanton clearly means by 'proof' something that compels assent, since he regards the fact of some people's rejection of Jesus in the flesh as a sign that his significance cannot be proved. Yet this kind of proof is impossible to attain anywhere and is certainly beyond the reach of science. Even logical contradictions are eagerly embraced by some, so truth cannot be confused with what as a matter of fact is universally accepted. Similarly, if historical proof is regarded as an appeal to what is self-evident, far too high a standard is being demanded of historical evidence. Since the physical sciences themselves cannot appeal to the notion of the self-evident, because they are empirical, we seem to be back with an implicit hankering for universal truths of reason. Yet by definition they are irrelevant when contingent matters of historic fact are in question.

Graham Stanton echoes Barth when he says 'The resurrection is not an historical event which can be investigated with historical methods.'[21] Yet the constant danger in this kind of assertion is that we slip away from Barth's insistence of the objectivity of the Resurrection. Stanton immediately goes on to say that the historian can comment on what happened as a result of the disciples' experiences but, as he says, 'the nature and reality of those experiences cannot be established by historical methods'. The absence of so-called 'proof' enables one to pass from the event to the experience of the event without having apparently changed the subject. Even reference to the 'reality' of the experience is ambiguous in that an experience can be genuine enough without it being of anything objective. My fear can be real enough even if its object is totally imaginary. The disciples may have been sincere in their reports about experiencing the risen Christ. Even if, however, they were not lying, that is a significantly different issue from whether they did actually see him. Stanton does not allow us to distinguish the two. The disciples could have had a real experience without it being of anything real. Because, though, the latter possibility is held to be outside the scope of history, it somehow cannot be examined on its own. As a result, it does not seem to be a claim to 'literal' truth, and certainly not one that can then be rationally examined.

Stanton, however, is unwilling to deny the relevance of history completely since he admits that 'in theory, at least, "Gospel truth" is open to falsification by historical evidence'.[22] For instance, he suggests (unlike Wittgenstein) that if Jesus were shown by historians not to have existed, that would disprove Christianity. He thus wishes to maintain a general connection between the reliability of the evangelists' portraits of Jesus and 'Gospel truth'. This is despite the fact that the Gospels do not constitute 'precise historical records'. There is thus an ambivalence about this position. It seems as if Christianity can be disproved but not proved.

Doubts about the relevance of historical narrative to faith may stem from the general worry that we have already encountered that we should base our whole lives on contingent claims that could turn out to be false. One retort would be that that is the human predicament in any context. More likely, however, is a continued distrust of the likelihood or the intelligibility of miraculous and supernatural events. If so, it should be clear that that is the issue, rather than doubts about historical proof. Anyone who reads the New Testament with the presupposition that certain kinds of events have been ruled out by modern science, will be likely to conclude that the documents are in a narrow sense unhistorical. They could not be 'literally' true, because literal truth has been reserved for what is approved by science. The temptation will then be to reinterpret them so that they still convey a message, without being understood to making startling claims. We can then concentrate on the fact of witness and the general meaning for human life which the narrative conveys. Whether an 'event' (such as the Virgin Birth or the Resurrection) can continue to have a valid meaning even if it may not have happened is a large issue. Stories and narratives can sometimes influence us, whether they are intended as historical descriptions or not. Myths can exercise their power over us. It is significant that all these categories have been invoked in an attempt to sidestep or ignore the issue whether the extraordinary events recounted in the New Testament occurred or not.

4   The New Testament as History

Once it is acknowledged that history is relevant to any extent and that Christianity needs some beliefs about the historical Jesus, even if of a somewhat minimal kind, we are still forced back to the texts with a critical eye. They have to be able to withstand the beginnings of a rational examination. Indeed, even Bultmann regards a doubt about whether Jesus existed as 'unfounded and not worth refutation'.[23] Yet because he believes that the words of Jesus meet us 'with the question of how we are to interpret our own existence',[24] the content of the message soon becomes more important than when it was said or by whom. Bultmann therefore quickly slips away from historical claims and even suggests that even though Jesus was probably the speaker, 'should it prove otherwise, that does not change in any way what is said in the record'. Yet this is itself a significant change in an understanding of the nature of Christianity. Is it simply a body of teaching or is it also a claim about certain events? The fact of the Resurrection, and not just its meaning, formed the foundation of the earliest Christian teaching. It would seem highly significant if the earliest witness was not just dismissed implicitly or explicitly as unreliable, but that its whole emphasis should be so radically altered.

It has become something of a truism that the Gospel writers could not be seen as writing history since their aim was a presentation of faith which was meant to evoke faith. Yet this ignores the possibility that they themselves regarded their faith as historically based. They may have seen themselves as witnesses to extraordinary events which they believed had a universal significance. It is at least arguable that the writers believed that they were preserving a record of what had happened which should be traced back to eye witnesses. That is what they said they were doing. The argument about how far this is actually so is what gives life to disputes about the dating of the New Testament. The assumption is that the more contemporary the records, the more perhaps they can be trusted. That would certainly be a normal presumption in history. Yet many philosophers and theologians are reluctant to place Christianity at the mercy of historical scholarship. The advantages, however, of not being proved wrong can usually only be obtained by never saying anything that can claim to be right. If Christianity so defines itself as not to be judged by historical scholarship, the danger is that it does so by ceding all the high ground to such scholarship and pretending that this makes no difference. In the end, however, there is a natural reluctance to pursue this programme wholeheartedly. Very few theologians want to break every link with history. The result is an uneasy compromise. Faith stands apart from history, and yet it still wishes to make some residual historical claims.

Whatever else they may be, can the documents of the New Testament be judged at all by the criteria of history? We are so often told that they were not written as history that we can ignore the fact that they were written in a known historical context about which there is a considerable amount of historical evidence. Even if the authors of the various writings were not attempting anything like an ordinary historical record, it may still be reasonable to wonder how far what they say meshes in with what else we know of this period. Once this question is raised, however, it becomes clear that philosophical assumptions can be brought to the issue from the very beginning. The very fact that historical evidence is thought irrelevant demonstrates that powerful presuppositions are at work.

The more that the role of interpretation is emphasized, the less the text and even less the authors of the text will be allowed to speak for themselves. The very idea of a text having a meaning independent of interpretation will be dismissed out of hand. If some trends in hermeneutics and postmodernism cast doubt on the accessibility of the author's original intentions and understanding, this is clearly a problem confronting all history. It is not the basis of a distinction between sacred and secular history. Indeed, if we cannot be allowed to read the New Testament in a way that distances ourselves from the assumptions of our time, no historical record can speak to us in its own voice. The possibility of history as such is being questioned and not just the distinction between the New Testament and 'proper' history. The very way in which the discipline of hermeneutics started with biblical criticism and then broadened out into a general philosophical theory about the interpretation of all texts bears witness to this.

The desire to put the New Testament into a category on its own often stems from a naturalistic attitude which rules out *a priori* any form of divine intervention or miraculous event. Many take for granted that if the New Testament is not to be dismissed out of hand, it cannot be taken at face value. It cannot really concern the events it purports to describe, but must have some other significance. If everything is to be made acceptable to the standards of 'secular' history, it is assumed that the categories of contemporary science should dictate what we can accept as a veridical report. Even in the seventeenth century Hobbes said that the alleged fact that God spoke to someone in a dream only shows that the person dreamt that God spoke. Thus extraordinary events become converted into mere extraordinary experiences.

Science, however, changes and develops and so it is dangerous to pin one's assumptions on where it happens to be at a given moment. The modern physical view of matter as energy bears no relation to that prevalent at the time of Hobbes. This suggests that all too often we may be governed not by a respect for science, but by philosophical assumptions about what science can and cannot discover. The world, it is held, does not admit of divine intervention. This is, however a philosophical presupposition and has little to to do with the function of history. The reason, it is said, that history cannot have recorded certain events is because they could not have happened, or be recognized as having happened.

Questioning the hold of naturalism does not imply that we should go to the other extreme and suppose that history can compel faith. If one takes mathematics as a paradigm, it is easy to assume that reason involves incontrovertible proof. This makes many fall back on the category of faith. Yet, as always, this is too stark a contrast. Kierkegaard said that it is not possible 'to conceive of a more foolish contradiction than that of wanting to prove . . . that a definite individual man is God'.[25] He goes on to say that 'the proofs which Scripture presents for Christ's divinity – His miracles, His Resurrection from the dead, His Ascension into heaven – are therefore only for faith.' The contrast goes deep in modern thought and can arise because too much is expected of reason. Reason cannot prove anything in science or secular history, but it can produce good and bad evidence, appropriate and inappropriate grounds. There is no doubt nothing so daft that somebody does not believe it. That does not mean that such a person is being rational or that what is believed can have any claim to truth. Photographs of the earth from space can doubtless be dismissed by believers in a flat earth as part of a campaign of disinformation by some organization. What is true and what people can be persuaded to believe does not always coincide. 'Proof', if it is taken to imply that it cannot, in consistency, be contradicted is unattainable outside mathematics and pure logic. Once we enter the messy world of contingencies, things are very different. Yet just because logical certainty is unattainable in most contexts, that does not mean that truth can never be claimed or that reasoning is irrelevant. That would be to suggest that any leap of faith is as good as any other, because they are all equally blind.

The acknowledgement of, say, Jesus as Lord has always been seen as a final step of faith which seems to involve more than a merely intellectual acknowledgement. Wittgenstein argues that even historic indubitability is not enough, because, he says, 'the indubitability wouldn't be enough to make me change my whole life'.[26] He says: 'Here we have a belief in historic facts different from a belief in ordinary historic fact. Even, they are not treated as historical, empirical, propositions.' Faith demands wholehearted commitment, sufficient to lead people to sacrifice their own lives. It seems markedly different from the mere acceptance that certain things happened. This is partly because I hold certain pictures in my mind which play a different role in my life from the rational acknowledgement of the historicity of other events. That is what Wittgenstein would say. Are, though, the pictures of anything? Are they based on anything real? Wittgenstein would hold that these are the wrong questions, and indeed describes religious belief based on historical evidence as superstition. The doubt which, for Wittgenstein, would be appropriate to any historical proposition, has no part in faith.

5   The Scope of Historical Reasoning

Even if it is granted that true religious faith involves a commitment that is all embracing, it is dubious whether doubt is excluded. Reason cannot be totally banished because faith is always directed at something or somebody. I must have a conception of what I have faith in. Someone's acknowledgement of Christ may involve an act of faith, in so far as it involves the will. It still involves a conception of who Christ was and what he did, which involves our reason. If Christ never lived or was significantly different from the way he is portrayed in the Gospels, any faith in him must be misplaced. This already demands some historical basis.

There still remains the question of how credulous we should allow ourselves to be about reports of miraculous events, and apparently supernatural happenings. Many would feel that once distrust about the historicity of the accounts in the New Testament sets in, it is difficult to know where to stop. There is a dilemma here. Are Christian believers to hold their beliefs because they believe in the independent truth of much that is reported in the Bible? Do they, on the other hand, hold to the truth of the Bible as a consequence and constituent part of their religious faith? Judged from within a Christian perspective, do Christians believe the Bible because it is true, or is it true because they believe it? The question is fundamental in that the former approach accepts that Biblical truth (or 'Gospel truth') is no different from other forms of truth. It is open to normal rational examination and criticism. Conversely this means that it could also receive rational support. The alternative position, on the other hand, fences faith from 'secular' reason and the possible depradations of historians. It can make Christianity invulnerable, but at a price. We make certain historical claims as a matter of faith and not 'proof' by agreeing with Wittgenstein that they are not ordinary 'historical, empirical propositions'. Yet this can result in ceding the category of truth to the empiricist who has a narrow view of the kind of event that can or cannot be perceived.

A rationalism that merely concentrates on what is universally established can restrict truth to what is logically true. At the other extreme, existentialists can approach history with the view that what is important is the meaning that certain stories gave for us. Both positions make it impossible to think that historic events may be important for us just because they happened. Any judgement about historical events involves an assessment of their significance. Some people rate certain events as more important than others do. The contemporary emphasis on the role of theory in science and elsewhere should remind us that the relevance of 'facts' and 'events' does not come ready packaged. It may seem incredible to some that events in first century Palestine should have any universal significance, while others may see in them the pivot of human history. Nevertheless, for an event to have any significance it must have happened. Some theologians are content to talk of the existentialist meaning of certain events whether or not they occurred. Yet for an event to have a meaning, when it did not happen, we would have to live in a world where Cheshire cats have grins but have lost everything else. The significance of an event is not the same as the moral of story. Unless there were real events in history, such as the Resurrection, Christian teaching has been profoundly misleading. There is no doubt scope for argument about the character of such happenings even if they are reckoned objective. One philosopher, for instance, draws a distinction between actually seeing and merely visualising, in the case of the Resurrection appearances and asserts: 'Anyone who had been there with Mary Magdalene could similarly have seen Jesus; a camera could have taken a picture of him.'[27] He argues that 'the risen Christ was a physical body that was objectively present to the witnesses in space and time'.[28] The issue may be partly whether, at least in this case, 'objective' must mean 'physical'. Could a 'spiritual' body be equally objective? Whatever position theology takes up, the reduction of all events to the experience, and possibly the imagination, of those who made claims about them would serve to undermine the Christian faith. St Paul certainly thought so, in his appeal to the Resurrection as the foundation and justification of Christian belief, and a sign of a life beyond death.

We seem, therefore, to be forced back into the world of the historian, although not necessarily that of a determinedly 'secular' one. There may be no such thing as historical proof in a strong sense. Any historian has to start with some preconceptions. Someone who already has a belief in God will be likely to be more prepared to see the marks of divine intervention in some events than would a convinced atheist. It is, however, the mark of rationality to allow all our preconceptions to be tested. Unless we deny that there is an objective world, in the end our beliefs must be constrained by what we led to believe is the case. At one level, there should be no distinction between the New Testament and ancient records of other contemporary events. The reports conveyed in the New Testament should be examined as history, just as much as if they had been included in the writings of Tacitus. They may well be intended to convey a greater message, but it does not seem irrelevant to inquire how far Roman history can make sense of them. They may not be mere history but it seems rash to assume that they are not history at all.

A generation ago, an eminent Roman historian wrote of the Acts of the Apostles that even taking into account the fact that it was written as propaganda, 'the confirmation of historicity is overwhelming'. His conclusion was that 'any attempt to reject its basic historicity even in matters of detail must now appear absurd'.[29] He gives as an example the way the book treats of Roman citizenship. As for the Gospels, he compares their treatment of Christ with Tacitus' history of Tiberius, the Roman emperor at the time of the Crucifixion. In both cases he thinks that it is possible for a critical historian to make progress in understanding the course of events.

Many would feel that this form of assimilation of religious writing to ordinary history begs large questions. Yet which are they? If it is possible to discount even Tacitus' hidden assumptions about Tiberius, why should the Gospels be treated differently? They are not written as 'neutral' history, but that is probably an impossible task. Even Tacitus' avowed intention to disavow partisanship and write *sine ira et studio* can be taken with a pinch of salt. Historians would certainly distrust his attribution of motives to Tiberius. No historian can be completely dispassionate and disengaged. The very fact that the subject matter has been chosen as worthy of attention already betrays some principle of selection. The choice of certain material as relevant to the historian's interests and the dismissal of other material as irrelevant demonstrates how total neutrality is an illusion. No one can passively soak up 'facts'.

We all need theories to determine what is to count as a relevant fact in the first place. In fact, much of the disparagement of the Gospels as history probably rests on a mistaken view of history. Even impartiality may be a dubious virtue for an historian if it turns out to be impartiality between truth and falsity.

None of this goes to show that the New Testament is right in its claims. The point is merely that it is making claims which can be subject to the same kind of rational examination as any other historical claim. The New Testament may be an expression of the faith of the Early Church, but it also set out to show what prompted that faith. The attempt to fence off such faith from the real world so that it is neither true nor false, reasonable or unreasonable, can be prompted by many motives. In the end, however, it is another example of the concentration on the fact of belief rather than on its content. It is not enough to know what the Early Church believed. The question can never be shirked of whether it was right to do so.

Notes

1 *Religion Within the Limits of Reason Alone*, p. 100.
2 *Ibid.*, p. 152.
3 *Ibid.*, p. 143.
4 *Ibid.*, p. 105.
5 *Church Dogmatics*, IV. 1, p. 333.
6 *Ibid.*, p. 335.
7 *Ibid.*
8 *Ibid.*, p. 336.
9 *Ibid.*, p. 335.
10 *Ibid.*, p. 375, III. 3.
11 *Jesus Christ and Mythology*, p. 37.
12 *Ibid.*, p. 51.
13 *Ibid.*, p. 61.
14 *Culture and Value*, p. 32.
15 *Ibid.*, p. 64.
16 Helms, *Gospel Fictions*, p. 10.
17 *Jesus and the Word*, p. 3.
18 *Ibid.*
19 *The Point of Christology*, p. 111.
20 *Gospel Truth?*, p. 192.
21 *Ibid.*

22   *Ibid.*
23   *Jesus and the Word*, p. 13.
24   p. 14.
25   *A Kierkegaard Anthology*, p. 389.
26   *Lectures and Conversations*, p. 57.
27   Davis, "'Seeing" the Risen Jesus', p. 147.
28   *Ibid.*, p. 146.
29   Sherwin-White, *Roman Society and Law*, p. 188.

6

Is a Religious Epistemology Possible?

1 Foundationalism

The question of whether historical evidence can be called upon to support religious belief raises the whole issue of the nature of 'evidence' and its relation to religious faith. We have seen how there is a tendency to cede the idea of evidence to the physical sciences, on the ground that they are somehow more objective and neutral. This is to go along with Enlightenment ideals of reason which tend to make it the antithesis of religious faith rather than perhaps a support. Reason should not, however, be neutral when it comes to the consideration of what is real. Its aim should be to align itself with whatever is the nature of reality, at whatever level. The perennial temptation for religious believers is to retreat to 'faith' or some such category, so that their beliefs can no longer be subjected to rational scrutiny. Yet a realist should not be afraid of reason. There should be a proper grounding of our beliefs in what is the case. We should aim at something better than merely being accidentally right. Moreover, reality should be common to all, whereas the category of faith is personal. The aim of reason should be to unify beliefs arising in different areas of apparent knowledge and to make claims that can be universally accepted. Whether they are or not will always be a separate issue.

Because the notion of evidence has become so caught up with a scientific vision, it has become a suspect notion in the area of religious epistemology. It is often felt that religion is being forced to comply with rational demands that are inappropriate. Bertrand Russell, whose atheism was widely proclaimed, was once asked what he would say if after dying he found himself after all in the presence of God. Russell's reply was that he would ask God: 'Why did you not give better evidence of

your existence?' This was presumably not meant to be a flippant reply
to the question, since it has often been taken for granted that the
question of evidence should loom large in our search for knowledge.
Russell himself regularly insisted that strength of belief in a hypothesis
should depend on the strength of the evidence. Both in an intellectual
discipline like history, and in the conduct of science, the basing of
conclusions on evidence has seemed to form the heart of the enterprise.

Nicholas Wolterstorff describes the so-called evidentialist challenge
to religious belief as the view that 'no religion is acceptable unless
rational, and no religion is rational unless supported by evidence'.[1] The
idea of rationality is thus firmly tied to that of evidence in a way that
demands some elucidation of what could count as proper evidence. It is
indeed for this reason that evidentialism is usually associated with
foundationalism. The main tenets of the latter are that some beliefs are
held on the basis of other beliefs, and others are held immediately. The
latter can be regarded as certain and incorrigible. The task must then be
to give an account of them. Some will be seen to be self-evident, such
as that two plus two are four. Others will be states of consciousness
about which I could not be in error. In this way a whole edifice of
knowledge – indeed, the whole body of human knowledge – can be
built up on foundations which seem to be rock solid, because we could
not be mistaken about them. The further our theories are from the
common base of agreed, incontrovertible data, the more room there is
for error. There is then a distinction between propositions which are to
be regarded as properly basic, and those which follow from them or at
least can be regarded as probable with respect to them.

This whole way of looking at what it means to be rational has been
very much under attack. Foundationalism has become suspect even in
the realm of science, because it has not seemed to give due account of
the role of interpretation and theory in the recognition of data. However, Alvin Plantinga has made another form of attack. He has pointed
out that the very thesis that 'A is properly basic for me only if A is
self-evident or incorrigible or evident to the senses for me' is self-
referentially inconsistent.[2] This is because anyone who wishes to be
rational in accepting the thesis must accept that it is itself self-evident,
incorrigible or evident to the senses. Yet not only is it not, but as
Plantinga points out, we run into tremendous problems when we encounter general beliefs in enduring physical objects, other persons, or
the reality of the past.[3] None of these appears to meet the criterion. It is

in fact significant that they have typically produced tremendous problems for empiricist philosophy. The notions of rationality and proof have been drawn so tightly that most of the beliefs that apparently form the bedrock of our lives cannot be judged rational. The assumptions which we bring to our experience, and according to which our experience makes any sense, cannot, it seems, be justified.

The idea of truth seems indissolubly linked to that of claims to universality. The alternative is a relativism which restricts certain truths to particular groups. Nevertheless, as we saw in the last chapter, that should not mean that we cannot talk of objective truth in connection with contingent historical events. It is a mistake to assume that only necessary truth can be universal, and the mistake derives from an inability to distinguish between what is the case and what humans are able to agree about. The problem of irresolvable disagreement about religion, both between atheists and theists, and between different religions, haunts discussions about the rational basis of religion. Empiricists solved the issue by an appeal to empirical foundations that implicitly ruled out religious claims from the beginning. Anything transcendent, lying beyond the empirical world, had to be ignored, and reference to it considered meaningless. The reaction against foundationalism in epistemology has been partly fuelled, at least in the philosophy of religion, by an unwillingness to let religion be judged by inappropriate criteria, usually those derived from the physical sciences.

Foundationalism is explicitly a thesis in epistemology and so it is perhaps not surprising that it is found to be an inappropriate view when facing the metaphysical claims of religion. The subject has been changed from existence to how we can build up knowledge of it. This line of argument cannot be pressed too far because it is apparent that we do need some form of religious epistemology to help us to distinguish truth from falsity and weed out superstition. Appeals to faith cannot be allowed to result in all so-called religions being granted equal status with each other or with what seems to be our most firmly based knowledge about the physical world. We need criteria of rationality within the sphere of religion as well as outside it, if we are to avoid being utterly credulous and gullible.

Nevertheless it is important to recognize that the claims of the foundationalist to have a proper grounding for our knowledge cannot be identified with the insistence of the realist that there is an objective reality independent of our knowledge. Many philosophers can all too easily assume that a realist must be a foundationalist. The confusion arises because the realist, too, wishes to talk of our knowledge being grounded in something, but in the realist case it is not necessarily something of which we are aware. If we do indeed possess knowledge it must by definition be associated with reality. We cannot know what is false, and much of our putative knowledge may not be knowledge at all. Yet it is crucial to recognize that the reality is independent of the knowledge and is not constituted by it. In other words, whether we gain a grasp of reality or not does not affect the status of the reality. It exists as a grounding, a basis or a foundation of our knowledge, if we want to use such metaphors. It is, however, essentially an external criterion in that we do not always know whether we have arrived at a knowledge of reality or not. As a result, we can even succeed in referring to reality, even when we are not in a position to demonstrate that that is what we are doing. William Alston points out that it is a confusion to conflate 'referring and showing that or how one refers'.[4] He concludes that if that is cleared up, 'the metaphysical realist is in no inferior position to anyone else'.

Reality is in no sense an indubitable foundation for knowledge as envisaged by traditional foundationalism. The certainty demanded by the latter cannot always be guaranteed by realism. Certainty is a state we aspire to and not a property of reality. As we shall see in chapter 7, D. Z. Phillips envisages realism as foundationalism without its certainty, but this is still a misunderstanding.[5] It runs together the reasoning by which we arrived at our beliefs with what our beliefs purport to be about. If we wish to retain the questionable image of foundations, the foundations of our knowledge may be said to be distinct from the metaphysical foundations on which our knowledge has to be built. For instance, the former could be internal to our knowledge, so that we have to be aware of them. A metaphysical conception of reality has to be logically distinct from our knowledge if it is to be its warrant. Yet this logical gap between myself and the object of knowledge could actually serve to cast doubt on claims to knowledge. In fact, there may be a justification for our knowledge even though we are not ourselves in a position to give one. We may be correct in our judgements and this correctness may not be a lucky accident but may be derived from my relationship with reality. That does not mean that I am aware of this or more crucially can stand apart from myself and my predicament and give an account of how this is so.

2 Doxastic Practices

The distinction between the metaphysical status of what we believe in and our own ability to give a justification for the belief is crucial. This provides the explanation for a point that is often emphasized, particularly by the practitioners of what has been termed 'Reformed epistemology', such as William Alston, Alvin Plantinga and Nicholas Wolterstorff. The approach of each of these is not completely the same. Indeed, Alston has playfully suggested that he should be known as an 'Episcopalian epistemologist'. They do, however, agree that an inability to give a final justification as a grounding for my most basic beliefs does not necessarily undermine their validity. As Alston puts it, there is a distinction between 'the state or condition of being justified in holding a certain belief' and 'the activity of justifying a belief'.[6] I can be justified without supposing that I am or being able to give a justification. Knowing something does not always mean that I know that I know.

It follows from this that we may start from certain basic beliefs, without being able to give a full justification for them. Indeed, the claim must be even stronger. We have no choice but to start somewhere. Unless we can produce self-evident foundations for knowledge, we are bound to be forced back to basic beliefs which cannot be given a rational justification even if they are justified. Even many of our most ordinary everyday beliefs, such as the memory of my having breakfast this morning, come into this category. As Plantinga points out, 'I do not reason to them from other propositions, or accept them on the evidential basis of other propositions.'[7] That does not mean that they cannot be corrected from other sources of belief, but it does mean that asking for a non-circular justification of memory as such is impossible. It is the main claim of reformed epistemology that belief in God is also 'properly basic' in this way. There is, they would say, no reason to give other apparently basic beliefs a privileged position, but to demand that belief in God rest on the evidential basis of other beliefs. We can start with a belief in God that does not rest on the foundation of a knowledge that is more secure. It can be corrected, but it need yield priority to no other beliefs by virtue of some appeal to 'evidence'.

Alston himself applies this approach to the whole practice of perception. He sees that perception as such cannot somehow be given a justification by reason of some firmer knowledge. He argues that in fact it is impossible to give a non-circular justification of our everyday contact with the physical world. We can justify one perception by means of another and the whole system of perceptual belief can gain a substantial degree of internal self-support. We can never stand outside it, however, and give it an external justification. Even if I rely on someone else, I am still relying on their perceptions. Yet that does not mean that we are not perceiving something real in an unmediated way. In a sense, Alston is a 'naive' or 'direct' realist about perception, in that he considers that we do obtain information directly from the external world. There is a difference, he believes, between thinking of a chair with one's eyes shut, and then opening one's eyes and seeing the chair. Yet even so there is no way of checking that I am seeing a chair without an appeal to somebody's perception. He writes:

> Try the following experiment. Close your eyes, and think about the things and people around you ... Then open your eyes and look at them. There is a world of difference in your cognitive consciousness before and after that eye-opening experience. What is the difference? It is felicitously put by saying that when you open your eyes, these things and people are presented to your awareness.[8]

There may sometimes be reasons for doubting that things are as they seem, but the point is that we need no further justification for the fact of presentation. Such perceptions form a basis for knowledge and, indeed, as Plantinga would suggest, if our perceptual organs are working properly in the environment for which they were designed, then we do have knowledge. Alston wants to claim that this puts our ordinary perception of the physical world in a similar position to mystical claims to have had direct awareness of God. He quotes examples of religious experience, and says that 'our sources take it that something, namely God, has been presented or given to their consciousness, in generically the same way as that in which objects in the environment are (apparently) presented to one's consciousness in sense perception'.[9]

Alston, however, does not wish to rely merely on the claims of individuals. He introduces the idea of what he calls a 'doxastic practice', 'a way of forming beliefs and epistemically evaluating them'.[10] In this way, what he terms the 'Christian Mystical Practice' can claim as much epistemological authority as other recognized ways of building up our knowledge, such as perception and memory. This places religious beliefs in a very different position from that envisaged from traditional foundationalism. They no longer have to measure up to a standard imposed from another context. It will be wrong to suppose that they can be justified by the standards of ordinary perception, just as it would be inappropriate to try and justify the latter by means of mystical experience. It is a mistake to look for one universal, secure foundation for all our knowledge. Instead, according to Alston, we must rather divide up our ability to gain and judge belief into different compartments. Mystical experience is of course only one facet of religious belief, but if claims to be able to have direct awareness of God can claim to be taken as seriously as our ordinary human ability to see the world around us, religious faith is in a very different epistemological position from that envisaged by the Enlightenment. Alston believes that just as we do directly perceive the world around us, we can equally have a direct experience of God. His main concern, however, is the epistemological one of how far we are able to obtain justifications for our beliefs. It is always possible that we are justified but we still need guidance in our decisions about what to believe.

He gives as examples of doxastic practices those 'involving reliance on sense perception, introspection, memory, rational intuition, various kinds of reasoning, and mystical experience'.[11] These are all various ways of apparently gaining knowledge. As a realist, Alston is merely proposing that such practices are innocent until proved guilty. We cannot be faulted for doing what we cannot help, but that still leaves the question of truth. We still have no guarantee that the practices concerned are properly reliable. The question may still arise as to whether we could be wrong all the time. This would always follow from the kind of realist perspective that Alston wishes to espouse. He writes that since each practice does not create its own reality, 'but rather seeks to tell it like it is with respect to the one reality (or segment thereof), there is a live possibility that the outputs of one practice contradict those of another'.[12]

This is a possibility that many philosophers would refuse to allow. Those influenced, for instance, by the later Wittgenstein could not envisage the idea that our practices could be radically mistaken, or that our language-games are somehow ill conceived at root. For them, the only alternative to the normal following of our everyday practices would be insanity. We could not be honestly in error as that would make no sense. There would be nothing external to the practice according to which such a judgement could be made. Pragmatists, in the American tradition, would similarly find it difficult to envisage a global scepticism about a practice. For them, scepticism and doubt must be parasitic on accepted practices, and cannot be used to undermine them.

One criterion that Alston seems to set store by is the fact that such practices are socially established. He argues that 'it is rational to engage in any socially established practice that we do not have sufficient reasons for regarding as unreliable'.[13] It is for this reason that he is able to hold that we can perceive God as directly as we can perceive the world around us. He says that the Christian Mystical Practice 'is rationally engaged in, since it is a socially established doxastic practice that is not demonstrably unreliable or otherwise disqualified for rational acceptance'.[14] Thus, it seems, the mere fact that it is socially established means that 'it is prima facie worthy of rational participation'.

The question still must be faced at what moment such practices have to be regarded as unreliable. Clearly the fact of the existence of different mystical practices in different belief systems itself may raise problems, and Alston is willing to confront these. Despite his avowed realism, the emphasis on social establishment is intended to invoke Wittgenstein's views about social practices, and similar criticisms can be levelled against the idea of doxastic practices as against such notions as language-games and forms of life. Dividing up our knowledge into distinctive areas so they can each provide a framework of justification raises the issue of how they should be individuated. In fact, Alston does not envisage practices to be totally separated from each other. For example, the outputs from one can be inputs to another. Yet he tells us that 'there is no appeal beyond the practices we find firmly established, psychologically and socially'.[15] It seems as if reference to such practices is not very enlightening unless we can decide where one ends and another begins. Indeed, at times the very notion of a practice becomes so attenuated as to be almost meaningless. Alston says at one point that mystical perception as a practice 'is best viewed as a fragment of the cognitive aspect of a larger religious practice that, on its cognitive side, makes use of all a person's faculties and wide stretches of the person's belief system'.[16] At that point, the notion of an identifiable practice risks becoming submerged in a generalized account of human reasoning.

The issue of what counts as a practice becomes of crucial importance when Alston refers to 'a plurality of mystical, perceptual doxastic practices with mutually contradictory output and/or background belief systems'.[17] Why should mystical experience itself be parcelled up into different practices? If the mere fact of major disagreement defines a different practice, doxastic practices are likely to multiply at a frightening rate. At the root of Alston's approach, and his wish to stress the epistemic autonomy of established doxastic practices, is the commendable wish not to let one set of beliefs be judged by the criteria appropriate to a completely different kind of belief. It is also a recognition of our inability of giving a non-circular justification of, say, perception. He wishes to stress that there is 'no appeal beyond the doxastic practices to which we find ourselves firmly committed'.[18] Yet the result is a splintering of our knowledge and belief into separate compartments in a way that may shield them from inappropriate criticism but which also seems to blunt their ability to claim an objective truth whose force transcends the limits set by the practice. The emphasis on practices can undermine the realism that Alston simultaneously wishes to promote.

We may have to start with our ordinary doxastic practices simply because there is nowhere else to start. We have to trust our perception, memory and so on, because that is all we have. We have to assume their reliability. Alston would wish to say that the same holds for the epistemic status of mystical perception. He says of it as a doxastic practice that provided it 'is firmly rooted in its devotees from early in life, interconnected with other practices in a form of life, and socially established, there will be the same argument against abandoning it as for more widely distributed practices'.[19] Yet this fails to get to grips with such fundamental issues as to why it should be 'firmly rooted' or 'socially established'. The best answer is because it is a vehicle of truth but this will, in many people's eyes merely bring us back to the question of the criteria of truth, and the very issues of rationality and justification that Alston is trying to confront. Nevertheless there would seem to be a significant difference between a practice such as perception that is recognizable as an essential part of what it is to be human, and more local practices, such as alleged experiences of God which are not so widely shared and may even be different in different religions.

Alston maintains that his theory, despite its debts to the views of the later Wittgenstein, is far from the relativist views being canvassed in some quarters. He does not want to hold that doxastic practices define distinct worlds. He writes:

My theory of doxastic practices is firmly realistic, recognising a single reality that is what it is, regardless of how we think or talk about it. The doxastic practice is a source of justification and rationality: it does not determine truth or reality. In other words, for me doxastic practices are crucial epistemologically, not methaphysically.[20]

Given this stance, the important issue will always be the link between reality and our understanding of it. What can prevent the success of a doxastic practice being anything other than a huge amount of luck? Will it always be a coincidence that what we take to be knowledge is properly grounded and that our attempts at justification are not totally illusory? The problem with any theory that breaks the link between apparent and real justification is not just the threat of scepticism. The danger is that the process of justification becomes detached, in practice if not in principle, from the real world. It becomes an artefact of our local social situation and reality can become so much of an article of abstruse metaphysical faith that it eventually drops out of account as being irrelevant. This is not Alston's view. He believes that it is through using our doxastic practices that we can establish metaphysics. Yet if a practice can in principle be wholly unreliable, it is far from clear how this can be done. Indeed, the very idea of a practice being untrustworthy itself depends on a prior realist metaphysics.

3   The Possibility of Trust

Whatever realist gloss may be given, flirting with Wittgensteinian conceptions of justification appears exceedingly risky. In *On Certainty* Wittgenstein roots epistemological certainty in our practices. He shows that argument has to come to an end somewhere, and that the foundations of particular language-games cannot in the end require some further external justification. Some assumptions are just part of our life, perhaps as humans but also perhaps as those, like physicists, with more specialized practices. Wittgenstein's inability to provide any argument as to why I am right to be guided by the propositions of physics rather than oracles is itself an indication of an incipient relativism.[21] He claims that 'to say: in the end we can only adduce such grounds as we hold to be grounds, is to say nothing at all.'[22] Instead of always wanting to ground a particular assertion, we have, he thinks, to see it in the context of the practice of which it is a part. A language-game cannot be shown to be justified or unjustified, reasonable or unreasonable. As he says, 'It is not based on grounds . . . It is there – like our life.'[23] A consequence of this would be that, in Wittgenstein's words 'it has no meaning to say that a game has always been played wrong'.[24] This would be as true of our language-games as of a game like football. Alston's willingness to accept that in the end a doxastic practice could be seen to be unreliable would not be accepted by Wittgenstein. There is nothing by virtue of which what he terms the 'unmoving foundation' of a game could be shown to mistaken. The context of the practice itself is to determine what can count as well founded: 'At the foundation of well-founded belief lies belief that is not founded.'[25] His point is that justification has to come to an end and finally we have to take something on trust. This is stated explicitly when he says, 'I really want to say that a language-game is only possible if one trusts something (I did not say "can trust something").'[26] In other words we have to come down to a question of brute fact of what we do in fact trust and not of what is trustworthy. The latter would itself require a further edifice of justification, which just cannot be built.

The problem with concentrating on practices is that there remains the question of how widespread they may be and what happens when we find different practices collide, as in the case of physicists and believers in oracles. If we are not very careful, truth and justification will be so localized that nothing can make any claim to universality. The plausibility of some of what Wittgenstein maintains lies in his implicit appeal to our common nature as human beings and to consequent practices which we all share (such as those connected with typical pain behaviour). The difficulties arise much more sharply when it is acknowledged that some practices are much more local. As Wittgenstein himself acknowledges, 'what men consider reasonable or unreasonable alters'.[27] Given this, who is to determine what is right, or are we always to assume that the latest view is the best?

The easy assumption that universal agreement is even likely is probably too optimistic. We may as human beings be normally starting from the same place when it comes to the working of our sense organs, and our contact with the physical world; but when it comes to other kinds of beliefs it may well be that different groups of people in different historical situations make very different assumptions. It is at this point that the 'Reformed epistemologists' wish to stress that some beliefs may be

properly basic for some people even though they are far from universally shared. The quest for secure, universal foundations itself must
come to grief, but that does not mean that different people may not
have different starting points which cannot be given some form of
universal justification. Wittgenstein's insistence that something has to be
taken on trust is relevant. His position involves a suspicion of philosophical accounts of our beliefs which seem to stray from our ordinary
use of words. Yet without the kind of metaphysics ruled out by
Wittgenstein, our practices cannot claim any universal significance. He
refuses to allow us to stand outside our language-games and observe
them.

Hilary Putnam sees metaphysical realism and relativism as aspects of
the same problem. He alleges that each demands that we stand outside
our practices and detach ourselves from our most basic presuppositions,
in order to pass judgement. The relativist somehow wants to survey all
conceptual schemes in order to tell us that truth is merely an internal
matter to each. The realist, on the other hand, might similarly see our
epistemological practices as totally unrelated to metaphysical reality.
Putnam discusses the question of whether Wittgenstein is a relativist,
particularly in the light of the latter's views about religious belief.
Putnam considers it wrong to see relativism 'as a cure or a relief from
the malady of lacking a metaphysical foundation'.[28] Instead, he argues
that we should see 'relativism and the desire for a metaphysical foundation as manifestations of the same disease'. He continues:

> The thing to say to the relativist is that some things are true and some
> things are warranted and some things are reasonable, but of course we
> can only say so if we have an appropriate language. And we do have the
> language, and we can and do say so, even though that language does not
> rest on any metaphysical guarantee like Reason.

Putnam goes on to quote with approval Wittgenstein's remark about
trust and he sums up the position by claiming that 'our language game
rests not on proof or on Reason but trust'. Putnam, in other words,
wishes to champion a common-sense realism which assumes that our
language means what it says when we use it in ordinary ways. We do
not need, and indeed cannot, resort to metaphysics to provide it with
some inaccessible foundation. According to Putnam, following his interpretation of Wittgenstein, 'the way to understand religious language

isn't to try to apply some metaphysical classification of possible forms of discourse'.[29] We should not look for some kind of transcendental justification, but should instead see what religious believers mean when they use their language by seeing in the context of a form of life. Putnam thus arrives at a position very like that of D. Z. Phillips, which we shall be examining in the next chapter.

Common-sense realism is all very well when we are dealing with common-sense beliefs, of the kind that Wittgenstein does for the most part deal with in *On Certainty* (such as the belief that that is a tree). In a religious context such realism merely obfuscates, since what is in question is precisely the notion of reality that is appropriate. A repudiation of metaphysics would immediately close off certain options, and in fact this is just what happens. In dealing with analogous issues in the philosophy of mathematics Putnam refers with approval to a remark by Wittgenstein that we think of 'reality' as something we can point to, so that 'it is this, that'.[30] This is of course reassuringly in agreement with common sense, but Putnam draws a large conclusion from this. He says that it does not mean that all reality has to be observable but that 'the less what we are talking about is analogous to the thises and thats we can point to the less sense it has to ask whether what we are talking about is or is not a "reality"'. Putnam is particularly concerned in this context with the idea of 'mathematical objects', and is sceptical about such an idea. They would, he says be causally inert and he suggests in that case that mathematics would have worked just as well if such intangible objects did not exist. He says: 'For, since the supposed mathematical objects are causally inert, the ordinary empirical objects would have behaved just as they do, and our applied mathematics would have succeeded and failed just when it does succeed and fail.'[31]

At this point it becomes crystal clear that philosophical concerns about the status, if any, of 'mathematical objects' will be very different from apparently analogous concerns in the philosophy of religion. The way that Putnam has set up the problem makes it look as if it is going to be very difficult to make much sense of the reality of a metaphysical God, so far removed would such a reality be from the world of this and that. Yet for many believers the whole point of believing in God is that He is not 'causally inert'. He is not an intellectual, rational construction, or some kind of abstract object, like a number. Deist views may have been tempted to portray God like that, but in Christianity and other religions, God is the very opposite of what is causally inert. Apart from the fact that He is regarded as the cause of everything, alleged particular divine revelation and intervention suggest to many a definite ground for belief. No doubt anti-metaphysical views like that of Wittgenstein are inhospitable to ideas of special divine action. They are too rooted in our everyday experience. As a result a disdain for the 'philosophical' as compared with the ordinary results in a questionable emphasis on the material world and by extension the world of physics. Putnam at first may seem to agree with this. He says:

> The Wittgensteinian strategy, I believe, is to argue that while there is such a thing as correctness in ethics, in interpretation, in mathematics, the way to understand that is not trying to model it on the ways in which we get things right in physics, but by trying to understand the life we lead with our concepts in each of these distinct areas.[32]

Putnam would no doubt wish to add religion to this list. It may look as if he is trying to reinstate the integrity of different types of discourse in the face of attacks from scientific realists who wish, he says, to impose the same pattern of what it is to be true on all types of language. They wish, Putnam thinks, to insist on the link between truth and the existence of 'objects'. The choice which Putnam repudiates is one which insists that judgements are either misguided or they have to be about 'objects which are causally efficacious, in the way in which magnetism is causally efficacious'. No doubt the merits of this approach may vary case by case, but it should be quite clear that the repudiation of any idea that religion is about a causally efficacious object will be fraught with difficulty. God is not normally thought to be a physical object nor one cause among other (physical) ones. Yet to go to the other extreme and to suggest that because any divine nature is not physical it has no clear objective reality is to deny for many people the heart of religion. Most people would think that if God is real, He can relate to people, perhaps as a person rather than as an 'object'. The problem is how to give an account of this which does not make God into one cause among many, or one 'object' among many. Yet that does not mean that it is wrong to think of God as causally efficacious and objective. The refusal, characteristic of Wittgensteinian approaches, to stray from our ordinary, everyday use of language is bound to challenge the very heart of religion. Yet even if it is conceded that normal uses of the word 'object' are connected with causality, that, as we have seen, is no reason to think that God is not an object. Of course, it will then be insisted that our ideas of causality cannot be taken very far from the everyday use of the word 'cause'. In the end the refusal to escape from the world of this and that embodies a latter-day materialism that will not let us entertain the idea of entities other than those of everyday experience. Wittgenstein's horror of the philosophical is not just anti-metaphysical. It must also be anti-religious, unless 'religion' is radically reinterpreted.

Putnam is particularly concerned with questions of meaning and justification. It is significant that he is critical of the possibility of giving 'a metaphysical foundation', and that he should consider it worth denying that Reason could be the source of any metaphysical guarantee. It is apparent that he at least implicitly would associate metaphysical realism with the quest for foundations. He also assumes that the existence of a metaphysical reality must be synonymous with its availability to us. What our so-called 'Reason' cannot underwrite cannot provide any kind of metaphysical guarantee.[33] Since he does not believe that this kind of detached, contextless 'Reason' is attainable, that entails the impossibility of metaphysics. Yet this is to confuse the nature of reality with what it is within the power of human reason to find out. It may indeed be true that much of reality is beyond our reach and thus human metaphysics will be limited. This is, however, to begin to reinterpret metaphysics in terms of epistemology. It is still to demand that reality be reduced to what we can give an account of.

4 'Basic' Beliefs

Foundationalism comes in all shapes and sizes, but it is a general characteristic of its approach that the certainty of the starting point, whether it be beliefs or axioms or whatever, provides a firm basis for the items which rest on them. It seems to be the case, too, that the basis and what rests on that basis belong to the same category. Belief rests on other beliefs which in their turn can claim certainty. This means that in epistemology the foundations of knowledge cannot be radically different from the knowledge that is generated. This, however, creates a problem since justification is thereby generated by items, such as beliefs, which are very similar in nature to what stands in need of justification. This is, of course, one reason why it is so easy to level the charge of circularity at foundationalist systems. The perceptions that appear to be able to justify beliefs can themselves be characterized as beliefs in need of justification.

The whole point of referring to 'properly basic' beliefs is to deny that there is a circle. They can be held to be related to experience in a different way from 'non-basic' ones. The Reformed epistemologists try to show that this means that religious belief is in no worse state than any other form of belief. They argue for a parity between, say, religious and perceptual belief. There may be no way of appealing to evidence to support either without begging the question. In the end we come down to basic propositions. The allegation could be that these are somehow arbitrary because they do not, it appears, rest on anything else. This would be, however to miss the point of what such epistemologists are trying to say. For them, basic beliefs are reliable sources of knowledge of a reality beyond. We have to take something on trust. The problem is how to give an account of such a position which does not become indistinguishable from Wittgenstein's position in *On Certainty*. It is interesting that even the latter has been described as foundationalist in that he does still talk of 'grounds'. One writer, in following this line, claims that 'Wittgenstein's genius consisted in constructing an account of human knowledge whose foundations, whose supporting presuppositions, were in no way like knowledge. Knowledge belongs to the language-game and certitude does not.'[34]

For instance Wittgenstein says, 'If the true is what is grounded, then the ground is not true, nor yet false.'[35] In this he departs from traditional forms of foundationalism in that he makes a radical distinction between the character of what is grounded and the grounds. The latter cannot be justified because they are what impart justification. Yet as is apparent from his example of physicists and oracles, they are not necessarily universally acknowledged. Wittgenstein tends to appeal not only to common features of human life but also the communal background, which by its nature can vary. He says that 'the end is not an ungrounded presupposition: it is an ungrounded way of acting'.[36] This blocks the possibility of an infinite regress of justification, but it leaves unresolved the fact that humans not only act in similar ways, as when they feel pain, but also engage in very divergent practices, as with religion. We should remember in this connection how Wittgenstein himself stressed how a child can be brought up to produce 'apparently telling grounds' either for or against the existence of a God.[37] When ways of acting differ at root, it seems as if Wittgenstein leaves nothing more to be said. Once again the ideas of a language-game, a way of acting and a form of life, remain tantalizingly unclear.

The source of all this confusion is the fact that Wittgenstein restricts the role of reason to inside a system or language-game. It is only within such a context, that as he put it 'arguments have their life'.[38] As we have seen before, he rules out metaphysics. How far, then, can philosophers follow a similar path emphasizing the priority of our everyday practices without lapsing into a denial of metaphysics and of reason, and an extolling of common sense which undermines religion? Putnam certainly seems in effect to be doing this. Alston protests that despite his emphasis on doxastic practices he is nevertheless a metaphysical realist. The perennial problem is how reason can be understood to have a metaphysical basis. Wittgenstein certainly recognized the problem in that he tried to ground our beliefs and practices in something of a different character. Naturalists try very often to ground them not in the fact of communal agreement, but in our shared evolutionary history. This though faces the undoubted problem that it may well have been in our genetic interests to have evolved sharing false beliefs. The founder of sociobiology. E. O. Wilson,[39] thought that religion – any religion – helped to foster an important sense of corporate identity and consequent urges to altruism. It persisted, therefore, because of its beneficial results. Yet Wilson believes all religion is false. Naturalism cannot easily distinguish between the true and the biologically useful.

These are problems that Reformed epistemologists with their lively respect for metaphysics have to address. They can emphasize that theirs is an epistemological position and not one which carries metaphysical conclusions. Indeed, Wolterstorff says[40] that the centre of the programme of Reformed epistemology 'has been the contention that often it is entirely right and proper for persons to believe things about God without doing so on the basis of propositional evidence'. He thus concludes that 'beliefs about God which are basic in a person's belief system may nonetheless be proper'. This goes back to the point that just because we cannot give any justification of our beliefs that does not mean that they are not justified. All this makes sense given a metaphysical framework. The recurring problem, however, is that metaphysics is going to get dragged back into epistemology, rather than underpinning it in some way. Even a particular metaphysical stance will be said to be properly basic to a particular view. When Plantinga insists that belief in God is properly basic, this may carry with it a realist view of God. Yet it is apparent that, to use traditional categories, a belief in God becomes a matter of faith and not reason. This may not imply some deficiency of rationality, since it is claimed that all structures of belief function in similar ways. The problem, though, with an appeal to faith is always its particularity. Because one person, or group, has faith in something, that may not seem an adequate reason for others to adopt a similar faith. The question still remains whether what is trusted is trustworthy. The mere fact that someone is fully committed to a doxastic practice, and indeed that it has become socially established, is not enough. Others will be committed to something entirely different.

The trouble with the response that there is a justification but we may not know it, is that it runs the risk of becoming indistinguishable from the Wittgensteinian response that that is just how the language-game is played. Even the appeal to faith or trust is reminiscent of the same move by Wittgenstein. If we all have to stop the process of justification somewhere, the problem comes when people arrive at different termi- nuses. The advantage of being able to appeal to reason lies far from the fear that religion is made subject to alien requirements. It is that with it I can give grounds that can at least in principle persuade others of the rightness of my stance. Without an appeal to reason, I cannot expect others to take my beliefs seriously, let alone adopt them. It is a matter of concern how similar some versions of Reformed epistemology can at first sight appear to the seemingly relativist position of the later Wittgenstein. It can look as if one's most basic commitments[41] involve the kind of leap of faith that is entirely personal and is not required of others. Yet if one is confronted by reality, one will be confronted by something that is the same for everyone.

Beliefs influenced by Calvinism, as some Reformed epistemology avowedly is, all too often concentrate too much on the gifts of faith rather than the claims of reason. The beliefs of a particular group are then made the starting point, rather than the universal claims of reason. Yet if it is true, any religion should be able to claim the attention of all and not just some people. Its claims may not be acknowledged but that is a different issue. Why, though, should we trust our reason? Clearly the question could itself land us in a vicious regress, and yet for those who take a doctrine of human sin seriously it is a serious question. Of course, like all such positions it can overreach itself. Doctrines about our total depravity could not in consistency be properly stated, because if we are that fallible we could not be sure even of knowing our fallibility.

Plantinga sees the problem of providing arguments for trusting our reason, even in a theistic context. It is tempting, for instance, for theists to say that because there is a God who has made us in His image we can trust our reason as God given. God is no deceiver, so Descartes thought. Yet even if this were true, the problem lies in trying rationally to prove it without begging the very question at issue. If we are afraid that we cannot trust our reason, it will not help to provide a rational argument as to why we can. Plantinga puts it this way:

> Suppose you find yourselves with the doubt that our cognitive faculties produce truth: you can't quell the doubt by producing an argument about God and his veracity, or, indeed, any argument at all; for the argument, of course, will be under as much suspicion as its source.[42]

Once one believes in God, one will have a reason for trusting our rational faculties. There would be every reason to suppose, as Plantinga says,[43] that our cognitive faculties have the apprehension of truth as their purpose and for the most part fulfil their purpose. As a result Plantinga concludes that 'naturalistic epistemology flourishes best in the garden of supernaturalistic metaphysics'. Once again we come back to the question of metaphysics and the question of its possible relation with rationality. Plantinga wants it to guarantee rationality, but the question of how one can establish such a metaphysics (as opposed to, say, regarding religious faith as the gift of the Holy Spirit), remains unresolved. If there is a God, it follows that we are likely to be able to trust the mechanisms for producing beliefs with which we have been designed. If there is a God, it is reasonable to assume that apparent presentations of divine reality in human experience are reliable. How, though, can any of this be established? At every turn, there seems to be a danger of begging the question. In a way, it is not very comforting to be told that all our belief-producing mechanisms are in the same position. We cannot, for example, as we have seen, justify perception without appealing to perception. Is reason then, so impotent?

Reformed epistemology appears to succumb to the temptation of retreating to a faith that is groundless. Its defence is that all its opponents are in the same position. Everyone has to appeal to 'faith' or 'trust' in some way or other. Yet this is to flirt with the subjectivism that is always threatening when a retreat is made to faith, or with the relativism that can accompany an emphasis on social practices. Protestations of a realist metaphysics have little impact unless they give us a grounding for reason. Mere reliance on such belief-producing mechanisms and practices as we have is insufficient. The repudiation of the notion of reasons for faith may have been an effective way of resisting the depradations of those who want to subject it to inappropriate criteria. In the end, however, the test of faith is whether it is rooted in reality. It cannot be insulated from other forms of belief, since they all purport to be about one world. It may be that religious experience can claim to provide as important a contribution to knowledge as ordinary perception. Such claims, however, have to be tested against the character of the real world. Because there is one world, and everyone is confronted by it, claims to truth must have a universal significance. They cannot be locked up in special compartments, however defined. As we shall see, faith cannot be insulated from the nature of the physical world, any more than it could be insulated from the discoveries of history.[44]

Notes

1 Plantinga and Wolterstorff, *Faith and Rationality*, p. 6.
2 *Ibid.*, p. 60.
3 *Ibid.*, p. 59.
4 Alston, *A Realist Conception of Truth*, p. 157.
5 'On really believing', p. 53.
6 Alston, *Perceiving God*, p. 71.
7 *Warrant and Proper Function*, p. 61.
8 *A Realist Conception of Truth*, p. 157.
9 *Perceiving God*, p. 14.
10 *Ibid.*, p. 6.
11 *Ibid.*
12 *Ibid.*, p. 155.
13 *Ibid.*, p. 6.
14 *Ibid.*, p. 194.
15 *Ibid.*, p. 149.
16 *Ibid.*, p. 188.
17 *Ibid.*, p. 7.
18 *Ibid.*, p. 177.
19 *Ibid.*, p. 169.
20 *Ibid.*, p. 165.
21 *On Certainty*, #609–12.

22 *Ibid.*, #599.
23 *Ibid.*, #559.
24 *Ibid.*, #496.
25 *Ibid.*, #253.
26 *Ibid.*, #509.
27 *Ibid.*, #336.
28 Putnam, *Renewing Philosophy*.
29 *Ibid.*, p. 168.
30 'On Wittgenstein's philosophy of mathematics', p. 267.
31 *Ibid.*, p. 247.
32 *Ibid.*, p. 263.
33 See my *Rationality and Science*, chapter 5, for a discussion of Putnam's views about a God's eye view.
34 Stroll, *Moore and Wittgenstein on Certainty*, p. 145.
35 *On Certainty*, #205.
36 *Ibid.*, #110.
37 *Ibid.*, #107.
38 *Ibid.*, #105.
39 See *On Human Nature*, 1978, p. 184.
40 *Divine Discourse*, p. 14.
41 See my *Reason and Commitment*.
42 *Warrant and Proper Function*, p. 237.
43 *Ibid.*
44 For further comments on the relation of reason to the world, see my 'The grounding of reason'.

7

Should Religious Forms of Life be Justified?

1 Concepts and Practices

We saw in the last chapter how even philosophers who wish to espouse a strong metaphysical realism can emphasize the role of social practices, particularly in our assessment of what is to count as knowledge. Yet the ensuing danger is that the fact of the practices, however defined, takes precedence. Somehow the reality that gives them their point becomes secondary. We believe in the reality because of our practices. We do not become committed to our practices, because of the nature of reality. What we regard as rational can become a construction out of our form of life, rather than a reflection of the way things are.

One of the major criticisms of seeing Christian mysticism as a 'doxastic practice' is the existence of different religions with different systems of belief and different ways of assessing religious experience. We may sit happily within our socially accepted way of viewing things, but then so do many others with radically different visions of reality. Can these differences be rationally assessed in ways that do not beg every question at issue? This might appear to be the province of the philosophy of religion, but it is significant that even the purpose of that is hotly contested in the contemporary world. There is a perpetual tug between those who wish to appeal to metaphysics and to an all-embracing rationality anchored in it, and those who concentrate on the local meaning and parochial rationality generated within the context of particular practices. It will then appear to be impossible to transcend all practices and local assumptions to talk of what is 'really' the case. There will, instead, be a concentration on describing the assumptions made within 'forms of life'. The idea of transcending what is said from the standpoint of a particular practice (perhaps so as to check its accuracy) will be ruled out.

There is a certain instability about such views. Those who hold them wish to deny that we can in any meaningful way detach ourselves from whatever practices have formed our thinking and acting. Yet they still appear to consider that philosophical remarks about the meaning of such practices can be made. Even an assertion that we are all bound to certain contexts itself bids to be a statement that is free of context. It appears to be a claim about forms of life, rather than one made from within one particular form of life. Philosophy perpetually runs the risk of becoming mere descriptive sociology. Yet the possibility of the rational detachment necessary even for the conduct of sociology is being denied.

Given all this, the issue becomes pressing as to what precisely is the subject matter of the philosophy of religion. An obvious answer is religion, but that may be misleading. To take a parallel case, the philosophy of science should examine the presuppositions and methodology of science. It is not automatically a sociological investigation into the practice of science. Some philosophical positions concerning the nature and role of science have provided a powerful impetus to the sociology of knowledge in general and of science in particular. The more that scientific reasoning is made to depend on the influence of a particular 'paradigm' or tradition within science, the more tempting it is to conduct a sociological investigation into the way such paradigms can get established. The less universal scientific reason appears, the less it appears to be its own explanation. Scientists are not, it seems, pursuing truth by means of a detached reason. They are historically situated in a particular social context at a particular time. Their concepts are rooted in identifiable social practices, and can be explained accordingly.

This is a controversial account of science which rapidly detaches it from the pursuit of truth. It stems from one philosophical account within the philosophy of science. One of the most pressing issues within the latter is precisely the role of reason within science. To return to the philosophy of religion, if the discipline is anything like the philosophy of science, it should examine the presuppositions and methodology of religion. The response may well be that religion is nothing like science, but that point may be one of the major questions facing the philosophy of religion. How far, for instance, is a religious belief like a scientific hypothesis? Yet just as the philosophy of science cannot assume without begging the question that scientific practice must be accepted at face value, leaving its rationale on one side, so the philosophy of religion cannot just take religion as a social phenomenon to be the object of its investigation.

This is not necessarily generally accepted. For instance, a Dutch philosopher of religion, writes of the demise of philosophical theology as a discipline. He argues that we are left with the fact of religious traditions or, as he says, 'the secularized postexistence of such traditions'.[1] His conclusion is: 'The object of the philosophy of religion is not so much of a logical or epistemological kind; rather it is a factual entity or plurality of such entities, namely the comprehensive cultural entities called religions.' His argument is that the philosophy of religion is in effect the heir of rational theology. He continues:

> Philosophy of religion thus expresses by its very name a serious rupture of the metaphysical tradition. This name signals that it is impossible to know God by reason alone: we cannot have knowledge of God other than we have of the contingent entities called religions.[2]

This view is no doubt expressive of a strong current in the philosophy of religion, although it is seldom expressed so clearly. Yet it is only one view within the discipline. Anyone studying the philosophy of religion who concludes that metaphysical presuppositions are built into the heart of all religion is surely not involved in a contradiction. Even the conclusion that it is possible to reason about God and obtain knowledge in that way (say through natural theology) would seem to be a perfectly legitimate one, whether right or wrong, within the problems philosophers of religion set themselves. The rational presuppositions of religion cannot necessarily be reduced to terms a sociologist would find acceptable.

Yet for those who become baffled by attempts to establish a rational basis for religion, let alone those who try to prove the existence of God, it is very tempting to shift the ground and to talk simply of the fact of certain practices and the existence of certain traditions. We have already seen how potent a temptation this can be in the field of the comparative study of religion. Yet the more it is emphasized that our concepts cannot be grasped out of context, and that the context is provided by our practices, the more it can appear inevitable that any religious understanding must be rooted in local ways of acting. The universal claims of metaphysics then seem to be forever beyond our reach. Does this matter? Can everything remain the same when we participate in traditional practices without claiming that there is any rational justification for them? To some the situation might appear comparable to expecting a child to go on writing letters to Father Christmas long after she has learnt that the presents on Christmas morning come from her parents. Some children may enjoy the ritual so much that they do go on with it. Is religion in a similar position?

Adriaanse recognizes the difficulty. 'How', he asks 'can the blessing of the heritage of theism be enjoyed without making the metaphysical claims implied in theism?'[3] Many may not, indeed, see theism as a blessing, but for those who do, can they continue to participate in their traditional way of life, even though they have ceased making any claims to objective truth? Christianity, like other religions, he recognizes, is used to assuming that it is talking about what is real. He thinks, however that we should dissent from that claim. 'Why', he asks, 'should it not be in a position to say the prayers, sing the hymns and tell the tales it has always cherished, just for the joy and the pleasure and the relief and the edification of performing them?'[4] Yet in such practices we will still use the word 'God' and, as Adriaanse recognizes, there appears to be no way of using the word 'without getting tangled in metaphysics'. The more we are encouraged to accept the use of religious language and the adoption of certain practices without questioning their assumptions, the more we are pulled back into a metaphysical stance. 'God' is not a term which can be lightly used. It carries with it the metaphysical baggage of the centuries. This appears intolerable for those who distrust metaphysics or question its meaningfulness.

The urge to metaphysics undoubtedly lies in the wish to transcend local circumstances and particular contexts, so as to make a claim that holds good in a universal and objective manner. Its truth does not then depend on anyone believing it, but rather demands acceptance by everyone just because it is the truth. There is a profound tension in such a position. It means that those who are restricted (as we all must be) to a particular social context, and tradition of thought, expect somehow to transcend it, so as to talk of what is true outside all contexts and all traditions. Put at its most general, it means that people are using the resources of one conceptual system to refer to something wholly beyond the system. The later Wittgenstein reacted against such views and realized that one should not judge claims by an inappropriate set of

criteria. An inability to discover God by means of the instruments in a
scientific laboratory did not thereby show that all language about God
should be given up. Each form of life had to be judged on its own terms,
against its own context. The assertions of religion could not be assumed
to function in the same way as other uses of language.

Wittgenstein says that we must make 'a radical break with the idea
that language always functions in one way, always serves the same
purpose: to convey thought which may be about houses, pains, good
and evil, or anything else you please'.[5] We cannot take it for granted
that reference to God is about an 'object' in the same way that reference
to Fido the dog undoubtedly is. For Wittgenstein the purpose of philosophy was to unfold the way we actually use words. A 'grammatical'
investigation would show us the nature of concepts. As he says, 'Grammar tells what kind of object anything is.'[6] Wittgenstein was fully aware
of the subtleties of language about God and the dangers of assimilating
it to everyday language about dogs and chairs and tables. Indeed, he
fleetingly raises the possibility of 'theology as grammar' at this very
point.

It will not be enough for anyone influenced by Wittgenstein to be
told that God is objective, let alone 'an object'. It will not be enough to
emphasize the importance of the 'object' of belief. As D. Z. Phillips
stresses, 'no grammatical work has been done to elucidate the relations
between belief and its object'.[7] He writes in the context of a discussion
about the debate between realists and non-realists in theology as to the
question of the existence of God independent of our conceptions. His
view is that 'theological non-realism is as empty as theological realism'.
To take Wittgenstein's point, it will be wrong to assume that language
about God works in a similar way to language about houses. Different
assumptions have to be made. One cannot ask what colour God has
been painted this year. Yet this simple point can be made to seem more
important than it is. Phillips says:

> The influence of our talk of physical objects is all too evident when we
> are told that the God whose existence is inferred is a disembodied spirit.
> The spirit seems to be the shadow of the absent body. Thus God
> becomes 'the invisible man' of theology.[8]

No doubt God is not a physical object. That, however is, for many,
precisely the point. We may be able to say what is not the case, but that

does not explain how any statements about the transcendent gain any meaning. At issue for Phillips is the same question that was posed so trenchantly by the verificationists of the Vienna Circle. What is the meaning of statements about God? It is easy to assume that, once we start talking about what by definition lies beyond our reach, our language loses its grip. One merit of verificationism was that it very firmly insisted that those who used metaphysical statements should know what counted for and against them. There is little point in making grand statements about the qualities of an ineffable Absolute, if by definition they are totally inaccessible to us. Anything that is said is then as good as anything else, and there can be no constraint on the wildest claims. Language must degenerate under such conditions to babble. It appears tempting, therefore, to anchor our statements in the here and now. What gives them their sense has, it seems, to be something in our present circumstances rather than a remote 'object' of which we can have no inkling. We must be careful to ensure that our religious language does not degenerate to pointing to something in the bright blue yonder, which is totally beyond our comprehension, and to ineffectual hand-waving.

2   The 'Grammar' of Spiritual Reality

One widespread reaction to challenges about the difficulties of talking about 'spiritual' matters is to change the subject in a subtle way. It is claimed that the word 'spiritual' does not refer to some ghostly substance, nor even some transcendent realm of reality. It refers instead to a dimension of human life. Even this interpretation can be given a further twist, so that it is not so much a 'real' dimension as the result of the attitudes we, as humans, bring to bear on whatever befalls us. This tendency can be seen in the readiness of many to invoke the word 'spiritual' to denote what is clearly nothing more than aesthetic experience. The appreciation of good music, or the cultivation of a love of literature, can then be said to comprise the 'spiritual' side of human nature. There need be no reference, explicit or implied, to God or any divine reality.

Even if religion is invoked, one ploy is to accept that just as science deals with what is objective, so religion deals with the 'subjective'. In other words, it deals with the inner life of humans, their hopes and fears and aspirations. It is concerned with values and purposes. In a sense, all religion is concerned with such things. The catch is, however, that if science has claimed truth, whatever religion is left with is certainly not truth, or at least not factual truth as understood by scientists. It looks as if all it can describe are our subjective responses to the facts. It cannot tell us what the world is actually like, as that would be to trespass on the domain of the scientist.

The image of science as the arbiter of reality remains powerful. One contemporary writer deliberately contrasts the 'knowledge' obtained by science with the 'insight' provided us in ways of life. He denies religious claims can be tested and says: 'I prefer to see religion as something dealing with conceptions and pictures of an ideal utopian state of human life. In other words, it concerns the realm of values.'[9]

This explicitly distinguishes the truth-seeking activities of science from the role of religion. It has the consequence of reducing religious claims to aspirations towards a better form of human life. Anything else, not least reference to God, can be seen as pictures guiding us in preferences. Values then have no objective status, but are, we are told 'created by us'.[10] In fact the aim of views of life is simply 'to lead us to insights about what it means to be a human being in the universe'. Yet because this is by definition not factual knowledge, these insights have to be pictures we construct.

This division between the world of facts and the lived world of human life in which we make our choices, can serve to delineate two different areas, one for science and the other for religion. Yet, as we have seen, science has already, in the eyes of many, obtained monopoly rights on truth, and so religion has to be restricted to 'values', or some such term. The very distinction, however, between 'fact' and 'value' reeks of positivism. The assumption is always that facts can be established scientifically, whereas values are the outcome of subjective choice and preference. It is recognized that we have to choose how to live and that our 'values' help us to orientate ourselves. No room is left for metaphysical claims or for reference to the transcendent. 'God' drops out or becomes a mere symbol representing what we consider most important for human life.

The influence of the later Wittgenstein in the philosophy of religion, with his emphasis on the different uses of language, ought to have ensured that at least different practices must be seen on a par. Science may not be judged by religious criteria or vice versa, but that should not mean that science can grab the notion of 'fact' for itself. Each should be judged by its own criteria in its own context. Things do not, however, seem to have worked out like that. Although Phillips is right to warn us against using the assumptions of everyday language in the context of religion, the inevitable result is that terms like 'object' or 'existence' have then to be restricted to our ordinary talk of physical objects. We saw in the last chapter that Putnam wanted to stress a common-sense realism, and this then raised questions about the status of 'mathematical objects'. Similar points can be made about 'fact' or 'states of affairs'. We know what they mean when we are talking about tables and chairs. If we rip them out of their context and use them in a language which has no context, we may think we are doing metaphysics. In reality we are, it is alleged, using language which has gone on holiday and is doing nothing. Phillips refers to those who have the kind of belief in God presupposed by the sentence, 'The Lord is my strength and shield.' He refers to the philosophic view that this is a belief in a state of affairs and continues: 'The seductive phrase "states of affairs" is being asked to have a magic mediation of sense, whereas in fact, it has been placed beyond all possible contexts of application.'[11]

We can certainly talk of states of affairs when we are in contact with physical objects. The question is what would give the corresponding meaning to the phrase in a religious setting. Phillips thinks that since God is a 'spiritual reality', the term states of affairs' can only be given sense in the course of such activities as 'praying to God, seeking God, reflecting on spiritual matters and so on'. Yet his philosophic opponents would say that such activities must 'depend on a logically prior belief in a certain state of affairs being the case'. In other words, we must have a prior conception of God, and a belief that certain things are so in order to justify our participation in religious practices. Phillips cannot accept that we could have obtained our concepts except in a concrete context of application. By definition, metaphysics has departed a long way from such contexts. It has transformed, he says, a religious transcendence into a metaphysical one. Metaphysics, however, makes distinctions and claims, without the constraint of them making any difference to our lives. Phillips says,

> Distinctions between sense and nonsense are not given to us in vacuo. We come to master what these distinctions amount to when we acquaint ourselves with the context of human practice in which they

have their natural home. This applies as much to religious contexts as
any other.[12]

Phillips gives an illustration of what he means, by discussing his belief
that his dead father watches over him.[13] He is happy to talk of 'spiritual
realities', and his conscious use of religious language adds to the power
of his writing. He talks of the person he knew, his father, being raised on
high. He points out that it is easy to be confused over the grammar of
such beliefs, but that 'what the convictions express may be incapable of
being expressed in any other way'. The confusion of grammar arises
when people take seriously references to spiritual realities. For Phillips
they have everything to do with the manner in which we live our
present life, and nothing to do with any transcendent spiritual realm.
He remarks:

> It would make no sense to conduct an enquiry into whether the spirits of
> the dead are real independently of the contexts I have described. When
> people begin wondering what happens to our particles after death they
> have gone badly astray.[14]

It is clear from such a statement that Phillips cannot begin to give any
credence to life after death, unless it is understood in the crudest
physical terms. Yet reducing it to that level reduces it to absurdity. He
believes that anyone who believes that such a life would involve some
'inner substance' called 'the soul' is pursuing a philosophical chimera.
He says elsewhere that 'whatever is meant by the immortality of the soul
cannot be the continued existence of such a substance'.[15] Any notion of
eternity must be one which gives sense to our temporal world. Instead
of earth being seen in the light of heaven, heaven must be seen in the
light of earth.

Although Phillips is more than willing to refer to God as a spiritual
reality, the grammar of such talk has still to be elucidated. We may wish
to assert that God is independent of us, but again Phillips will want us
to elucidate what is meant by 'independent' in a way that clearly links
such talk to our practices. It must make sense within our form of life, to
use Wittgenstein's phrase. The whole point of such a reaction is to link
our concepts with ways of acting. The meaning of the former gains its
sense from the latter. It will always follow, therefore, that once we use
language in a way that cuts it free of its base, once we project ourselves

and our concepts into the unknown and the unknowable, the language will lose its sense. Once, it seems, that belief and practice are separated, our believing becomes unintelligible. What, then, is it to believe something true? Phillips writes that 'the realist can give no intelligible answer to this question. His failure is due to his exclusion of the mode of projection within which the relation of belief to its object has its sense.'[16]

In other words, simply believing that God exists outside all possible ways of acting, sundered, for example, from the activities of worship and prayer, becomes a totally empty belief. Sense cannot be given independently of any context of application. Phillips criticizes realists for wishing to sever belief from its object. He is vehemently opposed to the kind of metaphysics which deals with the idea of a transcendent God. To be more accurate, he is intent on showing that what is meant by 'transcendent' is not what metaphysicians think. He is not saying that God is not transcendent or that there is no God. He even claims that he is not taking sides in the debate about religious realism and anti-realism. Because he is above all concerned with questions of meaning, he tries to elucidate the kind of picture that is being invoked in such contexts. After all, to deny transcendence is to admit that one knows what is meant by the term and finds it unacceptable. Phillips claims that he is, like Wittgenstein, merely trying to clarify the use of language. How does a phrase like 'divine transcendence' get its meaning? Phillips would deny that the notion of transcendence can transcend the use we make of it. He continues:

> If it made sense to claim otherwise, which it does not, the meaning of religious concepts would be said to be beyond our practices; that is, beyond what we do with them. In thinking this, we would be turning away from the practices that we need to be clear about.[17]

We cannot, Phillips maintains, treat God as 'a being among beings'. He concludes[18] that 'the reality of God cannot be assessed by a common measure which also applies to things other than God'. Elsewhere he defines foundationalism as 'the claim to possess a rational measure by which all our practices must be assessed'.[19] This definition makes no distinction between the metaphysical vision of reality as the ultimate measure (even if beyond our reach) and an epistemological search for a certain foundation within the framework of what we take to be knowllge. The result is that he is able to refer to realists as foundationalists, 'for whom beliefs never yield certainty'. He holds that they fail to capture the conviction involved in a confession of faith, and comments that 'Penelhum and Trigg, along with other foundationalists, turn the conviction into mere probability.'[20]

The result of all this is to conflate realism which, as we have seen, has to be a metaphysical theory about the status of reality, with foundationalism, which is an epistemological view about the basis of our knowledge. Yet realism and foundationalism are distinct views, which may indeed be in conflict with each other.

3   The Shadow of Verificationism

Phillips arrives at a conclusion about the meaning of our concepts which appears to have far-reaching metaphysical consequences. Because the meaning of words like 'transcendence' or 'God' is rooted in particular contexts, their mode of application is determined by those contexts. They cannot then be held to gesture to anything which is outside our grasp. In other words, because the meaning of language is made the yardstick, and because that is linked with local practices, questions about the reality of God become issues not of metaphysics nor even of human understanding. They are linked to particular modes of understanding which certainly may not be shared by all humans. To say that Phillips makes questions about God anthropocentric is thus to understate the case.

The dismissal of metaphysics and the insistence that sense be given by the use that is made of language, means that public standards of meaning can be upheld. No one can say what they like about God, but their words must spring out of practices which many can share and teach to others. The whole point of Wittgenstein's arguments against the possibility of a private language was to anchor concepts in the public, shared world. There must be rules, and not just personal impressions of rules, which we can all see kept or broken. Yet the rules cannot gain their legitimacy from another world to which we have no access. They grew out of our practices.

There is a clear parallel between Wittgenstein's reluctance to treat pain as a private object which our language attempts to label, and Phillips's protests that God is not a being. Both fear that the object may recede beyond our grasp, pain into the inner recesses of a private world and God into the higher reaches of a metaphysical one. A gap is thus opened up between our judgements and what we make the judgements about. The subject and the object are separated. This forms the nub of Phillips's objection to realism.

> It is the realist who severs belief from its object. Such severance is unavoidable, since realism ignores the context in which the relation between religious belief and its object has its sense.[21]

The result, Phillips feels, is that religious belief becomes a matter of hypothesis and probability. Yet for him, tentativeness in the expression of faith seems inappropriate, just as Wittgenstein thinks that the expression of doubt in the language-game about pain has no place at all.[22] I cannot, the latter considers, be tentative about my pain. The whole notion of trying to identify a sensation and perhaps getting it wrong, is thought empty by Wittgenstein. If pain is totally private, no one could ever catch me out and demonstrate that I was wrong. Yet for Wittgenstein, if I cannot be wrong then I cannot be right either. The expression of pain has thus to be viewed not as a simple claim to truth but more like an exclamation. The point is that the model of meaning being invoked is a mistaken one. We are not talking about separate objects. The 'object' cannot be sundered from our beliefs and from our practices. If we think that the grammar of all expressions has to be interpreted on the basis of 'object and designation', then, Wittgenstein says, 'the object drops out of consideration as irrelevant'.[23]

Meaning cannot be derived from inaccessible objects. It might be objected that pain seems all too accessible to many. At this point it becomes clear that the emphasis on the social character of concepts, and the repudiation of 'private' objects, is driven by an implicit allegiance to a verification theory of meaning. What cannot be publicly checked is deemed meaningless, or at least irrelevant for our concepts, which have, according to this view, to be established and transmitted by social practices. Wittgenstein's emphasis on rule-governed behaviour only serves to stress that his idea of rules is of what is firmly grounded in public procedures. When, for instance, he talks of the possible relevance of a private experience of red when we see something red, he points out there can be no proper transition from what I privately see to the use of the word: 'Here rules really would hang in the air, for the institution of their use is lacking.'[24] The only reason for this, though, is that they are uncheckable. There appears to be no difference between my thinking that I am following a rule and doing so regularly, and thinking so but making a new one up every time. Yet the reason why Wittgenstein cannot allow that there is a difference is because any such difference has, he imagines, to be verifiable. The only reason there is no difference between the two scenarios (which appear to be described coherently and distinctively) is the insistence on public checking. Hence Wittgenstein gets himself in the curious situation of denying the relevance or importance of the felt quality of a sensation of pain.[25]

When a verification theory of meaning is applied to concepts of the mind, distortions are bound to appear. The same thing happens when it is applied to religious belief, not in this case because the belief is necessarily an inner process, but because of the nature of its object. Theism has posited a transcendent God and thus an epistemological gap is opened up between religious belief and its object. The metaphysical world of the theist becomes as problematic as the private world of introspection. Both are verification transcendent, if verification implies intersubjective checking. Other people cannot have access to my pain, and we do not seem to have the ready and reliable access to a transcendent world which scientists have to the physical world. Much of the force of objections made to notions of God as a being come from the feeling that God should not be viewed as a physical object. There seems something illegitimate about talking of God as one object among many, like a chair in a collection of furniture. Phillips, therefore, denies that the language of facts is appropriate to religion. He says 'that it makes as little sense to say, "God's existence is not a fact" as it does to say "God's existence is a fact."'[26] He enlarges on this by claiming: 'When God's existence is construed as a matter of fact, it is taken for granted that the concept of God is at home within the conceptual reality of the physical world.'

Because God is not a physical object, many questions about issues about size, location, age and so on which we would naturally ask are totally inappropriate. Yet the point is that this refusal to see God in physical terms only becomes problematic if a tacit assumption is made that all reality is physical, or that we can talk merely about a physical reality because we are embedded in a physical world. It may be claimed that the realist's insistence on objective reality is heavily influenced by the pictures which are inherent in a conceptual scheme geared to a world open to scientific manipulation. If it is nevertheless maintained that God is real in a way that totally transcends our understanding, we will be told that a familiar idea of physical reality is being employed, by being uprooted and used in a context in which by definition it can have no application. Yet why should our concept of reality be tied to that of physical reality, and our view of facts be determined by our understanding of physical facts? Verificationist demands are being smuggled in, so that all our uses of words are constrained by situations with which we are familiar. The refusal to call God's existence a matter of fact is in effect to cede control of what are to count as facts to the scientist.

Even if the context in which religious language finds its role is convincingly shown, the tying of meaning to this context ensures that it can never reach out and attempt to describe any metaphysical reality. The meaning of the language has to be found within the context and the rules for its use must be publicly checkable. Verificationism runs very deep. It proscribes metaphysical entities and also makes internal acts of judgement, and personal mystical experience, highly problematic. Nothing is tolerated that is not fully open to public access. Metaphysical realities, and private rules, are equally deemed beyond the reach of language. The realist separation of subject and object becomes unintelligible. The idea of an object is regarded as empty if it lies outside our grasp. Only the possibility of intersubjective verification by humans within their present practices can, it seems, give the content that is necessary. Entities that are transcendent thus lie by definition beyond the reach of language.

On Wittgensteinian (and postmodernist) assumptions, the very idea of a pure rational subject examining a world that is radically independent has to be dismissed. We are set, it is claimed, in a particular linguistic and social context, products of a form of life. The notion that I can abstract myself, even partially, from a concrete context so as to examine possibilities by the aid of a free-floating reason is regarded as metaphysical and hence vacuous. The intersubjectivity beloved of empiricism is itself challenged because subjectivity is itself undermined. The picture that stems from Wittgensteinian emphases on language-games and forms of life is rather one of definite, social situations in which public practices determine the fundamental criteria of meaning. What reality is and who we are are questions that can only be answered be reference to the public world. I do not start with myself and then attempt to avoid solipsism and scepticism. That is the Cartesian way which is challenged by the later Wittgenstein. Instead I have to be content with the language that is used in our dealings with each other and realize that there are no shadowy realities lurking behind as a form of inaccessible justification. At the least, the assertion that there are can make no sense. Wittgenstein's insistent question of any assertion is 'What difference does this make to their lives?'[27] Yet this refusal to allow apparently deep philosophical questioning and a search for justification, by grounding our practices in something beyond themselves, is not meant to be glib. In talking about the certainty (and trust) that appears to undergird so much of our language, Wittgenstein asserts 'Now I would like to regard this certainty, not as something akin to hastiness, or superficiality, but as a form of life.'[28]

4 The God of Reason

An insistence on the priority of the concept of a form of life has major consequences. We have to accept our everyday use of language and refuse to allow that there is any possibility of a context-less rationality, detached and impartial. All reasoning, it seems, has to be linked to a concrete situation. Otherwise it is divested of any meaning. Phillips argues at one point in connection with beliefs about God, which might form the justification for a religious commitment, that 'what Trigg is left with is a free-floating conception of proposition'.[29] Given a Wittgensteinian conception of meaning this is bound to seem objectionable, because propositions are supposed to be linked closely to the use of language in specific contexts. Yet this view of meaning is not just verificationist and anti-metaphysical. It is avowedly anti-realist. By refusing to allow realism to be properly stated, it may claim that somehow it is demonstrating the vacuity of the debate between realist and anti-realist. Typically what happens is that philosophical worries about the status of a particular way of speaking are met by a mere reiteration of the language. For example, Phillips quotes an expression of religious belief: 'Hereby we know that we dwell in him and he in us because he hath given us of his Spirit.'[30] He challenges the realist who wants a justification for such a statement and thinks of such a belief in terms of 'acting as if there was a God, or acting on the assumption that one is not mistaken about this'. He asks what has happened to the God who is said to dwell in us and in whom we are said to dwell. Yet the very fact that

Phillips can ask this question shows how he has failed to engage in what is at issue in the debate about realism.

The mere use of language with conviction and sincerity, the mere embedding of it in a way of life, cannot of itself show that the language is being used correctly. The reply will come that it must since the criteria for correctness come with the language. In a sense that is Wittgenstein's whole point. There may be a superficial plausibility about such a position when we are talking about tables and chairs, and even of pains and tickles. The issue in such cases is how such language is to be understood, its grammar interpreted, not whether we should go on suing the language. Conversion from realism to idealism, or vice versa, does not stop people talking to each other about the ordinary, shared world. Yet religious language is clearly not like this. The pressing question is always why one should adopt it in the first place or go on using it. What happens when worshippers become convinced that they have misunderstood the idea of a God, to whom they prayed so as to intervene in human affairs, and whom they would meet in a life beyond death? What happens when a realist, metaphysical view is replaced by a Wittgensteinian one that we should go on using the language, but that we have mistaken the grammar? God cannot then be regarded as some kind of super-Person. Yet if not that, what? It is hard not to see views that wish to go on using the language while rejecting its traditional philosophical basis, as deeply incoherent. The traditional pictures of God which are contained in our inherited religious language seem to imply that there is another realm beyond this one, and that talk of spiritual reality is saying something more than attempting to view our present life in a serious, even an ethical, light. The problem is how we can both use traditional language and deny the way it has been traditionally understood.

Talk of God as transcendent epitomizes the dilemma. For Phillips this is itself an internal move within a language-game. It gains its sense from its context. For others, it points to the limitations of language and of human understanding, and yet affirms that human beliefs and practices can be grounded in something surpassing anything they can properly comprehend. There is often the conviction that we are trapped within a conceptual scheme and pressing against its limits. For Wittgenstein, the very idea of being trapped is ludicrous. We say what we say and there is no way we can somehow transcend our limitations even to say that we are limited. The metaphysician will yearn to move beyond all possible contexts and to use language in ways that go beyond all possible contexts of application. This is self-evident lunacy to many. Yet one is left wondering whether such a yearning is not the very springboard of religion (and at another level a motive for progress in science). Once again we are forced back to the issue of whether positivism is correct and the physical world as we experience it is all that can be meaningfully described. Positivism was avowedly atheistic and it would seem curious if its most basic assumptions could be applied to religion without fundamentally altering the latter's character.

Just how radical a Wittgensteinian understanding of religion can become is illustrated by Gareth Moore. He says firmly, 'The presence of God is not the presence of a thing (or person) called God, a thing undetectable because invisible, intangible, bodiless. There is not one more thing in thing in the universe than atheists think.'[31] He says this because he believes that 'the question of whether God exists is not a factual question, a question of what we might find'.[32] On the contrary, 'it is a question whether to adopt the concept "God" (the word and its use) into the language or to retain it'. He says later that 'religious beliefs are related to reactions to things and to the way life is lived, in a different way from scientific beliefs'.[33] Once again we see how the assumption that somehow science establishes facts and deals with 'literal truth' bedevils much of this kind of discussion. 'Evidence' is consigned to the world of the scientist, and as a result ordinary conceptions of truth and reality are ceded to science. Moore can say that 'spiritual things are not the same as ordinary material things only different'.[34] The very vocabulary we feel drawn to use to describe God as object, thing, existent and so on, is thought inappropriate or at least as dangerously misleading.

The result of all this is to restrict the language of reason to the language of science. Even many Christian believers feel compelled to concede that science sets standards for rationality, that scientific evidence is the only kind of evidence on offer, and that the truths of science exhaust the possibilities of 'literal' truth. Yet once one has restricted notions of rationality to science, the status of science itself is brought into question. Unless it purports to inform us of the character of a physical world that exists independently of scientific practice, it is hard to see its purpose.[35] Unless one has been seduced by the verification theory of meaning, there seems little reason to suppose that religion is radically different. It, too, is surely concerned with what is true. Like science, it could go wrong. This possibility of error is precisely what many find objectionable. The idea that religious faith carries a risk, and might be totally misplaced, seems incongruous when measured against the certainty and confidence that so often characterizes it. Judgements about probability, tentative assessments, leaps of faith based on partial evidence, can seem laughable to those who believe that true faith is unswerving and doubt free.

Yet removing the possibility of error also removes the possibility of being right, since there is nothing to be wrong, or right, about. Religious belief can buy protection but only at the cost of itself being seen to assert nothing. The Wittgensteinian may wish to show the vacuity of metaphysics. In the end, this can only be achieved by showing the vacuity of religion, so that it claims nothing and is about nothing. It is simply part of a fossilized way of life which can be described and not justified.

The sundering of subject from object was thought by Phillips to be the vice of realism. Its significance, however, stretches beyond theological issues about the status of God. The possibility of rationality as such is being challenged. Our reason always assumes a certain distance between ourselves and what we are reasoning about. The possibility of mistake cannot be defined away. Similarly the idea of reason assumes a distancing of ourselves from our immediate context. If I just mouth the assumptions of a particular form of life, I am not reasoning about them. I am just expressing them in an unreflective way. The possibility of seeing something as a form of life or language-game implies the very ability to abstract ourselves from our immediate context that is apparently being put into question. The unreflective believer in tables and chairs may not reflect on their status any more than the unreflective participant in a religious way of life may wonder about the reality of God. Once, however, they describe their own predicament and consciously put their language in its context, the assumption is being made that it is possible to pull back from the use of language and reflect on how it is being used. The subject is then already distinct from the object at this level. The possibility of a gap between how a group conceives things and how they actually are is thus raised.

Arguments have raged through the centuries about how far human beings can comprehend what appears to be incomprehensible. It is not surprising that anti-realists try to change the subject and concentrate on the fact of belief, rather than what is believed. Yet it is not just the question of the existence of God or the validity of religion which is at stake. It is the possibility of reason itself. It is not enough to accept religion as a social phenomenon to be taken at face value. We cannot escape the issue of the justification of religion. If rationality is not to be the province of science alone, or dismissed as am impossibility, we must recognize that religion as much as any other human activity must be subject to rational constraints. Attacks on the idea of a free-floating rationality detached from a particular conceptual scheme have taken the form of attacks on the possibility of a so-called God's-eye point of view. Since humans cannot be omniscient the linking of reason to such a goal seems to make the task of reason a forlorn one. Yet the linking of the possibility of reason to the existence of God may not be as far-fetched as it seems. It is certainly significant that attacks on any meta-physical conception of God, existing independently, also appears to involve attacks on the possibility of a context-free rationality.

The epitome of such rationality is God as traditionally conceived. If the concept of such a Being is meaningless because it has been torn from very context which could give it meaning, for the same reason the notion of rationality is put at risk. We are all trapped in conceptual schemes without any ability to distance ourselves from them and question their grounding. The fact that in such circumstances it may not make any sense to talk of being trapped, because we could know no better and cannot recognize or express our limitations, seems of little comfort. Our vision has been limited and our reasoning circumscribed. The very considerations which make it impossible genuinely attempt to refer to God as an independent entity make human rationality a mirage. The possibility at least of there being such a God marches hand in hand with the possibility of rational selves being able to recognize truth and search for reasons and justification for our basic world-views. So far from a commitment to the possibility of rationality ruling out the possibility of God, we have to recognise that the two issues are inextricably entwined.

Notes

1   Adriaanse, 'After theism', p. 144.
2   *Ibid.*, p. 144.
3   *Ibid.*, p. 153.
4   *Ibid.*, p. 155.

5   *Philosophical Investigations*, #304.
6   *Ibid.*, #373.
7   Phillips, 'On really believing', p. 35.
8   Phillips, 'At the mercy of method', p. 6.
9   Herrmann, *Scientific Theory and Religious Belief*, p. 23.
10 *Ibid.*, p. 103.
11 Phillips, 'Between faith and metaphysics', p. 150.
12 *Ibid.*, p. 146.
13 *Ibid.*, p. 153.
14 *Ibid.*, p. 157.
15 Phillips 'Dislocating the soul', p. 450.
16 'On really believing', p. 40.
17 'Religion in Wittgenstein's mirror', p. 239.
18 'Religious beliefs and language-games', p. 62.
19 'Authorship and authenticity', p. 200.
20 'On really believing', p. 53.
21 *Ibid.*, p. 55.
22 *Philosophical Investigations*, #289.
23 *Ibid.*, #293.
24 *Ibid.*, #380.
25 See my *Pain and Emotion*.
26 'Philosophy, theology and the reality of God', p. 2.
27 *On Certainty*, #338.
28 *Ibid.*, #358.
29 'On really believing', p. 38.
30 *Ibid.*, p. 55.
31 Moore, *Believing in God*, p. 20.
32 *Ibid.*, p. 39.
33 *Ibid.*, p. 100.
34 *Ibid.*, p. 178.
35 See my *Rationality and Science*.

8

Does Theism Need Dualism?

1 God and the Self

Rationality has to be grounded in the way things are. In the case of religion, without a metaphysical conception of a transcendent God, religious reasoning has to be envisaged as a much more parochial enterprise. What it is appropriate to believe becomes a function of the form of life of which one is a member. Yet a global conception of rationality not only demands the idea of a reality to which everyone in principle has access. It demands the notion of a self which can detach itself from its most immediate physical and social surroundings at least sufficiently to be able to assess what it is reasonable to believe. It must be able to do more than simply embody the assumptions and prejudices of a particular historical period. Yet this is to raise in an acute form the issue of the metaphysical status of the self.

The relationship of God and the world, and that of the self to the brain, not only produce parallel problems. Some would hold that in the end they pose the same problem. Certainly both issues are metaphysical, and invite the same controversy between those who would reduce everything to physical terms and those who would be prepared to countenance two different kinds of substance, 'spiritual' and physical. There is then a major problem as to what, if anything, unifies them. The problem of God's relationship with physical reality will be discussed later, but there are analogous issues concerning the nature of the self. Who am I? What is my relationship with my body? Even to pose the question in this way will already seem to many to be treading a dangerous path. Since the days of Hume, empiricists have been quite ready to deny there is anything uniting all experiences, with no one or nothing in charge. At the present day, many attack the very idea of the self from different philosophical directions.

Some appeal to the discoveries of science, particularly neuroscience. There is a prevailing impression that a dualism of mind and body does not fit in with a growing understanding of the functioning of the brain. The more that particular neural activity is linked to specific mental events, whether perception, sensations or more general cognitive states, the more it seems as if the brain can tell us the whole story about ourselves. Yet the challenge to dualism is not that we need our brains after all, or that the mind and brain are closely correlated. It is that all reference to mind, self or soul is illusory. There is, it is claimed, nothing true of us that cannot be put into scientific language and attributed to our brains. The very same urge to a monistic picture of the world would insist that talk of God is superfluous. People who believe in God, and people who believe in a self are equally in the grip of an outdated piece of folk belief, as quaint and misguided as a belief in some 'vital force' to account for the fact of life.

Since God has been conceived as in some sense a self, a rational agent with purposes and intentions, we should be alerted to the fact that God and the human self are to some extent mirror images of each other. That is not to compare humans and God in a hubristic way. It is to point out that the idea of a rational self, able to abstract itself from its immediate context in order to reason, is an image that, for theism, inevitably invokes the model of the superior rationality of the Creator, as source of all truth. In the same way, the idea of God as a person must to some extent reflect the only experience we have of persons, namely each other. Attacks on dualism, therefore, can take two forms and are related to each other. One can refuse to distinguish the human self from the brain. The other would refuse to accept that there was any spiritual realm, separate from the physical world. There would thus be no possibility of a transcendent God.

However, the demise of dualism cannot yet be finally celebrated. We should realize that the proposal that we give up our 'folk psychology' in the face of the onward march of science is a matter of expectation and not achievement. It relies on the future success of a research pro-gramme rather than a settled record of agreed understanding. In other words it betrays an ungrounded faith in the progress of science. More-over, if the issue is not simply an empirical one, but a metaphysical one, an appeal to science, present or future, will simply beg a large question.

Certainly an appeal to a rational self does not seem to be a claim about the workings of the brain. Whatever future neuroscience tells us, there will remain the issue whether the brain is the vehicle by which the mind expresses itself, or whether any appeal to such an apparently ghostly entity should be instantly repudiated.

The conduct of science itself presupposes the ability of rational, self-conscious scientists to weigh and assess evidence. Science itself needs the rational subject, who is able to transcend a particular context and make judgements about what is true.[1] This links the concept of the self to those of reason and truth. It suggests that science cannot destroy the idea of rational subjects without calling into question the status of its own practitioners and hence itself. The issue is whether the rational self can be envisaged as separate from the brain, however closely it may as a matter of fact be linked to it. Yet for many, the question is already illegitimate in that it assumes the existence of a unitary self, of a centre where 'it all comes together'. Yet if 'I' am an illusion, the ideal of rationality also recedes. When I cannot abstract myself from my circumstances and context sufficiently to make judgements about what might be true, I am no longer aspiring to rationality. I am merely the outcome of causal chains, and different sciences will compete in trying to demonstrate which ones are significant. Paul Churchland says, 'Without a neural network in place, there can be no self, neither an emotional self, nor a perceiving self, nor a deliberating self, nor any other kind of self.'[2] It is, he maintains, the brain that is the 'engine of reason', and the 'seat of the soul'. A dualist could accept such language, in so far as the exercise of reason needs a functioning brain, and the souls, in this life, are physically embodied. Churchland, however, would refuse to distinguish rational processes from events in the brain. He would certainly deny that the former are the explanation for the latter.

There is a simplicity about a monistic approach that may appear attractive when compared with the multiplication of kinds of entities advocated by dualism. That is, at least, the contention. Yet if 'folk psychology' is mistaken, what guarantee could we have that any scientific theory, even about the working of the brain, does not similarly rest on an illusion? If all our reasoning is but the froth on the surface of neural activity, our understanding of what is the case, even apparent truths about the relationship of the mind and the brain, would seem to be governed by processes that are totally independent of rationality. In the end, scientific theories gain their cogency from the rational conviction of scientists that they can provide good evidence for their truth. Yet the demolition of the rational self removes the possibility of scientists genuinely doing such a thing. Like everyone else, they are merely at the end of processes that are guided by noone. They are certainly not under the direction of reason.

2 The Hermeneutics of Suspicion

The ties between reasoning, the self and the pursuit of truth are not only under challenge from some areas of science. Merely because they have been seen as the ingredients of our modern understanding of the world, they have also been called into question by those who suppose that we have moved into a postmodern era. We have already seen how a constant theme of such thinkers is the fact that all human thinking is historically situated. The result can be a dismissal of metaphysics on the grounds that it is trying to anchor everything in something that does not change. Yet, as is often pointed out, that can be very convenient. Some might find it in their interest to persuade others of the unalterable nature of things. Paul Ricœur has referred to the 'hermeneutics of suspicion' encouraged by writers such as Marx, Nietzsche and Freud. What people think, and the reasons they produce, may not be the real reasons at work. It then becomes easy to become suspicious of the motives of everyone, whether as the representative of an economic class or the purveyor of a morality, or just as an individual with psychological problems to resolve. The removal of genuine rationality from the stage leaves open the possibility of accusations of rationalizations for ulterior motives. This form of analysis (leading us to think of groups or individuals 'what is in it for them?'), is not only corrosive of trust in society. It is bound eventually to undermine itself. Why are such views themselves being propagated? What are those spreading them going to gain?

While rationalization, and the concealing of one's real reasons even from oneself, can be a major human failing, it must be parasitic on genuine reasoning. I cannot deceive myself all the time. If everyone is always lying, there can remain no such thing as truth. Yet the hermeneutics of suspicion can be taken to extreme lengths. Even the assertion of realism as a philosophical theory, (particularly about God) has come under this suspicion. Don Cupitt, in arguing for anti-realism in religion, has attacked realism for inculcating 'an ethics of "my station and its duties" such as is suitable for a well-ordered class society'.[3] He refers to realism as 'cosmic Toryism' and claims it is highly political. Yet this kind of jibe merely invites the retort that the writer must be in the grip of an alternative political vision. The result is the breakdown of the ideal of rationality into the rancour of mutual name-calling. The problem is that once any basis for rationality has been destroyed, all that can be left is mutual abuse and, ultimately the use of power.

For Cupitt himself 'truth is human, socially produced, historically developed, plural and changing'.[4] As a result, he says, 'we are nihilists',[5] and both the human subject and God are seen as the product of the thought of particular historical periods. For Cupitt, the 'death of God' occurred as early as 1730 at the end of what he terms 'the last generation of realistic, metaphysical theists'. He says of such thinkers as Locke, Leibniz and Berkeley that 'they are clearly all of them referring to and talking about one and the same public Object, established in the public realm outside their respective philosophies, in a way that has not been true of any subsequent generation of major thinkers'. Thus it seems that the establishment of realism and of a metaphysical view of God, depends not on reason but historical circumstances. It becomes a sociological fact of what was acceptable in the public domain. On this view, the world we live in is historically constructed and changes regularly. It follows that ideas of God and of the self are similarly constructed. For Cupitt, 'selves and worlds are all optional'.[6] We have to choose a 'fiction', a 'story to live by that suits us'. It is perhaps unkind to ask who is able to opt for a self, let alone a world, or who chooses the story. If we are what language and history have made, we cannot abstract ourselves sufficiently from either to make a choice. We are what we have become.

The idea of a human subject as a metaphysical subject is, for Cupitt, as dependent on an epoch of history as a realist view of God. He writes:

> The human subject as a metaphysical subject, a rational soul more-or-less prior to an independent of history and the body, was already in dire trouble before Darwin, but in William James and Nietzsche it clearly disappears. With it go unchanging Reason and Truth out-there.

The idea of a subject has to be contrasted with that of an object. The believer, the subject who believes, has to be distinguished from what the beliefs are about, the object. This is indeed the archetypal dualism. I am set in the world, and soon discover that it does not always conform to my will or understanding. The real world is not a dream-world under my control, a fiction my language has created and can mould to suit my convenience. Reality is more resistant. At many levels, things are not always as I want them to be, or conceive them to be. Realism has to start with the realization that I, or anyone else, can be wrong. Fallibility is part of the human condition. Any view which denigrates reason, and the possibility of truth, and which even doubts our identity, is in fact saying that there is no way we can be mistaken, either individually or collectively. Each epoch will have its own views, its fictions, and even that view will be a fiction. Even the notion of a fiction collapses, since there will be nothing left to contrast it with. If we cannot be right, we cannot be wrong, and if we cannot be wrong, we cannot be right. When everything is linguistically constructed, language itself will collapse. So far from the differentiation between subject and object being the consequence of a concentration on language, language itself depends on it. The self cannot be constituted by language. It is presupposed by it.

According to Cupitt, abandoning 'the old philosophical and religious dream of absolute, timeless and story-transcending knowledge . . . has been called the death of God'.[7] The possibility of detaching ourselves sufficiently from our circumstances to reason about them is denied in a way that rules out both the rational self, and God as the source of such rationality. Once a historicist position is adopted which roots us wholly in a particular historical epoch, the concept of a rational self, able, to some extent, to transcend local circumstances is thereby denied. Similarly, the notion of a God who is by very nature independent of particular locations becomes impossible. The idea itself will be wholly formed by special historical circumstances.

Cupitt is to some extent reflecting the views of Richard Rorty,[8] who opposes the aim of the Western philosophical tradition to break out of the 'world of time, appearance, and idiosyncratic opinion into another world – into the world of enduring truth'. Yet one does not need grandiose metaphysical schemes in order to distinguish between subject and object, self and the rest of reality. All that is necessary for rationality is to be able to detach ourselves sufficiently from our context to reason about things as they are, and not simply as we have been conditioned to view them. Yet Rorty himself is quite clear both that there is no God, and that this has important repercussions for our view of ourselves and of the world. He considers that the idea has to be ruled out that selves, human nature or even the world as such, each have some kind of 'intrinsic nature' that makes each what it is. He considers that this is a remnant of the idea that the world is a divine creation, the work of 'someone who had something in mind, who Himself spoke some language in which he described His own project'.[9]

There is thus no possibility that, without God, the world has a distinct character, other than that imputed to it by varying human vocabularies at varying times. The repudiation of the divine and of the transcendent, according to this view, results not just in taking leave of God, but in repudiating the independence of reality from human beings. The whole idea of language as description becomes problematic. Rorty's conclusion is that 'to drop the idea of languages as representations, and to be thoroughly Wittgensteinian in our approach to language would be to de-divinize the world'. The historicism of all this repudiates the possibility of rational understanding. Rorty is perhaps rather quick in assuming that it is impossible to hold to any form of realism from an atheist position. Nevertheless, his conclusion is that there is, in the abstract, nothing to understand, and no one to understand, even if there were anything. We are not allowed to 'divinize' the self. Everything is the product of contingent circumstances. Yet that is precisely what gives rise to the hermeneutics of suspicion. We must still wonder how the social world, which by definition forms us, has itself been formed. What interests and purposes have been at work in its construction?

Nietzsche's attack on Christian morality as the means by which the weak can exact benefit from the strong is an example of such an approach, looking at the genealogy of various methods of social control. The exercise of power, and not the rational pursuit of truth, is then seen to be the key. I can very often get you to do what I want more effectively if I do not threaten you, but induce you to believe that you are doing it because you want to do it yourself, or because you think that it is the right thing to do. Thus, it is claimed, the inculcation of beliefs and assumptions is a reliable way of one group in society dominating another. Those exercising such power do not even have to be conscious of what they are doing. They can be as much in the grip of an ideology as those they are exploiting. The difference is that they derive benefits from the situation. Marx's notion of false consciousness draws attention to this phenomenon. Such self-deception is part of the human condition, and the force of such an analysis derives in part from the fact that we recognize that we may sometimes act like this. Yet the point of such accounts is not that this occasionally happens, but that is the nature of human society. We are all totally conditioned by circumstances, and are warped in a way that makes us systematically grasp power and advantage for ourselves.

Without the possibility of rationality, a struggle for domination and power is all that can be left. Yet like all such global theories, this one is bound to undermine itself. Presumably those putting it forward are in the grip of the same will to power as anyone else. The thesis itself is clearly in no position to claim to be true. Marxists have always had to face this kind of difficulty. If everything, religion included, is designed to further class interests, how can philosophical theories about this situation themselves escape global condemnation? Where could Marxists stand, in order to dismiss religion as the opium of the people? The problem is why they can stand beyond economic interest while religious people cannot.

Yet without the idea of a self that can be detached from its physical and its social environment and yet remain itself, it would be impossible for anyone to rise above their circumstances and make any global claim. Without a conception of such a metaphysical self, everything we can be is given us by our context. We are creatures of it and cannot be divorced from it. We have no independent existence. As a result, it will appear that the most important feature about somebody is race, class, gender, nationality and so on. It then becomes possible to assume that we can accurately describe a person by classifying their historical position. It is perhaps significant, however, that there is little agreement about which feature is the operative one, or whether they all make a contribution.

3 Feminism, Self and God

Nowhere are views like this more forcefully expressed, since the demise of Marxism as an effective force, than by radical feminists. 'Feminism' is a blanket term which can cover many positions. It can, for instance, imply little more than a laudable aim to ensure that women are able to play their full part in public life. It can simply stand for an attempt to ensure that they are not denied the opportunities in education and elsewhere which have traditionally been available to men. The more radical versions, however, can be seen to follow Marxist patterns of explanation, even though for them the operative factor is not so much economic class as gender. Society has been constructed, they would maintain, in such a way that we all, male and female, have been conditioned to see certain ways of living as natural and right. Yet the allegation is that these ways have been systematically built up to further the interests of males. The fact that many, both male and female, would reject such an analysis is to them merely a further demonstration of the power of ideology. Such an attack on traditional modes of understanding inevitably becomes directed at Christianity in Western society. The view is that religion has been the source of most of our basic assumptions about the role of the sexes. Once again, claims to truth become suspect, since the suspicion must be that many such claims have been put forward with the idea of perpetuating the power of some group. Yet it will not always be easy to decide how a particular group is to be delineated. If, for example, the power of the medieval clergy is pointed out, is this an example of the domination of laity by clergy, or of females by males?

Underlying controversies about radical feminism are assumptions about the self and about God. Clearly, for many who believe that gender is the defining feature of a person, any notion of a sexless rationality or of an ungendered rational self must be ruled out. Similarly, the idea of a God who is always referred to in male terms will be deeply suspect. Some may feel that this is merely a linguistic problem. Some languages, such as Finnish, can refer to persons without attributing a gender. Other languages, such as Ancient Greek, Latin and, of course, English find it impossible to refer to God as personal without doing so. Yet refusing to view God as personal is itself a significant philosophical step to take. We have already seen an example of this when Hick's talk of 'Reality' is explicitly intended not to imply personality.

Many wishing to subject Christianity to a feminist critique, however, are often not content with protesting about the English language. Merely to change language or symbols will be regarded as tinkering with superficialities. Thus Daphne Hampson writes: 'Simply to name God as female, while retaining the conception of a transcendent God, would seem too superficial a change which will fail to stick.'[10] In fact swinging from seeing God as male to seeing God as female would to some itself seem a radical change. For those who believe that God, though personal, is truly transcendent, both may seem wide of the mark, the only difference being that the one has been sanctified by tradition and the other brings in new and perhaps disturbing resonances. Yet this reference to tradition would to many feminists seem precisely the point. Our images, it would be claimed, are the outcome of a social structure in which men have always dominated women.

Luce Irigaray has been in the forefront of those who have tried to expose the link between belief in God and a male-dominated society. Referring to the belief in a transcendent and unique God-Father in differing religions, she says that sometimes his name is Zeus, sometimes Jupiter, but that 'he is also God the Father of Judaeo-Christian tradition'. She continues:

> Respect for God is possible as long as no one realizes that he is a mask concealing the fact that men have taken sole possession of the divine, of identity and kinship . . . It becomes obvious that God is being used by men to oppress women and that, therefore, God must be questioned and not simply neutered in the current postliberal way. Religion as a social phenomenon cannot be ignored.[11]

Her argument is that at the moment the divine goal set for woman is in fact to become man. She says: 'If she is to become woman, if she is to accomplish her female subjectivity, woman needs a god who is a figure for the perfection of her subjectivity.'[12] The link between the nature of the self and God is here made again, but Irigaray clearly sees the divine as a reflection and projection of human needs. She quotes Feuerbach's statement that 'God is the mirror of man'[13] and retorts that 'woman has no mirror wherewith to become woman'.[14] Feuerbach was doubtless thinking of humanity and not just males, but a feminist rejoinder would be that unconsciously the two were regarded as synonymous. Irigaray holds that a 'female god is still to come'. Above all women must be 'capable of autonomy,'[15] and the function of a god must be to provide woman with that goal. Freedom and the opportunity of fulfilment 'as individuals and members of a community' depend on a 'God in the feminine gender'.[16]

In all this, metaphysics has been discarded and, following Feuerbach, God is seen only as a projection from human societies. It follows on this view that, in a male-dominated society, God will inevitably reflect the nature of that society. One remedy might seem to be to project deliberately an alternative view of the divine which could serve feminist ideals.

Yet projections gain their force when they are unconscious. A deliberate mirroring of perceived needs by some manufactured deity would hardly create a god capable of being worshipped. No god artificially produced to serve the aspirations of a group could call forth the devotion characteristic of religious worship. A feminist critique of traditional conceptions of God cannot fail to be atheistic in its effects, if what is being attacked goes deeper than the mere images which we use to describe a transcendent God.

Any discussion of the relation of the self and God has to appeal to metaphysics. Both categories are essentially metaphysical, and the dissolution of the one will inevitably raise questions about the status of the other. Irigaray wishes to talk of autonomy and freedom, but it is reasonable to ask just who it is that will be autonomous and free. Clearly such a notion still depends on a strong view of the self, able to transcend the influences which go to shape it. Feminists, in a post-Kantian manner, are often eager to attack 'heteronomy', a subjection of will to that of another. That is a concept which is clearly the opposite of feminist ideals of autonomy, and it opens the way for women to be systematically subjected to the will of men. Daphne Hampson, for example, advocates an explicitly 'post-Christian' feminism, which, she says, implies 'an ethical position in which I do not give over my being to any person or to any God who lives outside myself'.[17] She even repudiates any ideal of self-sacrifice, which Christianity has preached, and which, she holds, has been a useful ideological tool in the subjection of women by men. She maintains that 'a transcendent monotheism comports ill with the society which feminists seek to create'.[18]

It is not only on feminist grounds that Hampson wishes to reject any idea of God as a separate being, an 'anthropomorphic agent'. She does not regard Christianity as compatible with scientific knowledge. This makes it much easier to see religion as a human projection, based largely on male aspirations. She does not extend her analysis, as some feminists do, to reason in general and the pursuit of science in particular. Yet, once the hermeneutics of suspicion are unleashed, any masculine claims to truth can become suspect. The very notion of impersonal reason and objective truth can itself be attacked. It could be argued that a halfway house that undermines some claims to truth, as being instruments of subjection, but accepts others, is a very unstable position. There would seem little reason to trust the pronouncements of male scientists, and yet to distrust male theologians. One may have rational grounds for preferring scientific to religious claims, but there might not seem any good reason to trusting one group of males rather than another. Theologians have had more time over the centuries to have had an influence, but modern science could well have a more devastating impact.

Central to a radical feminist critique of Christianity is an attack on the possibility of divine transcendence. It is alleged that this is a cloak for the legitimation of male hierarchy. Hampson claims of Christianity that 'the whole shaping of the religion – the way in which God is conceptualized, the relation between God and humanity, and the internal relations of the Godhead – reflects the problems and aspirations of men living within patriarchy.'[19] She sees the idea of a transcendent God, as Creator, lying at the root of the problems. The very notion reflects 'the concept of a being who, exists as separate and as more powerful than humans'. She couples this concept with the idea of a self, as a self-subsisting discrete entity, which 'will continue to exist not only in time but through all eternity'.[20] Her conclusion is that 'both of these would seem to embody deeply masculinist presuppositions'.

Hampson, like Irigaray, does not dismiss the notion of God. Hampson wants to retain it to refer to a dimension of our present reality. Yet the danger is that this itself is a mere projection of current attitudes, such as a search for purpose. The nature of God is then being made to conform to human wishes, in this case feminist ones. Yet if this is so, questions of truth are discarded, and the issue becomes a mere struggle for power. Whose attitudes are to prevail, those of males wishing to dominate, or those of feminists wishing to be free of domination?

Once metaphysics is set aside, and ontology (or its surrogate) becomes explicitly a matter of projection, it is inevitable that issues about the nature of reality, including the nature of the self, become changed into ones about who holds the power. Who is to be in control of the projection? The basic issue is whether disinterested reason is possible and whether we can talk of what is true. If everything is the pursuit of power, as philosophers allege who are influenced by Nietzsche, metaphysics as an enterprise falls. Yet it is not just that a concept of a transcendent God must be regarded as a tool in the pursuit of sectional interests. All claims to truth must be viewed as disguised attempts to achieve some other aim. Metaphysics and the pursuit of reason, however, may not be that flawed, since even the arguments of feminists presumably attempt to be rational. It ought to be possible to distinguish the issue of the truth of particular claims from that of possible baleful effects of believing those claims. Whether there is a transcendent God is one problem. The fact that a belief in such a God may sometimes have been used in the pursuit of the interests of a sex, an economic class or some other grouping such as the priesthood, is interesting and important. It is, however, utterly distinct. The reality of God and its effects should not be confused with the question of some effects produced by belief in God.

Feminists would no doubt claim that the character of the belief is such that it is impossible to divorce its content from its effects. Given a theory of projection, which itself relies on a Kantian view of the anthropocentric character of concepts, this is easy to explain. Hampson can say that 'the objectivity of the male religion, Christianity, may be nothing of the sort, but rather a projection of male needs, hopes, fears and sexuality'.[21] The issue is not so clear, however, if we retain a notion of an objective reality to which we have at least a degree of access. What is believed can then be considered apart from the motives of belief. What is real is not the same question as the face of its being believed to be real. Hampson herself has to assume this in order to say that the Christian religion is mistaken. She has to stand somewhere to make this judgement. She then has to face the question why she can make judgements about truth that somehow can claim to surpass her own needs, hopes, fears and sexuality, while men have never been able to. Even if she were right in saying that Christianity is a 'male' religion (a view which is certainly not true from a sociological standpoint), she still has to explain why this disqualifies it from making claims to truth. Yet it appears that women themselves still can claim truth. Once, however, the hermeneutics of suspicion sees people as wholly driven by vested interests, this will have to apply to women as well as to men.

4   Dualism and Power

If it is generally held that what passes for knowledge in a society is socially constructed, it will be natural to ask which groups are in control of the construction. The obvious feminist question will be whether this is not intimately connected with questions of male domination. Grace Jantzen remarks that 'it is a commonplace of postmodern philosophy that knowledge and power are interconnected'.[22] Her own thesis is that issues about mysticism, both who are mystics and what counts as mystical experience, are socially constructed, and at the mercy of battles for power. Certainly anyone with access to special knowledge is likely to gain authority and influence. It may not be surprising that an authoritarian Church would be wary of challenges to its position from individuals who might claim privileged access to transcendent truth. Yet there is always the danger of confusing the issue of what people experience, and may even know, with the social recognition given this. Knowledge may grant authority but that does not mean the two should be identified. Authority may be seen as a sociological concept, but to treat knowledge in the same way as a social construction is itself to deny both the role of a rational self as the subject of knowledge, and of a knowable reality as its object.

Jantzen attacks contemporary philosophers of religion in their treatment of mystical experience, typically treating it as detachable from its particular social context. She denies that 'any discussion of mysticism and religious experience can avoid taking a stand on the issues of power and gender, since to be silent about them means colluding with the ways in which they have operated, and with the triumph of the dominant'.[23] Yet once even religious experience is viewed as socially constructed, a major challenge is mounted for traditional views of the relationship between humans and God. A possible source of knowledge of God has been blocked off, at least if God is considered as belonging to a spiritual realm. The possibility of gaining knowledge through mystical experience might be viewed as parallel to the manner in which we gain knowledge of the ordinary physical world through perception. We have seen how an epistemologist such as William Alston draws precisely this comparison. Yet this itself raises the question of the relationship of the individual and society. My perception of the world around me would seem to be typically a matter for me myself and not a result of social construction. Similarly, a mystical experience would seem to be preeminently an individual and not a social phenomenon. The more that 'social construction' is emphasized, the more the role of the individual recedes. It can soon be held that the very notion of an individual is itself the product of particular societies. Thus the modern view of the isolated individual trying to obtain knowledge can be held to be the mere product of Enlightenment thinking.

Once the idea of the individual is made secondary to that of society, and reason to the control of vested interests, it is not surprising if our whole way of viewing human spirituality is bound to change. The idea of the response of the individual soul to God will be supplanted by a different vision. In fact Jantzen is herself opposed to the whole picture of an individual self seeking what she terms 'a privatised, inward spirituality which soothes and tranquillises and promotes an inner harmony that is content to leave the public and political as it is'.[24] A preoccupation with self is, of course, always dangerous and has been the antithesis of what is generally perceived as a mystical approach to God. Nevertheless too much stress on empirical experience has in the past encouraged a philosophical phenomenalism which makes it appear that the physical world is constructed out of the sum of individual experience. As a result the threat of solipsism has never been far away. In the same way, an excessive stress on the fact of religious experience can produce an undue emphasis on the privacy and subjectivity of religious experience. Religion can then be made to appear an individual and personal matter with little relevance to the public world. Jantzen resists the contrast between spirituality and embodiment, and between spirit and world. Otherwise, she thinks, one is likely to view the intellect, and pure rationality, as 'somehow more god-like than the body and the senses'.[25] This, she argues fits in with a male tendency to view men as intrinsically more rational than women. God is contrasted with the material world, and, in a similar way, the spark of divinity in humans, the image of God, is identified with the active, rational aspect of human nature. This is then contrasted, she claims, with 'the physical, un-godlike, bodily and sexual aspect'.[26] She concludes that the spiritual and the rational is then valued over and above the bodily, the emotional and the sexual. The point of these remarks is, of course, to demonstrate how what is valued is identified with the male, and the reverse with the female.

The picture again emerges of a parallel dualism of God and world, and self and body, which is claimed to be deeply ideological in that it has served to promote the interests and power of males over females. Linked with this is the whole contrast between individual and society. We thus have a situation in which it seems that God as spirit can only be known by spirit, and this spirit or mind was viewed as the very essence of each individual human person. This was certainly the view promulgated in Greek philosophy. Since it was believed that like had to be known by like, it appeared that for humans to know God, they must be like God. If God is Spirit, it seemed to follow that humans must be at least partly spirit. Jantzen says,

> This dualistic understanding of human personhood, with the body and its senses and sexuality serving at best as an allegory and at worst as an hindrance to union with God, is constant throughout all the male writers of the Christian tradition, as is also a deep division between God as spirit and the material world.[27]

The hermeneutics of suspicion is clearly operative here in that Jantzen assumes that because the prominent writers of the Christian tradition were male, it follows that their beliefs have had everything to do with the pursuit of male domination. She contrasts this with a stronger female stress in medieval mystics on the role of passions and emotions, but has to admit that such mystics may use different imagery but do not challenge the basic orthodoxy. Certainly, once dualism is challenged, and attention is directed at our embodied, physical nature, then, by definition, the differences between male and female become particularly relevant. Similarly once the distinction between God and the world is removed, the physical world can become of paramount importance. It is, too, hardly surprising that a split between spirit and matter can seem to involve a devaluation of matter. The quest for 'spirituality' can appear to involve a repudiation of the world around us and even its neglect. Those concerned with the depredations constantly made on our physical environment may well think that a concentration on a spiritual realm undermines our concern for the physical world. An undue preoccupation with private spiritual concerns can induce a pietistic withdrawal from the public world. These are all undeniable dangers, though there are equal ones attendant on the repudiation of any form of dualism. Once metaphysics is given up, the issue becomes, as so often happens, merely a matter of human attitudes.

Christianity, as a religion, has traditionally been well aware of the dangers of exalting the spiritual at the expense of the physical. The doctrine of the Incarnation has often been used to demonstrate God's concern for the physical world. A vision of eternal life, too, can be used to illuminate our present form of existence rather than to bring it into contempt. It could be said, too, that it is precisely because of the eternal destiny of human beings, and the fact as claimed by Christianity that there is life beyond death, that what happens here and now is seen as being of supreme importance and of eternal significance.

The issue of male domination has still to be faced. Yet it is difficult to see that a dualist conception of human nature itself lends support to discrimination against females. Since its whole point is to separate the essential part of what makes a person from his or her body, dualism can make no distinction between male and female. Arguing that it does, requires an assimilation of spirit or soul to a particular conception of intellectual rationality. It demands further that we hold that the latter is somehow the prerogative of the male. This may have been possible for Greek philosophy, but it could never be an option for Christianity which has always maintained that 'in Christ' there is neither male nor female. Women cannot be seen on any Christian view as somehow less than persons. Nevertheless, some feminists may repudiate dualism just because they are convinced that being female is of crucial importance, and that they – the persons that they are – could never be envisaged without their female body. This can then lead to a view of this physical world as the only possible one.

5   Dualism and Theism

Any blanket assertion that religion is an ideology serving the interests of masculine power can overreach itself. Reason and truth soon get trampled underfoot when everything is viewed as simply a struggle for power. The arguments of feminists themselves lose any rational force they may wish to claim. This is always a dilemma for feminists who want to argue against injustice, while arguing from a philosophical position that all conceptions of rationality are the product of ideology. If their own idea of injustice is itself a matter of construction rather than discovery, their own motives have to be put as much under scrutiny as that of their opponents. Richard Rorty points out this tension in some feminist thought. He says that 'pragmatists and deconstructionists agree that everything is a social construct'.[28] This may appear, to be an effective way of exposing claims to what is 'rational', and of showing that it can never be finally distinguished from what is culturally specific. It suggests that no social arrangements are immovable or based on 'the way things are'.

We are back with the view that since everything is contingent, everything, including our conception of ourselves and of reality, is subject to change and indeed can be changed. The problem is that according to this view there is no extra-social standard to which we can appeal, nothing which can serve as a justification for social arrangements. The very notion of 'justice' becomes problematic. People cannot then be viewed as individual recipients of justice and fairness when they are abstracted from their social context, since it is the latter that has created them. Without some idea of a self which is not defined by its place in society, the view that people are being treated in ways they should not be becomes self-contradictory. If their allotted role is to be oppressed, that is what constitutes who they are. It is only when we see that people that are not social constructions, that we can see that they matter wherever they are located in time, place and society. The dualist view of a self which is not the creation of local circumstances is what makes appeals to justice possible.

Rorty himself is impatient with any rational appeals to justification, and in true pragmatist fashion holds that 'all that matters is what we can do to persuade people to act differently than in the past'.[29] The problem is why they should make any effort to do so. Given Rorty's position that our practices are grounded in nothing deeper than contingent historical fact there would seem no conceivable reason to change the existing states of affairs. If justice is merely the interest of the stronger, and cannot be grounded in anything transcending local circumstances, merely pointing this out does not seem to solve the problem. It is hard to see what the problem is, unless one is numbered among the weak and oppressed. Rorty points out about relations between men and women how, as he puts it, 'the people with the slightly larger muscles have been bullying the people with the slightly smaller muscles for a very long time'.[30] Yet without an appeal to justice, the only issue seems to be how they can fight back, not their rightness in doing so. The matter is a mere power struggle, which by definition those with the power are going to win. It is possible to appeal to justice as a rhetorical ploy, but justice on this bleak view will be an irredeemably ideological concept. Once it is recognized that this is the case, even its rhetorical force will wane.

Feminists have a choice. They can apparently demolish their opponents' position by stressing the fact of social construction and its ideological basis. They then cannot themselves appeal to the support of any morality. Alternatively, they can be fired with a notion of justice, but must accept that this must be grounded in some way. They have to realize that contingent social arrangements do not tell us the whole truth of ourselves or the world in which we act. We must accept that who we are and how we should be treated are matters that must transcend our present circumstances. If each conception of justice can be challenged and put under suspicion as serving the vested interests of some entrenched group, we will in the end not be able to go on talking of justice at all.

Derrida faces this problem. He wishes to appeal to justice and such a notion as that of human rights, while simultaneously attacking the concept of the human, and putting all appeals to justice under suspicion. Jantzen sees this as a problem in Derrida's thought and suggests that any idea of justice 'must itself be subjected in the name of justice to deconstruction'.[31] She significantly draws out the links 'with the God of western religion, the God who is above all names and yet is named'. Symbols can become idols and must be shattered, but the implication is that there is a reality grounding them. This is a precarious position, since, as has been remarked before, a reality that is beyond knowledge becomes as irrelevant as no reality at all. This is equally obvious whether the appeal is to God, or an abstract conception of justice.

We are forced back to the role of reason and its ability to grasp truth. However shaky and imperfect it may be, without it human beings sink into the abyss of power struggles and eventual violence. Yet positing the very possibility of such a rationality is to look beyond the world of physical processes and of social arrangements to one where reasons can guide us in a search for justification that is not a mere rationalization of our own particular interests, whoever we may be. It does not follow that allowing for the power of human reason leads inevitably to the idea of God. It does, however, suggest that the rational subject can abstract itself from circumstances. The ability to reason itself draws attention to the fact that none of us is defined totally by our physical make up or our social role. Rational protests about injustice can themselves make no sense unless those making the protest can transcend their immediate situation and still be themselves.

It may still be objected that by detaching the idea of the self from its physical and social context, one is in effect accepting some form of dualism. Not all forms of dualism are theistic, and it certainly does not follow that allowing for the power of human reason leads inevitably to any idea of God. To assert the rationality of atheism is not a contradiction. It is possible to say that the idea of God as some supernatural Self has been constructed in our own image. This would be the obverse of saying that our rationality is the imperfect reflection of that of the Creator, in whose image we have been made.

Charles Taliaferro argues that dualism and theism are powerfully linked, but does recognize that dualism does not entail theism. He argues that dualism may be compatible with a non-theistic naturalism which sees the mental as an emergent property of the physical, to be distinguished from it, but in the last resort not ontologically distinct.[38] He qualifies this by saying, however

> A theistic outlook will provide a fuller model of explanation in which the natural emergence of the mental from the physical, and indeed the very constitution and powers of the physical world itself, is seen as stemming from a deeper underlying cause.

Monism may always appear by definition a preferable view, on the grounds that an explanation in terms of one kind of entity will always appear simpler than one in terms of two. Once, however, it is accepted that the idea of an explanation involves notions of reasons and justification which in turn depend on the existence of minds able to recognize them, we may feel forced to recognize the inadequacy of the mere recognition of brute facts that monism encourages. We may recognize that even such recognition involves more than a physical process. Taliaferro's point is that different kinds of processes, both physical and mental, can be seen in a unified picture if we invoke the idea of God. Dualism need not be a profligate multiplication of types of entities or processes occurring inexplicably alongside each other. When coupled with theism, it can provide a unified account of the cosmos. The reality of God will ground both the physical and the non-physical. In a sense, a dualist notion of the self, and a strong view of rationality, needs theism to prove an overarching rationale for the apparent division of reality. Without a dualist framework, which allows room for the spiritual and the supernatural, theism itself, as traditionally understood, cannot be intelligible. At the very least, it would have to be heavily revised in an attempt to fit it into a naturalist framework. This is bound to destroy it. Theism without dualism is empty. Dualism without theism would seem pointless.

Notes

1 See my *Rationality and Science*, chapter 10.
2 Churchland, *The Engine of Reason, the Seat of the Soul*, p. 308.
3 *Creation out of Nothing*, p. 54.
4 *Ibid.*, p. 45.
5 *Ibid.*, p. 188.
6 *What is a Story?*, p. 64.
7 *Ibid.*, p. xiii.
8 *Contingency, Irony and Solidarity*, p. 29.
9 *Ibid.*, p. 21.
10 *After Christianity*, p. 182.
11 *Sexes and Genealogies*, p. v.
12 *Ibid.*, p. 63.
13 *The Essence of Christianity*, p. 63.
14 Irigaray, *Sexes and Genealogies*, p. 67.
15 *Ibid.*, p. 68.
16 *Ibid.*, p. 72.
17 *After Christianity*, pp. 38ff.
18 *Ibid.*, p. 128.
19 *Ibid.*, p. 166.
20 *Ibid.*, p. 239.
21 'On being a non-Christian Realist', p. 94.
22 *Power, Gender and Christian Mysticism*, p. 2.
23 *Ibid.*, p. 278.
24 *Ibid.*, p. 347.
25 *Ibid.*, p. 122.
26 *Ibid.*, p. 122.
27 'Feminism, ideology and deconstruction: a pragmatist view', p. 98.
28 *Ibid.*, p. 100.
29 *Ibid.*, p. 101.
30 Jantzen, *God's World, God's Body*, p. 352.
31 *Consciousness and the Mind of God*, p. 84.

9

Does Faith Need Reason?

1 The Priority of Faith

Underlying questions about the rationality of religion lie issues about the very propriety of reasoning about God. Should we not rely on 'faith'? Is it not presumptuous to imagine that we can do otherwise? In the first place we will be told that because of God's utter transcendence, the very possibility of relying on our own efforts must be questioned. William Placher asserts that 'If God is really transcendent, then there is no epistemological path from us to God, and everything we know about God comes at God's initiative.'[1] We are in other words totally dependent on revelation, and thus on God's own choice to be revealed. This explains the emphasis of so many theologians on the grace of God, and our dependence on a divine initiative. Placher himself maintains that this has been somewhat lost in modern thinking from the seventeenth century on. He writes that

> Theologians before the seventeenth century often better understood, first, that our coming to faith is also not our own work but something for which we must be grateful to God, and, second, that since God is transcendent, this work of God too remains ineluctably mysterious.[2]

We shall return in the final chapter to the problems created by the notion of transcendence. For the moment, it suffices to point out that the more impotent human reason is made to appear in our understanding of God, the more 'faith' will appear to be some necessary but mysterious gift from God (perhaps obtained, Christians may think, through the working of the Holy Spirit). Not only will what we have faith in appear mysterious, but as Placher indicates, the manner in which faith is achieved is made equally so. It is not surprising that for many faith and reason seem totally opposed to each other. Yet there are great dangers in Placher's approach. It can make faith appear the prerogative of a fortunate few, perhaps selected especially by God. It appears to suggest that even if the claims of the Christian Gospel were objectively true and thus worthy of universal attention, this could only be grasped by those to whom it was revealed. Yet even that is a statement that cries out for some kind of rational justification. Why should truth and the possibility of understanding such truth be separated in this way? Why should not human rationality itself be seen as a gift from God? The belief that we were made in God's image has often been viewed as asserting precisely this. We soon get to a position where it cannot be said that someone without faith ought to have it, since that would seem to be a matter for God. The great problem is that the more that the emphasis is placed on an inner, subjective faith, whether granted by the Holy Spirit or not, the more we begin the slide to a subjective notion of truth. No religion can accept that it is 'true for' those who believe in it, and not equally true even when it is rejected. Once the distinction between appearing true and being true is lost, religion becomes an idiosyncratic choice of style of life, and nothing more. It can certainly not be thought to be making claims about the living God.

We will be told that, as a project, reasoning about God is not only beyond human capabilities, but is presumptuous. Moreover, because of human fallibility it will be flawed, perhaps totally so. The true response, it will held, is a submissive openness to the grace of God. Faith is a gift which cannot be acquired by our own efforts. Such an approach only makes sense given belief in God. Placher was writing consciously in the tradition of Karl Barth.[3] The latter says that the type of thinking that wants to begin with questions about how God can be known 'is not grateful but grasping, not obedient but self-autonomous'.[4] In stressing that the possibility of the knowledge of God springs from God, he wishes to focus on the revelation of God in Christ. He sternly maintains that any thinking which begins elsewhere, and rests on the power of human reason alone, cannot coincide with our knowledge of God. It has changed the subject. Philosophical arguments about the possibility of God will never produce a belief in the God who is Father, Son and Holy Spirit. This is the God, in Barth's words, 'whose revelation and work is attested by the Holy Scriptures and proclaimed by the Church'.

God, the Redeemer, cannot be encountered by an alternative route. The God of the philosophers, or the God approached through the natural world, may be a mere intellectual construction, and is not thereby shown to be the Father of the Saviour.

Barth is fully aware that in all this he is diverging from a basic theme in Roman Catholic theology. He quotes the First Vatican Council which condemns those who say that God as Creator and Lord, cannot be known by the 'certain, natural light of human reason'.[5] Thus Barth champions a strand of Protestantism which particularly looks to the consequences for humans of the Fall, particularly the sin and error in which it is alleged we are caught up. He wishes to rule out the possibility of natural theology, of reasoning from the nature of the world to the fact of God without recourse to specific Christian revelation. We cannot, he believes, directly discern the works of God in nature: 'This direct discernment . . . has been taken from us by the fall, at least according to Reformation ideas of the extent of sin, and it is restored to us only in the Gospels, in *revelatio specialis*.'[6] In the last phrase, Barth draws attention to the traditional distinction between general revelation through the created world and human reason, and special revelation, in the Christian case in Christ. For him, there can be no 'natural' knowledge of God. He holds that while there is a way from Christology to anthropology, there is no way from anthropology to Christology.[7] Our faith may illumine the world, but the world cannot ground our faith.

Not only is natural theology undermined by the fact of human sin so that we cannot trust our judgement. It is itself, according to Barth, a symptom of sin. It aims to deal, it seems, with an independent world, and is therefore 'not only to fail to assert the unique sovereignty of Jesus Christ in this sphere but even to contest it'.[8] Christ, we are told, 'has ceased to be the measure, but is Himself measured by the other'. Looking at the world as independent of God, even in preparation to reasoning to God, is to question the lordship of Christ. Our judgement is made the arbiter. Human presumption has gained its hold. Yet the trouble with this position is that it is itself a product of human reasoning. Theology, itself, purports to be a rational discipline. Even if it is to remain true to the object of faith, the question still remains as to why we should have faith in that, rather than something or someone else. In the Christian case, given that Christ is the Son of God, diverging from that insight and even questioning it might indeed be culpable. Yet the issue is how it can be established that it is indeed true. Otherwise theology will appear to rest on a blind commitment. Asserting that it is made by the grace of God merely begs the whole question. How are we to distinguish between beliefs implanted in us by the working of the Holy Spirit, and those that merely appear to have been but are themselves the product of human corruption? It is not enough to assert that we have a belief, and of rely on a putative divine source for it. Some process of discrimination between true and false beliefs is still necessary, and that would seem to be preeminently the role of reason.

2 Natural Theology

'Natural theology' has sometimes been thought to be that to which all rational persons could subscribe. It thus can seem to be less demanding than revealed theology. Yet if God has also been revealed in a special way, as many religions, including Christianity, claim, that is an assertion about what has really taken place. If something has happened, it is rational, given evidence, to believe that it has. It has not thereby moved beyond the bounds of reason. No doubt some have thought so, because it makes inevitable reference to divine intervention in the affairs of this world. A deist reliance on natural theology needs no such view. The issue, however, is whether something is true. Barth would still say that human attempts to establish such truth will be undermined by sin. Yet why should an attack on the possibility of natural theology be any more likely to be true than a statement upholding it? If each is made by humans, they might both appear to be liable to the same condemnation. Retreating to specific revelation ignores the fact that that too needs to be confirmed by human reason. No claim to divine revelation can be accepted untested. There are false prophets. The contrast between God's revelation received through grace, and reasoning in presumptuous independence of it, may point up an important issue about human dependence on God. It cannot show that human reason is to be decried, not least because such a move is itself made with the resources of such reason.

There is, as has already been indicated, in fact a surprisingly short route from a denial of the role of reason, through an emphasis on 'faith' to a retreat from claims to objective truth. It is not one that Barth himself travels since for him faith is in an objective God. Once, however, it is conceded that my faith is my faith, and I cannot give grounds which may convince others, there is an emphasis on the subjective which can quickly corrode all claims to truth. The alternative, as we have often seen, is for science to claim a monopoly of such truth (and hence of rationality) and for religion to retreat into a ghetto of arbitrary commitment.

Arguments about faith and reason are not necessarily the same as arguments about special revelation and God's general revelation in the created order. Barth contrasts faith in Christ with reasoning from the natural world. Yet faith in Christ should not be blind, and reason must play its part. As with all faith, we must have a conception of what we faith in.[9] It is not necessarily wrong to argue from historical evidence to a conclusion about the person of Jesus. Similarly, the fact the we reason from facts about the nature of the physical world, which ought to be available to everyone, should not undermine the claim that it is God we are reasoning about. The claim that God is revealed in Christ alone and not in the world around us is itself a theological claim that must be scrutinized. It is one about God and not the scope of human reason.

There is in all this a continuing concern that God is Redeemer and not just Creator. Religion should, it is thought, change human lives and not be like the answer to a geometrical theorem. Intellectual argument, it is feared, can become destructive of true religion. Certainly once reason became detached in the eighteenth century from the upholding of particular Christian revelation, and a quest for 'universal' truth instituted, it seems that atheism was an inevitable consequence. Such at least is the thesis of Michael Buckley who argues that religion turned to philosophy for validation in the Enlightenment, and made nature the subject of its arguments. 'Christianity', he says, 'in order to defend its god, transmuted itself into theism.'[10] His view is that Christianity built up for itself a series of contradictions. It made impersonal evidence the evidence for a personal God, and it based religion on something beyond itself, namely philosophy. Instead of the personal encounter with God, which Buckley sees as fundamental to religion, there was a resort to a philosophical appeal to evidence. Instead of being the result of religious experience, religion became the product of a process of inference, the result of a series of arguments about the physical world. Yet the more that the material world was seen to operate in its own right, according to its own laws, the easier it was to dispense with God altogether. As Buckley argues, 'philosophy eventually developed into natural philosophy, which became mechanics'.[11] What started as a search for inde-

pendent evidence for God, became a materialist concentration on the
workings of the physical world in their own right. Religion, it seemed,
put itself into the hands of philosophy. According to Buckley, 'philosophy spoke, and its final word was no'.[12]

Natural theology thus turned away, it is alleged, from any encounter
with a personal God. The more it became entwined with the impersonal workings of nature, and the more evidence for God was sought
apart from God, the more the seeds of atheism were sown. It could be
argued that the very notion of 'evidence' for God's existence involves a
turning away from God to something independent and even alien. The
material world could be seen to exist in its own right without any need
of appeal to anything or anyone beyond it. The idea that philosophy
could stand in judgement on religious belief might seem inappropriate.
Buckley maintains that 'another discipline cannot be made more fundamental and religion its corollary or epiphenomenon'.[13] The only consequence, he feels, will be the dissolution of religion. Similarly, he says,
'the Christian God cannot have a more fundamental witness than Jesus
Christ'.

The allegation is that, particularly through the influence of natural
theology, Christianity became 'theism', a philosophical doctrine about
God, and this itself bred atheism in reaction to it. Once appeals to a
reason that might be able to make universal claims supplanted the
Christian Gospel centred on the person of Christ, reasons for belief
became vulnerable to contradiction. Reasons for the existence of God
could be replaced by reasons against, and the whole hypothesis of God
as a means of accounting for apparent evidence could be discarded.
Some would conclude that the right policy is not to be seduced by
philosophy or the discoveries of natural science in the first place. If we
believe in God, we may see the world as God's creation, but we cannot
begin without belief and hope that human reason can establish anything about God. We will always be confronted with the challenge that
the conclusion has nothing to do with God, as revealed in Christ.

This view can gain strength from the observation of arguments in the
eighteenth century which looked to human reason to establish the
universal claims of a 'natural' religion. The very project of a natural
theology might appear to be a contradiction in terms. If humans rely on
their own resources and their own reason, how can their theology be
genuinely centred on any God? A theology that starts with the physical
world can, it will be alleged, all too easily end with it. A theology that is

centred on God must, it may seem, start with God. The contrast between the impersonal forces of the physical world and the Father of Jesus Christ might appear too vast.

Yet the physical world is our home and we cannot pretend that its nature is irrelevant to us. Starting with a faith derived from a particular revelation may seem to avoid many problems, but it never faces the question why we should start with any faith, and in particular that one. If faith is the gift of God, which some are to receive and others not, that implies a partiality on the part of God which fails to take seriously the claims of truth on everyone. As we have repeatedly seen, the question should never revolve round who believes, but whether what is believed is true. The whole point of an insistence on the role of rationality is that the objective nature of truth is upheld with its universal claim on everyone to believe it.

We must be careful not to become involved in circular reasoning. We will, it is said, believe in God as Creator because of a previous commitment to a particular revelation. Yet revelation has to be recognized as such. The concept of God should already be grasped before we can say that it is God who is being revealed. Some would say that this presupposes our membership of a community in which the concept of God has been taught. That is important but it still does not face the question of the origin of the idea in the community. The problem is that if we need a particular revelation to interpret the world as God's creation, and the concept of God to acknowledge a revelation as such, we still have not explained where we obtain our idea of God in the first place.

We could have been born with the concept of God already implanted in us. In that case, a religious answer to the question of how we obtain knowledge of God would be similar to Plato's notion of the recollection of innate ideas. Yet it seems unlikely that humans naturally share a concept of the same God, or the same concept of God. There may be a predisposition to search for an object of worship or a focus of meaning, and it is often alleged that religion is universal among humans. Monotheism, though, did not come naturally. Some would say that this demonstrates the need for revelation, but this brings back the circle of argument that threatens us. We believe in a God because of revelation, but accept the possibility of revelation because of a prior conception of God.

A conception of natural theology as a source of a common discourse about the world may appear attractive. It may seem a if particular doctrines from particular religions lack the universality required of reason while an appeal to a common world could supply it. Yet the idea of such a common discourse is more sociological than the product of reason. There would seem as great an obstacle to finding common ground between atheists and theists about the need to go beyond the brute facts of the natural world as between the proponents of particular religions about the rival claims of alternative revelation. In the eighteenth century, putting aside the particular claims of Christian revelation in favour of some 'natural religion' may have seemed a promising way of finding common ground. Natural theology could then be resorted to as a form of 'polite' discourse which could avoid some of the more troubling controversies of the day. In such circumstances, it could appear a retreat from Christian doctrine, and even antagonistic to it.

In fact, however, natural theology should not be regarded as a substitute for any particular revelation but as the necessary rational underpinning for the acceptance of any. Without some conception of a Creator, there must be considerable doubt about what, if anything, or who, if anybody, is being revealed. Just as the atheist can refuse to acknowledge the need for any explanation of the brute fact of the world, any revelatory experience, or extraordinary event, can be accepted at fact value as mere experience or event. We can always refuse to go beyond appearances unless we have a powerful reason for doing so. Religion can easily be pressed back into a ghetto where people take particular ethical stances or have a distinctive policy for living, but where no universal claims are made. In fact, the idea of universality should always be tied to that of objectivity, and not to the sociological question of what happens to be accepted at any given time. What is rationally acceptable may not coincide with what is accepted. If it is retorted that this is a clumsy device for imposing one group's set of beliefs on everyone, that merely questions the possibility of human reason (and does so in what purports to be a rational manner).

3   The Unity of Knowledge

Once we accept that blind and arbitrary commitments must be ruled out,[14] and that all our most basic beliefs must be under rational control, we have to be prepared to give reasons for belief in God. Personal religious experience can feature as much as pure reason, but the concept of God must be rooted in something that is in principle available to everyone, even if it is only through report. Otherwise we shall be driven to the view that belief in God is only available to some people and that only they will be able to grasp what is meant by God. Natural theology can provide an explanation as to why the possibility of belief in God can precede actual belief. The idea of God can be available to anyone able to reflect on the nature of the world around them.

Nothing perhaps could illustrate this ability more than an example quoted by Wittgenstein from William James's *Principles of Psychology*.[15] The immediate issue is how far there can be thought without language and James gives an example of a Mr Ballard, a deaf-mute, who was able to remember in detail his own early thought.[16] He remembered how 'some two or three years before my initiation into the rudiments of written language, that I began to ask myself the question: how came the world into being'. Wittgenstein himself was sceptical about how much reliance could be placed on a translation of a wordless thought into words. Putting aside, however, the dogma that thought is impossible without language, the example indicates an apparently spontaneous ability to reflect on the nature and origin not only of particular things but of everything. It did not arise in the context of a particular tradition, but rather raised a series of questions, as a result of observation of the world, most particularly about 'the source from which the universe came'. Ballard recounts his feelings of inadequacy in grappling with the subject but significantly does not refer explicitly to God. Wittgenstein reports the recollection as being about 'God and the world' but this is itself already to crystallize the questioning too much, and makes it easier for Wittgenstein to challenge the memory of the thinking. Without the aid of any social institution or language, Mr Ballard, as a boy, had apparently taken the first steps towards natural theology.

Reason begins with the individual, but is constrained by, and has ideally to conform to, the nature of the objective world. This is not to deny the role of tradition, but it is to suggest that traditions gain their hold because of their perceived ability to answer questions that are antecedently meaningful. If one accepts that the traditional arguments for the existence of God fail to prove God's existence in the way that a geometrical theorem is proved, it will be seen that we cannot know God through the working of *a priori* reason. Natural theology, however, claims that reflection on the nature of the physical world, and not least on the mere fact that it exists at all, can lead us to ask whether it has

been created. The question 'Why is there anything at all?' at least raises
the issue as to whether the physical universe does have a particular
origin, and makes us wonder what that might be. Clearly, if the discussion is left at this, we may well decide that there is no answer. Alternatively we can resort to a pantheism that in effect deifies the world we see,
or a deism that posits a rational explanation for the existence of the
world in a manner that makes it remote from human affairs. Pantheism
appears to validate an ethical and aesthetic approach to the world,
while deism neatly solves an intellectual problem with an intellectual
solution.

   None of this can be irrelevant to any revealed religion. At the very
least, a God worthy of worship has to be identified with the Power, if
any, that has created the universe. The source of human salvation
cannot be separate from any purpose underlying the reality in which we
find ourselves. Some would seize on the ambiguity of arguments from
natural theology to demonstrate their weakness. One writer says: 'Natural theology breaks down because, given the fact of evil, it cannot prove
that our world is intelligible in a way that unambiguously points to
God.'[17] Yet this is to demand far too much for natural theology on its
own. A reliance on it by itself would only serve to indicate that there was
no need of any further revelation. A fully plausible natural theology
would thus actually undermine the particular claims of revealed religions. They would have been shown to be superfluous. This is no doubt
what many opponents of natural theology, and of the incursion of
philosophy into theological concerns, are afraid of. The demand, however, for unambiguous proof is not one that can be made in any area of
science, and should not be expected in natural theology. We have
several times come across the idea of 'critical realism'. Whatever its
defects in confusing metaphysics and epistemology, it does draw attention to the way in which our purported knowledge, not least in science,
must remain open to revision.

   What is necessary in the field of rationality is that we should be
willing to combine all our purported knowledge, and not lock it into
separate compartments. The content of faith cannot exist securely apart
from the conclusions of rationality. We may not be able to prove that
the world was created. Yet it is hard to deny that knowledge of the
nature of the physical universe must be relevant to the establishment of
a belief in a Creator. If we conclude that everything, from the origins of
the universe to the development of humans as a species, has been the

product of chance, it would be difficult simultaneously to believe that everything had been created for a purpose. That is not to say that there may not be room for an element of chance in the evolution of organisms. That is precisely the kind of issue that natural theology can discuss. Purpose and chance may operate at different levels, but just as different branches of the universe cannot be allowed to produce conflicting pictures of the universe without reference to each other, so science and theology should not ignore each other. Just as reality is not parcelled into separate compartments, neither should our purported knowledge be. The demand for a unity of knowledge to reflect the unity of reality must lead to attempts to integrate the understanding of different disciplines. Leaving theology insulated from other forms of understanding is particularly dangerous, since it is in effect to concede that it is not actually a type of knowledge at all.

Yet because of the inability of natural theology to do more than point to the possibility, or perhaps the probability, of creation by a God, we are still far from understanding what the nature of such a God might be. A natural theology may create a space for the notion of a Creator, but it is still not much more than an empty space. We may conclude from the apparent unity of nature that it would have to be one reality rather than a series. It is still unclear, however, whether such a Being is personal. Is it indifferent to human beings? Is it even good? Questions are raised but not answered, unless we conclude that the nature of the physical world is such that it cannot allow any belief in a purpose within it. In other words, natural theology provides a case for thinking that, if there were a God, humans still need a further source of knowledge about the character of such a God. God has to be revealed in a more specific and direct way. Revelation is thus not a substitute for 'natural' reason. It is an answer to the questions such reason produces.

Yet how far does an appeal to revelation take us? If all purported knowledge is revisable, because humans are fallible and possess imperfect information, instances of apparent revelation may also fall under the same doubt. They have to be interpreted, and it may be claimed that revelation is not an alternative source of incorrigible knowledge. If all human judgements are fallible, them so may be a judgement that something is a divine revelation. The Barthian distrust of natural theology can then be generalized. Because, it may be said, all purported revelation has to be accepted and judged by humans, will not teaching arising form it be infected by the same human weakness that is liable to taint all our judgements? The proponents of critical realism in theology would agree and wish to make a distinction between the ultimate reality we are trying to refer to and historically conditioned judgements about its nature. The bridge between humans and God that revelation allegedly provides then becomes as clouded in fog as any other human advance towards knowledge.

Reality in these circumstances can once again recede, with the possibility of God becoming a mere Kantian noumenon beyond all understanding. Theology can then appear mere cultural construction and one which of its very nature can be revised as circumstances change. It then splinters not just into the insights of different religions, but into the presuppositions and prejudices of a succession of cultures. Theology may then appear not so much to reflect the nature of God as of the society that produced it. God, if there is such a Being, can never be allowed to break into human reality since every such revelation becomes reduced to mere interpretation, telling us more about the character of those who interpret, than what is interpreted.

4 'Constructive' Theology

This emphasis on the historic situation of particular groups of people can, as we have seen, give rise to the hermeneutics of suspicion. It is the very antithesis of the notion of a natural theology that reasons from the fact of the world to God in a way that would claim truth across place and time. Arguments about natural theology are themselves as much at risk from attacks on the possibility of a transcultural and transhistorical reason as are any claims to special revelation. The very idea of a 'natural world' is not one that sits easily with a view embedding all meaning in the particular circumstances of particular human culture. The very idea of a revisionary or a constructive theology may seem a contradiction in terms. If theology is concerned with the reality and nature of God, how can it be deliberately constructed or changed, rather than be discovered or revealed? What kind of religious truth can be the product of humans, particularly if bound tightly into a cultural context? Once we adopt a post-Kantian view of the relationship of concepts and reality, we assume that reality must be veiled. The human face of reality is stressed so that reality becomes reality as we conceive it or interpret it. We than have to face the question of whether we are rational subjects able to recognize truth, or historically conditioned in a strong sense.

Theology as a human construction, rather than as the pursuit of knowledge, may seem a notion that is self-destructive. How could theologians talk of God if they believed that they were merely reflecting the prejudices and presuppositions of their age? Any theology has to aim at being explicitly ahistorical if it is not to deny its own validity. Natural theology, for instance, cannot be seen as merely an interesting byproduct of some parts of eighteenth-century society. That is merely to dismiss it as irrelevant to us in very different circumstances. Once forms of rationality are viewed as simply the creation of particular societies, human understanding becomes a mirage. Even a revelation apparently made to one group of people becomes transmuted into what that group took to be a revelation. The beliefs of previous societies are made to look irrelevant to ours.

Gordon Kaufman insists on a strong form of historicity and puts forward what he significantly calls a 'constructive theology'. He says that humans are in a special way 'historical' in that they 'create and shape' themselves through unfolding historical processes.[18] His work is imbued with Kantian assumptions about the way reality is constituted for us through our experience and discourse. His views demonstrate the effects of a repudiation of realism in the field of religion. He sees great religious traditions merely as processes 'through which humans apprehended and shaped and reshaped themselves by means of certain practices and according to certain images'. The inevitable consequence is that we appear to be imprisoned within whatever conceptual scheme we happen to hold at the time. There is no question of transcending the special conditions of our culture.

The consequence is that it will appear important that our views and categories of thought reflect life as it is lived today and not as our predecessors once lived. With the idea of the historicity of theology can easily go the belief that it is vital that it is related to contemporary concerns. Kaufman does not dismiss appeals made in other ages to authoritative divine revelation as mistaken. Such a view, he considers, 'could have been an expression of the actual cultural experience and life of a whole people, and in those contexts they are legitimate and proper moves'.[19] His theological programme, on the other hand, is to work 'from within widely accepted comtemporary assumptions'. We can have no choice in the matter if he is right. When we are the creatures of our age, how could we reason in a different idiom?

There is, though, a tension in such thinking. Kaufman, for instance, may assert our historicity but he still provides lengthy arguments as to why we should not go on thinking in ways that clearly many still do. The argument slides from how we have to think because of our historical context, to how we ought to think regardless of context. It becomes a question of what is appropriate rather than what is necessary. So far from being moulded exclusively by the forces in our history, it becomes apparent that we have a choice in the matter. We can, if Kaufman's argument is correct, reason about what we ought to think, and that is precisely what a strong view of historicity should in all consistency deny. According to him, what we know or think we know about the world makes a traditional picture of a God as a divine super-Self outside the universe 'literally unthinkable by us' and unintelligible. Yet he accepts that some do still hold this picture, and we are left wondering why if it is unthinkable that this is still thought. Kaufman's view of the task of Christian theology is that 'theologians should attempt to construct conceptions of God, humanity and the world appropriate for the orientation of contemporary human life'.[20] The issue is which understanding of God, which 'human imaginative construction', is appropriate to the world in which we happen to find ourselves. Yet this question seems fraught with difficulty for a genuine historicist. According to any historicist position, people cannot remove themselves sufficiently from the constraints of their historical situation to decide rationally what they ought to think. They just find certain ways of thinking appealing, and that is all that can be said.

Philosophy and theology are left with nowhere to stand, if it is impossible to reason about our circumstances, as opposed to merely from them. The most that can be aspired to is superior form of cultural commentary, but one which is itself the product of the culture it purports to describe. The problem comes when someone both wishes to espouse historicism and yet to go beyond description and to prescribe. Kaufman, for instance, is quick to use the language of rational argument to persuade. He says, for example, of a belief in a spiritual realm that 'this dualistic way of speaking . . . is fundamentally incoherent, leading us to know something(s) which we cannot possibly know'.[21] In other words, he is not talking of what people happen to believe but of what is believable at any time. Similarly, he dismisses understandings of any transcendental reality distinct from this world saying: that 'there seems no good reason for such a postulate – except that that is the way these ancient myths, regarded as authoritative in our religious traditions, spoke.'[22]

This encapsulates the problem of both stressing the embedding of belief in a particular historical context, and of referring to good reasons external to that situation. Either we are to be wholly creatures of our time or we can step outside our systems of belief, and question how well grounded they are. No historicist view can allow us to say that a set of beliefs, open to us to hold, is somehow no longer appropriate. Kaufman provides philosophical arguments, derived from Kant, against the idea of transcendence, when he ought to be content with pointing out that no one can believe in a transcendent God any more. His view is that 'our concepts of God and of Christ must be reconceived with attention to our modern understandings of ourselves and of the universe'.[23] Yet we must face the question why this should be so. If it is merely that such understandings are modern and religious traditions ancient, we can have no choice. We are not inhabitants of the ancient world. If, on the other hand, it is because we have knowledge not previously possessed, that suggests a view of revelation that subordinates it to the requirements of a substantive natural theology. Yet the notion of an independent natural theology must be ruled out by historicism, on the grounds that it will always involve a tacit appeal to a rationality transcending the circumstances of a particular age.

The emphasis on our historical situation and the simultaneous revisability of our judgements must be an unstable one. If people are conditioned to have certain beliefs, it seems incoherent both to note this and suggest that they ought to be revised. That would appear to imply that they are mistaken. Yet the more that a religious outlook is seen as a mere ongoing tradition, the less can it be criticized on rational grounds. It may as a matter of sociological fact find the going more difficult in ages other than those that produced it. It may look more and more like a social fossil, preserving the insights and customs of a generation long gone. What cannot happen is that we are given reasons why it ought to be revised. Kaufman is quite content to see the great theologians of Christian history not as setting out the truth, but as 'articulating and reconstructing one particular perspective on life among many'.[24] Yet if Christianity merely provides a perspective, the question why it should be revised becomes pressing again. If one really accepts a form of pluralism, why should any perspective be reinterpreted? If its adherents remain content, there can be no other grounds for change. They believe what they believe.

A retort may be that a tradition which exists in a self-contained compartment, alienated from other perspectives, is not likely to survive. That is arguable from a sociological point of view, although it might also be that a very separate body is more likely to keep a hold on the allegiance of its adherents. This kind of sociological speculation is not the issue. The problem is not the best technique for survival, but the issue of whether beliefs can be rationally revised. Sociological commentary slips almost imperceptibly into the judgement that religious belief is somehow not rationally acceptable in the present age. Reality, it is being implied, is not as traditional Christianity has claimed it is. Yet if such a global assertion is not being made and we are left with incommensurable perspectives, there can by definition be no rational ground for change whatever the cultural pressures.

5 Faith and Reality

The idea that Christianity is rationally revisable must go hand in hand with a view that there is an objective reality to which our judgements should conform. Yet if we all confront the same world, a unity of knowledge becomes imperative. We should aspire to consistency between all our different judgements and we should be concerned about disagreement with others. Without the notion of a common reality, there cannot be a common measure against which our views can all be calibrated. This is particularly relevant when matters of faith and reason are debated. Faith cannot be prised apart from the claims of reason, if it is to claim truth. The God who seems to have been revealed cannot be detached from the God who allegedly created the world. If we live in one world, the object of faith and what we reason about cannot be totally distinct. If reason is inconclusive, it is possible to go on trusting, but the object of trust cannot somehow be locked away in an area inaccessible to rational understanding. Many religious believers cannot accept even the logical possibility that the object of trust is illusory and that their faith is in error. That in the end, however, will be to reduce talk of truth to issues about the meaning for us of symbols.

Theology cannot be in the business of construction rather than discovery any more than the physical sciences can. It is no doubt trivially true that, in Kaufman's words, conceptions of God 'are our ideas, not God's'.[25] The point is, however, whether our ideas can also be about reality. It may be thought that what is real is somehow always veiled by our concepts, our understandings and our interpretations. If so, the focus must shift from what is conceived of, or what is revealed, to something else. Indeed, Kaufman argues that we should avoid reifying our ultimate point of reference.[26] This would allow it 'to be appropriately transformed as new circumstances arise in human life'. Such a statement embodies the view of theology as human construction. Yet any understanding of God should be based on a view of reality as existing independently of our circumstances. There is instead a systematic and deliberate confusion between what is believed and the mode of belief so that if it is thought desirable for the latter to change, it follows somehow that the former does. If the way we think alters, so does what we think about. The 'mystery' at the heart of things then becomes shorthand for human aspirations. The traditional dualism expressed in traditional Christianity between the natural and the supernatural can be made to appear mere dissatisfaction with the way things are and an aspiration for something better. To suggest that the infinite, which seems by definition to be beyond our grasp, can actually be grasped will, we are told, be to reify the unknown.

Underlying all these problems is a belief that somehow we can never break through to a genuine understanding of reality. The latter is thought to be transcendent in such a strong sense that the world we live in can only be thought to be the shadow cast by our thoughts. Such a view would make nonsense of the project of natural theology, since 'nature' would recede beyond our grasp. We might have a theology of nature, in the sense of building up a picture for ourselves of the world we inhabit. We could not, though, imagine that we were reasoning about its intrinsic nature. The quest for an objective unity in the world would become a search for coherence in our understanding.

This all brings us back to the problem of metaphysical realism. The more the realist stresses the logical independence of reality, the more our concepts can appear to be separated from the reality we conceptualize. It can seem as if our ideas are ours and can bear no relation to what they are ideas of. Yet this is itself a philosophic picture, and there seems little reason to suppose that entities are forever veiled and inaccessible, because we are 'trapped' within a particular conceptual scheme. We can be mistaken in what we think, but it does not follow that we can never be right. The idea that the human mind is incapable of grasping the nature of any reality is a form of scepticism which undermines both religious and all other forms of belief.

William Alston attacks this kind of insulation of the real world from our conceptual categories. He writes:

> The real, independently existing world, the nature of which makes our statements true or false, is one with which we are in contact already through our experiences, thought and discourse. The constituents of the world – people, trees, animals, buildings, oceans, galaxies, God – are things we perceive or otherwise experience, think about and talk about. They are not wholly external to us and our cognitive and linguistic doings, though they don't depend (for the most part) on those doings for what they are.[27]

This explicitly opposes any idea that we are always imprisoned in a world of our own construction so that somehow we can never break out of it to face any objectively real world. Yet it is the latter position that underlies most views stressing the importance of our historical situation. If we are never in contact with reality, previous understanding is bound to have little relevance to us. It will reflect circumstances long gone and will tell us nothing of what may confront us now. Once we realize that reality may not always change, and that we may have partial access to it, it will follow that ancient knowledge may still be knowledge. In particular, the view that we cannot know anything of God is a philosophical dogma of questionable origin. There seems to be little reason why as a result of natural theology, we cannot entertain the idea of a Creator, nor why the nature of that Creator may not have been further revealed.

Arguments against any possibility of obtaining any ahistorical knowledge inevitably involve a retreat by religion into a ghetto where in the end it can claim nothing. It can be endlessly revised, not least because there can be no external reality to act as a constraint on such beliefs. It has to become a mere reflection of changing historical contexts. A realist position does raise the possibility that our judgements about an independent reality are mistaken. Atheism has to be a possibility. All claims to truth are subject to error and must be subject to rational examination. On the one hand lie the dangers of an unsustainable dogmatic certainty. On the other lies the paralysis of a self-stultifying scepticism. We must recognize that in any sphere, including those of religion and science, we have an opportunity to achieve a knowledge that may not be complete or unquestionable, but which is rationally sustainable.

Some wish to change rather more of what has been traditionally held in religion than others. For Iris Murdoch, religion itself has to be demythologized, while morality, and in particular the idea of Good, remains central. She holds that 'this Good is not the old God in disguise, but rather what the old God symbolised'.[28] Good, she thinks, represents the reality of which God is the dream.[29] Thus there is such a thing as Goodness, in a Platonic sense, even if there is no God. The authenticity of our moral experience is insisted upon, even though it can no longer be said to be grounded in a belief in what Murdoch calls 'a supernatural person'. She writes:

> Perhaps (I believe) Christianity can continue without a personal God or a risen Christ, without belief in supernatural places and happenings, such as heaven and life after death, but retaining the mystical figure of Christ occupying a place analogous to that of Buddha: a Christ who can console and save, but who is to be found as a living force within each human soul and not in some supernatural elsewhere.[30]

She wants to renew the Christian tradition through its being changed 'into something that can be generally believed'. Yet the question is whether the combination of realism in ethics with a non-realism in religion can be stable. How can goodness be built into the structure of things if there is no Creator and no underlying explanation for the existence of goodness? It is but a short step from the repudiation of metaphysics in one area to its disappearance in another. As it is, the grounding of our moral judgements in reality is left unutterably vague and becomes little more than the projection of our moral consciousness. The problem must always be how in a world where there is no settled agreement on moral matters, the absolute claims of morality can be justified. Murdoch may claim 'that the idea of perfection haunts all our activity'[31] but it is easy to see this as the legacy of a religious outlook. Once the claims of a religion to truth are removed, there seems little reason why its images should be allowed to guide our lives. When we know that they do not reflect a genuine reality, the power of inspiration would seem to evaporate. How can Christ console, let alone save, if he is seen as the product of imagination? Dreaming that one is consoled is not the same as being consoled. How can he be still a living force if he is not in any sense alive?

Iris Murdoch is in the 'revisionist' camp of those who want to change traditional Christianity. Yet the basic issue should always be not whether what remains is recognizably Christian or not. It should be whether it reflects the character of the world we inhabit. We should not be simply concerned with how much or how little of traditional teaching which we have inherited from previous generations is acceptable or credible to our present age. That can easily degenerate into a sociological question of what certain groups of people at a particular time happen to find easy to believe. Clearly the mere fact that it is traditional teaching is not enough either to make it acceptable or to disqualify it from serious attention in changed circumstances. We are inevitably forced to examine the grounds for such belief. We cannot avoid looking at the rational basis of faith.

Notes

1 Placher, *The Domestication of Transcendence*, p. 186.
2 *Ibid.*, p. 198.
3 *Ibid.*, p. 183 note 3.
4 *Church Dogmatics*, II: i, p. 63.
5 *Ibid.*, p. 79.
6 *Church Dogmatics*, I: i, p. 130.
7 *Ibid.*, p. 131.
8 *Church Dogmatics*, II: i, p. 163.
9 See my 'Reason and faith'.
10 *At the Origins of Modern Atheism*, p. 346.
11 *Ibid.*, p. 358.
12 *Ibid.*, p. 357.
13 *Ibid.*
14 See my *Reason and Commitment*.
15 *Philosophical Investigations*, #352.
16 *Principles of Psychology*, I, pp. 267–8.
17 Dalferth, *Theology and Philosophy*, p. 97.
18 *In Face of Mystery*, p. 103.

19 *Ibid.*, p. 110.
20 *Ibid.*, p. 31.
21 *Ibid.*, p. 325.
22 *Ibid.*
23 *Ibid.*, p. xi.
24 *Ibid.*, p. 40.
25 *Ibid.*, p. 31.
26 *Ibid.*, p. 328.
27 *A Realist Conception of Truth*, p. 148.
28 *Metaphysics as a Guide to Morals*, p. 426.
29 *Ibid.*, p. 496.
30 *Ibid.*, p. 419.
31 *Ibid.*, p. 428.

10

Does Religion Need a Transcendent God?

1 God and the World

[A dualist picture of reality suggests that God is in a spiritual dimension wholly other than the physical world in which we situated. Any attempt to replace this with a theological view of one world either ignores the material world or reduces reference to a spiritual world to talk of something else. There have been times when the importance of the material world has been ignored, but in our present day the reverse temptation is more obvious. We can be led to assume that reality is comprised by what can be perceived, measured or otherwise manipulated. References to any other dimension of reality are then ruled out as meaningless or thought to be merely a picturesque way of talking about what may be especially important to us here and now. This policy is no doubt aided by the difficulties of finding any link between different dimensions of reality. The ease with which any dualist conception can be characterized as a 'two-world view' illustrates the dangers. If we are in one world, how can we gain any knowledge of another? Plato had to explain our knowledge of the other world through his doctrine of recollection. The point is not that this is a plausible view, but that some special explanation seems inevitable once an ontological split has been made.

The position of God in Christian theology is in some ways not unlike that of the world of Forms in Plato's philosophy. Given Plato's influence, that may not be a coincidence. The same problem, therefore, recurs. If God is totally separate ontologically from the physical world, and not bounded by our spatio-temporal framework, how can knowledge of Him be gained? What bridge can there be? The more apart God is seen as being, the less we can hope to understand of His reality.]

By definition, He seems to be beyond human comprehension, and language appears inadequate to describe Him. We have already seen how writers such as Hick want to empty the Godhead of the attributes accorded in any particular theology. The 'Real' somehow grounds everything but stays beyond our grasp. Yet, as in the work of Gordon Kaufman, the more the incomprehensibility and ineffability of God is stressed, the more it becomes obvious that even assertions of mystery become vacuous. We seem to be pointing into a fog, unable to discover whether we are in fact pointing at anything. Hume makes Cleanthes object to those who insist on maintaining the mysterious, incomprehensible nature of the Deity. He says:

> If our ideas, as for as they go, be not just and adequate, and correspondent to his real nature, I know not what there is in this subject worth insisting upon . . . Or how do you mystics, who maintain the absolute incomprehensibility of the Deity, differ from sceptics and atheists who assert that the first cause of All is unknown and unintelligible?[1]

This is a perpetual challenge to those who wish to insist on the mystery of God's existence. If God is transcendent, His mode of being must be mysterious to us. Yet we still have to face the challenge of how we can obtain even enough knowledge to talk of God's mystery.

Not only, however, would a God who is utterly transcendent be beyond knowledge, He would have no contact with this world. Something totally transcendent might, it seems, exist in some parallel universe, but there could be no interaction between the two realms. An intermediate position would add that if there was, we could never recognize it. Yet the whole tenor of such arguments is atheistic. A God who cannot be known or recognized, a God who cannot intervene because He is utterly detached from our world, seems remarkably similar to no God at all. We could ourselves never be in a position to say that such a God existed.

It is partly for these reasons that a transcendent God must also be conceived as immanent. He must be present in the world as well as being separate from it. This tension is reflected in the Christian doctrine of the Trinity which itself accepts that a wholly transcendent God is also a God who revealed Himself at a particular time and place within this world, and through His Spirit works within it still. This is already to suggest that a mere philosophical account of God's existence will be inadequate, and has to be supplemented by some form of revelation. That does not mean that rational understanding is irrelevant or impossible. It does imply that our own unaided reason could never be sufficient to grasp what is by definition beyond our grasp.

In the face of such problems, the temptation is to change the subject. If we cannot cope with the idea of a God beyond human understanding, it may seem as if we should think of God in some other way. An alternative may be to close the gap between God and the physical world. Otherwise it might seem as if nothing material could be revelatory of God if He is utterly to be distinguished from anything physical. Grace Jantzen says on this point: 'This means that we have a split between God and the world of such magnitude that we could not learn anything about the nature of God from the nature of the world.'[2] A dualist system that made God so wholly other that the physical universe would seemingly be unrelated to Him, is consigning God to oblivion at least from our point of view. Jantzen claims that if divine transcendence is understood as complete otherness, 'nothing revelatory could in principle occur within the natural order, since it is by definition utterly different from God and hence could not reveal him'. The Christian doctrine of Incarnation explicitly repudiates such a view. God is said by that to be both wholly other and to have been revealed in space and time, and indeed within the confines of an ordinary life. The problem is that a strong doctrine of transcendence has to be able to uphold God's ontological distinctness while not implying his total separation from (and even indifference to) this world.

Jantzen's own solution is explicitly aimed at the kind of metaphysical dualism which was referred to in chapter 8. She considers it to be as unacceptable in the case of God and the world as in that of persons and their bodies. She writes:

> If we affirm the transcendence of God, what we are affirming is that God is not reducible to the physical universe: ultimately reality is not describable in solely mechanistic terms. But, just as human persons are embodied but yet transcendent, so also the universe can be the body of a transcendent God.[4]

Thus transcendence becomes the opposite of reductionism rather than of immanence. We may not see the universe as a mechanism but that still does not entitle us, according to Jantzen, to posit two distinct substances or two realms of existence. One allegation will be that this is tantamount to pantheism. Jantzen rejects pantheism if it is merely a species of reductionism, but she does see much good in its rejection of two sorts of reality, 'one of which is God and the other ontologically opposite to God'.[5] Thus she says: [A theist who takes the doctrine of creation seriously must finally affirm, with the pantheist and against the reductionist, that all reality is from God and is ultimately not separable from him.']

Yet if reality is not separable from God, God it seems is not separable from reality, and one arrives at a repudiation of dualism that leaves the ontological status of God far from clear. The analogy with the human person suggests that we are to regard divine reality as somehow more than physical processes and yet ultimately 'supervenient' on them. In other words, just as, according to monist views, one cannot have a disembodied person, so God cannot exist apart from the physical universe. Jantzen accepts that 'if God were to will the annihilation of the universe, then he would be willing his own annihilation'.[6] The response to this must be that the role of God runs the risk of becoming superfluous. Monist approaches to the human personality can lead on remorselessly to an eliminative materialism which concludes that physical processes are the only genuine reality. All else is 'folk psychology'. In the same way, it would be quite easy to be drawn from a view of the world as God's body to an explicit pantheism and on to atheism. This is despite the fact that the very notion of 'God's body' invokes a classical notion of a personal God, which would be repudiated by pantheism.

What, though, is wrong with pantheism? Ever since Thales, the first philosopher, held that 'all things are full of gods', there has been a temptation to attribute divine characteristics to the physical world. As the history of the pre-Socratic philosophers demonstrates, this has inevitably led to an explicit materialism. [Once the separation of God and the universe is repudiated, there is a tendency to see the world as embodying the divine, and this is in turn transmuted into mere veneration of physical processes. This may be important for those concerned with the misuse of the material world, but the veneration can be just an attitude to nature, an expression of human awe and wonder, when faced with its intricate workings. It says nothing about why the world should be venerated in this way.]

The true pantheist would deny that pantheism is merely a matter of holding certain attitudes, the possessing of a romantic delight in the

Defines "true" pantheism.

beauties of nature. Although it denies God's ontological separation from the world, there would in pantheism be a strong sense of the divine Unity present in all things. It is a doctrine of immanence without transcendence. As one writer on pantheism puts it 'The Unity is not independent of (i.e. cannot exist apart from) the cosmos and it cannot create the cosmos since it is not independent of it.'[7]

As such, pantheism is not dualist, and cannot regard divinity as in any sense personal. Because of its repudiation of any other realm, it cannot allow personal immortality. All theology will have to be natural theology, and, what is more, a natural theology that cannot move from the world to God. There would be no scope for revelation in the sense of God actively revealing Himself. We could, when confronted with nature, respond as if something of the basic unity of things had been revealed to us. Yet there would seem little difference between the Unity being revealed and our recognizing the Unity. The idea of the divine as an initiating, active force would seem hard to retain once the notion of a personal God, with intentions and purposes, has been jettisoned. The mystical recognition of the inherent oneness of things (a oneness of which we are apart) would seem the heart of pantheism. This could easily degenerate into a merely aesthetic attitude to the physical world. Once anything apart from our cosmos is repudiated, it would seem all too easy to acquiesce in a scientific account of the world and merely cultivate certain attitudes towards it. Certainly the idea of the divine unity as an active force would appear questionable if it were identified with physical processes. What, indeed, is the difference between seeing the material forces of change and development as a brute, inexplicable fact at which we are moved, and somehow ascribing mystical properties to them? There may be an argument as to how intertwined the different processes of the physical world are. Physics could, however, discover they are linked at some deep level, without the need for any mystical gloss being put on this. The urge to be rid of superfluous entities or characteristics might prompt the wielding of Ockham's razor.

Some writers have been particularly influenced by a 'process theology' which stresses that to be real is to be in process. This stems from the philosophy of A. N. Whitehead and has been elaborated by Charles Hartshorne. Many are reluctant to accept the traditional conception of a God who appears to be remote and unaffected by the events of this world. How, they ask, can God be compassionate and loving if He is absolute and unchanging? Does not the ability to respond in a gracious way to human need imply that God is part of the processes of the world and not totally separate from them? Must He be so detached from the world as to be impassive? This might seem a particularly attractive view to those who place stress on the evolutionary character of the world. God could, then, in some sense be a part of the dynamic unfolding of greater complexity. The evolutionary process is the action of God. Yet such a position resists pantheism because, while emphasizing God's identification with the physical world, it still wants to stress His independence of it. All reality is embraced within the divine, but the divine nature is not co-extensive with the physical world. It includes it, but exceeds it.

This position has been given the name of 'panentheism' and it has obvious pantheistic overtones. David Pailin, who explicitly endorses this kind of view, describes the relation of God and world as 'two interdependent entities that mutually affect each other'.[8] He says, 'If God is not to be identified with all reality, the only appropriate way to describe the divine is as a reality that . . . is affected by and affects all events.'[9]

Process theologians tend to think of this divine influence as a generalized 'luring' that respects the autonomy of the non-divine. It therefore runs the risk of appearing somewhat ineffectual. While it may preserve the idea of divine action, it limits God by the placing of the divine within the events of the physical world. A God who suffers alongside us may seem a more compassionate God, but He is certainly not transcendent in a traditional sense. As a result, He is a part of the processes of the world to such an extent that He is within time and subject to all its limitations. It appears that the unfolding future will be as great a mystery to the divine nature as to human nature. God, it is said, cannot know what is still unknowable, because it has not happened. It is also hard not to conclude that, on this view, God is as involved with the evil which happens as the good. Unless He can be conceived of as genuinely distinct, in an ontological sense, from the events of this world, it seems difficult to demarcate the processes that are in accordance with the divine will and those that are not. At best, God may seem rather bungling, eager to lure people and events to the good, but somehow incapable of doing so very effectively.

The traditional problem of evil is no less a problem for those who believe in a transcendent God. The point is, however, that the ontological gap posited between God and the world gives the latter an independence which may help to explain its lack of conformity to God's will.

Once the two are identified, in whole or part, there seems no way of differentiating what happens from what God wills to happen. God, it seems, is to be identified with a cancerous growth in a body, as much as other processes. They are all equally embraced in the divine reality. Panentheism tries to stress the identification of God and the world, in the sense of a divine presence in, and love for, its processes. Yet it does not wish to say that the divine reality is bounded by the reality of this or any world, even though it must include some such reality. God cannot be self-sufficient, but needs, it seems, some world to love, even if it does not have to be this one. God, it appears, is distinct from this world, and yet at the same time cannot be. In trying to steer a middle course between pantheism and traditional theism, panentheism only succeeds in making what appeared to be a clear choice totally incomprehensible. God may be identified with this world, or He may exist in ontological separation from it. Either He is or He is not distinct. Panentheism seems to want to say that He is to be identified with this world's processes, but at the same time He is not to be. Ontological separation does not entail lack of love, and it is perhaps this that is leading panentheism astray. A distinct God need not be a remote, uncaring one.

2 Spirit and Matter

A classical belief in God has always placed great emphasis on the role of God as Creator. This has to be linked with a notion of God as personal, as a Being with purposes, as well as to the fundamental idea that the Creator is ontologically separate from what he has created. Attempts to talk of God as Being itself or the Real may try to show how everything is ultimately grounded in something, but its nature and the character of the grounding becomes obscure. The more that God is simply identified with reality, the less easy is it to talk of God's purposes and will apart from the continuing flux of events. Only if God is truly separate from creation can any sense be made of the claim that much of what happens goes against His will. Without an ontological separation, the conclusion must be that evil cannot be real, if God or Reality is good. The other option would be to say that ultimate reality is neither good nor evil, and we have then lost another of the traditional attributes of God, namely goodness. There is little difference between grounding everything in some ultimate reality which has no apparent purpose or preference, and merely accepting everything that happens in the world as a brute fact without a possibility of further explanation.

Paul Tillich warns against the assumption that God, according to pantheism, is simply the same as everything that is. He writes, 'If God is identified with nature, it is not the totality of natural objects which is called God but rather the creative power and unity of nature, the absolute substance which is present in everything.'[10] Yet once this step is taken, the question of transcendence reappears in at least one form. The pantheist will deny the ontological separation of the divine but there may still be a sense in which the divine unity could transcend our knowledge. There is no guarantee that simply because an ontological dualism has been repudiated, we can fully comprehend the nature of the all-embracing unity, the inherent essence of all things. The reason for our deficiency of knowledge may be different, but the more that the unity is distinguished from the apparent plurality, the more it is clear that there may be significant obstacles in reaching the unity from the plurality, the reality from the appearance.

The pantheist may be part of the unity and so there may seem less ontological distance between the subject and object of knowledge than in a dualist system. It could be claimed, however, that in the latter, the split is not just one between God and world but one between spirit and matter. Humans themselves encompass such a duality within themselves, or so a thorough-going dualist would claim. As a result, each person is an example of a bridge between the spiritual and the physical. This is an inversion of the argument that the relation of God and world should be seen on analogy with a monistic understanding of person and body. Dualism can accept the parallel but insist that is works the other way. The dichotomy between God and world is replicated within the human personality.

The problem of ontological distance between 'spirit' and 'matter' thus comes very close to home. It can be a problem within ourselves as well as about the relation of the cosmos to God. Both in the philosophy of mind and of religion, a widespread reaction is to reinterpret the concept of the spiritual so that it no longer refers to a non-physical mode of existence. A classic example of this is provided by Ludwig Feuerbach. He wrote that 'the historical progress of religion consists in this that what by an earlier religion was regarded as objective, is now recognised as subjective: that what was formerly contemplated and worshipped as God is now perceived to be something human.'[11]

Religion is thus merely a projection of human needs and desires.
Feuerbach, in particular, has influenced many modern thinkers with
this view, not least Marx and Freud, and more recently in feminist
thought, Irigaray. Feuerbach held that 'man projects his being into
objectivity'.[12] Our conception of God is then a mirror of human nature,
and not a glimpse of some objective reality. He repudiates Kant's
distinction between an object in itself and 'as it is for me'.[13] He thinks no
sense can be given to the former notion if the object cannot appear
other than the way 'the absolute measure of my nature determines it to
appear'. If our conceptions are shaped by our nature there is no possibility of imagining that they refer to anything beyond themselves. This
notion of projection relies on the idea that the source of our ideas about
God lies wholly in ourselves. Our 'knowledge' is a human product and
there is no reason why it should bear any relation to the real character
of a transcendent God. It could be pointed out that we may still be right
in our beliefs, but this would be a lucky accident and not one we are in
a position to know anything about.

Feuerbach goes much further than merely rooting our 'projections'
in human nature. His reductionism explicitly changes the subject from
the nature of a transcendent God to the nature of the people who
produce beliefs about God. He regards his task as the reduction of 'the
supermundane, supernatural, and superhuman nature of God to the
elements of human nature as its fundamental elements'. This form of
reductionism is rife in contemporary thought with the added complica-
tion that a disbelief in a general 'human nature' can link concepts not to
the human predicament, but to different sets of cultural circumstances.

In some studies of religion, religion can be explicitly reduced to a
mere set of cultural practices, organized around what one writer refers
to as 'objects deemed superhuman and sacred'.[14] The point is that what
is sacred is 'de-reified'. Just because all religions treat something as
sacred, it is claimed that it does not follow that the Sacred is what all
religions are concerned with. We are told: 'The description "sacred"
here refers not to a mysterious other force, ontologically postulated, but
a class term for a distinctive set of ways humans relate or respond to
those objects.' The reductionism is clear, however such ways are to be
identified. Once again the fact of belief is being stressed at the expense
of what, if anything, the belief is about. Indeed, it is made explicit that
the beliefs are not about anything at all, but are projections of attitudes,
social arrangements and the like. Analyses of this type do not give a

neutral account of religion. They undermine it to the extent that anyone accepting them cannot go on believing what they did. They are made to accept that their belief has been guilty of 'reification', of taking to be real what is merely being projected. As we have seen, this is a recurring issue in the contemporary philosophy of religion.

The notion of transcendence makes religion vulnerable to such moves, but the main problem is the realist attempt to separate reality from our concepts of it. The temptation is to place meaning exclusively on the conceptual side of the division, so that reason seems to be only at home in the conceptual arena. The result is that reality drops out as inaccessible, a Kantian noumenon. Because reality does not seem to be actually doing anything, but seems to be a passive and inert object of inquiry, the inquiry becomes everything and the target nothing. It may still have a regulative function, which should not be ignored. The role of target in archery or a goal mouth in soccer gives the game a point it would not otherwise have. Nevertheless a game in which one can never know whether one has hit the bull's-eye or scored a goal would seem a futile one. Similarly, the idea that we can continue to hold beliefs while being unable to distinguish truth from falsity would seem to threaten the very point of belief. That is not an argument against realism, but rather a warning not to be seduced by a Kantian picture. In the religious case, this will remorselessly lead on to Feuerbach's view that God is a mere projection.

3 Forms of Transcendence

The transcendence of reality over our conceptual scheme is a more general problem than simply the question of our knowledge of God. Even sub-atomic particles could be considered transcendent in the sense that their nature outstrips our understanding and our ability to describe them. In quantum mechanics, as in the field of religion, there are those who claim that we can refer to the basic reality and those who wish to confine themselves to human interactions with it.[15] The problem with the latter strategy is that once we confine ourselves to such interactions, the very idea of an interaction becomes problematic. We have lost our grasp of what it is we interacting with. In the case of quantum mechanics, all we will be left with are measurements and observations, without any notion of something being measured or observed. Simi-

larly, if the 'sacred' is reduced to our interactions with it, it will not be
long before the notion of the sacred is dismissed as a reification. We are
left with ideas of construction, projection and even of 'world-making'.
We can no longer talk of a personal God or even an objective abstraction called the Holy, the Sacred or whatever. The idea of anything
beyond our conceptual schemes seems impossible, and so we are left
with the mere fact of people's schemes.

[If we lose any idea of a reality which interacts with us, this can be
calamitous when we are talking of the physical world, since we are in
danger of losing any idea of an independent causality. Such a position
is also destructive of religion.] Religions typically make cognitive claims
about the nature of reality. Such a reality, however, should not be
thought of as an inert object. In the Judaeo-Christian tradition, for one,
religion concerns human relations with a God who is active and who
can enter into relations with us. The concept of God always has to be
distinguished from the reality of God. The former is intimately related
to our limited abilities. The objective reality of God, however, transcends our concepts in just the same way that quantum reality, at the
microscopic physical level, is not itself limited by our limitations in
trying to understand it.

We have already noted how the all-inclusive unity of the pantheist
may surpass our conceptual grasp, despite its lack of ontological separation from the physical world. It is clear, therefore, that there are two
forms of transcendence at issue here. One is conceptual transcendence,
where reality for various reasons may be said to outstrip our abilities
to comprehend it. That is the transcendence which equally affects
quantum mechanics and pantheism.] There are many other examples
where what is inaccessible to humans, must still be thought to be real.
Whether or not the observable universe constitutes the universe, the
possibility that it may comprise only part of it illustrates how the real
world cannot be bounded by the limits of our observation or indeed of
our theoretical understanding. Even physics has to take conceptual
transcendence seriously.

Anti-realist views characteristically resist the very possibility or
meaningfulness of anything transcending the understanding made possible by whatever concepts we have. [The project of understanding
something beyond our understanding appears self-contradictory, even
in the attenuated sense of understanding that there is something beyond
our understanding.] Yet this is an epistemological problem, concerning

our knowledge of reality. The ontological separation of God and the world is a quintessentially metaphysical one. William Alston has distinguished this from the conceptual transcendence we have been discussing. His claim is that the most basic feature of 'metaphysical transcendence' is distinctness. He defines this in relation to God as the fact that 'God is not identical with the natural world or any part thereof'.[16] He thinks, on the other hand, that conceptual transcendence is, in the case of God, mainly concerned with 'otherness'. He says: 'In the strongest form of the doctrine, otherness is so extreme as to render it impossible that any of our concepts can strictly apply to God.'

Much energy in the history of philosophical theology has been expended in deciding how we might be able to conceive of God, despite the 'otherness of the Creator from creatures'. Such otherness is more than just a matter of the independent existence of God, but is also a matter of the limitations placed on human understanding, implied by both this contrast and that between Infinite and finite. 'Otherness' is not a simple metaphysical category so much as an indication of our epistemological limitations. God is 'other' from our point of view. This is not something that inevitably follows from the independence of God from the world. God's distinct ontological status makes Him different from the natural, physical universe. He does not share in the change and decay we see around us. He is not contingent and therefore He is not dependent on anything else. The universe could be destroyed without God's reality being affected. All this is implied by a traditional Christian view of God. Yet even if we question the possibility of such absolute separation, we are still not meeting the distinct issue of conceptual transcendence. There may, though, still be a feeling that even if conceptual transcendence does not imply the metaphysical kind, the reverse may not be true. In other words, does the metaphysical distinctness of God lead to a total inability to understand anything about Him?

There is a sense in which this might seem inevitable. How could a God existing apart from the physical universe in which we are at home, and which itself appears to condition the way we think, be anything but wholly 'other' from us? There is a continual temptation to assume that we are imprisoned in our own conceptual world. From assuming that the world provides the circumstances in which we think, it is surprisingly easy to slip into assuming that the only reality we can know is itself constituted by human concepts. This is the Kantian position, which effectively fences off the 'space of reasons' from any brute reality. Yet the concentration on actual human reasoning can easily lock us in a world of our own making, since we have lost contact with any world beyond the space made possible by our own reasoning. More important is the fact that this is an implicitly anti-theistic position since it makes humans, and not God, the source of all reason and truth. If on the other hand we resist the Kantian emphasis on the centrality of human categories, we may realize that we can have access to a reality that has not been shaped by our own conceptual understanding.

This is all crucial for theism since God is the exemplar above all of an objective reality, which, if He exists, exists apart from human understanding. Theism needs realism, even if realism is not necessarily theistic. As a metaphysical thesis, anti-realism removes the possibility of God being ontologically separated from the world. It is opposed to ontological transcendence. Yet once we see for ourselves that our beliefs are mere constructions or projections, as opposed to our giving an analysis of the status of other people's beliefs, there is a problem. We are unlikely to feel impelled to enter into a relationship with the shadow of our own thoughts, let alone fall down in worship of it.

The issue is not just the status of the reality we confront or construct. It is also its nature. The idea of a target for our beliefs may give direction to scientific research but the idea seems somewhat anaemic when compared with the God of Judaeo-Christian belief. God is not merely some kind of intellectual terminus which we may never reach. God is not just an ideal like the settled final opinion of scientists that according to Peirce, the American pragmatist, would constitute the scientific millennium.[17] There are moments when some theologians come close to envisaging a convergence of religious thought, presumably on the lines of an ultimate convergence between scientists. Keith Ward, for example, insists that theology is never closed and says that[18] 'if truth is indeed one . . . and if there is a Supreme Reality which wills all to be consciously related to it, then one will hope for a convergence of beliefs between the great religious traditions'. Yet even here one can see an allusion to a crucial difference between religion and science. God is not an inert, passive goal of contemplation, so situated that human endeavours alone can produce knowledge of Him. Ward's reference to 'will' points up a difference. God Himself is regarded as active and personal, at least in traditional Christian theology. The view that ontological separation logically entails conceptual transcendence ignores this and concentrates on the insuperable obstacles to understanding apparently restricting all human effort.

One problem is that philosophical arguments about the relation of knowledge to reality can easily treat God like any other piece of reality, waiting inertly to be discovered by the powers of the human mind. As we have seen, many philosophers and theologians have protested at treating God as one object among many, one being among others. He must certainly be separate from other realities, since He is their Creator. Yet the fact that He possesses objectivity in this sense of ontological transcendence does not mean that He is just one more physical or abstract object. His reality is of a unique kind, because He is not dependent, causally or logically, on anything beyond Himself. The immediate accusation will come that these are mere words, themselves gaining their meaning from the circumstances of human life. It will still be alleged that ontological transcendence results in a conceptual distance that can never be traversed.

This is a problem for any religion which wishes to deal with ontological transcendence. How can God bridge the gap between the infinite and the finite, the Creator and His creatures? The minute that the question takes this form, we are in a different realm from the abstract question of the relation of human knowledge and objective reality. We are no longer dealing with an abstract target but, supposedly, with a God who acts and can reveal Himself. It is no coincidence that the ontological distance seen by the Enlightenment between God and the world was aggravated by a deist understanding of a God who did not intervene in the created world, did not reveal Himself in any special revelation and did not relate with us on a personal basis. In other words, ontological transcendence was coupled with an assumption of indifference on the part of the Godhead. Metaphysical separation was assumed to involve a lack of involvement in this world. The opposition of panentheism to a traditional view of a detached God is in some ways a reaction against this tendencey. A progressive depersonalization of God leads to a denial of God as being active in any way, with neither intentions or purposes.

4 An Active God

The notion of a God who acts raises its own difficulties. Why does He act here and not there, reveal Himself then and not now, intervene in this way and not that? It may seem easier to assume that concepts of providence, revelation, intervention, miracle and so on, are all human constructs expressing the beliefs and attitudes of varying groups of people. Yet, as Feuerbach's position demonstrates, such an attitude soon leads to atheism. A God who cannot act soon becomes indistinguishable from no God at all. A God who does act, however, is also the answer to the question as to how humans can gain at least partial knowledge of Him. Such has been the import of the Christian faith, not to mention the Judaic and Islamic traditions. God, it is thought, has actively revealed Himself in ways in which we can understand something about Him.

Ontological transcendence need not imply absolute otherness, since God, despite His distinct existence, can actively make Himself known in ways that can be grasped by us. Otherwise it does certainly become mysterious how we can refer to God. The concept of mystery, as we have seen, is often appealed to, particularly by those who are influenced by Kant's dichotomy of the phenomenal and noumenal worlds. Again and again, we have noted how our judgements about God become a fact about us, and the reality we are allegedly in contact with recedes behind a veil. Feuerbach himself makes this transition, and takes it to its logical conclusion. He first points out that 'in the scheme of his revelation God must have reference not to himself but to man's power of comprehension'.[19] This could be a profound insight, if the concept of a God with intentions and purposes is retained. Once, however, we shift our attention from the alleged reality of God to the manner of our understanding, it can be a short step to claiming that how we understand is a fact of human nature and nothing to do with what is apparently understood. In fact, Feuerbach, immediately after the passage just quoted, goes on to say that 'the contents of the divine revelation are of human origin, for they have proceeded not from God as God, but from God as determined by human reason, human wants'.

There will still be difficulties even if we retain a strong conception of a God acting and modifying His revelation so that it is intelligible to human beings. The idea that God shapes His revelation to fit our minds can invite the retort that it is itself the product of our minds. More fundamentally, we may wonder how we can start from the view of an active God as a means of justifying and validating revelation. Where does such an assumption come from? Our knowledge of God is being invoked in an effort to show how we can gain an understanding of what is ontologically transcendent. In other words ontological transcendence does not imply conceptual transcendence, if we assume the impossibility of the latter in the first place.

All apparent instances of revelation face this kind of difficulty. We cannot, without begging the question, appeal to revelation by God, whether of a special or general kind, in order to show how knowledge of God is possible. A favourite challenge by sceptics will be to accept whatever empirical facts are brought forward and then refuse to go beyond them. This is one reason why in the struggle between 'faith' and 'reason' many would feel that faith is the starting-point, since it would seem that revelation cannot be used to justify revelation. Something has to be taken on trust. Yet what is at issue is not just revelation but also the power of human reason. Why should it be assumed that human rationality cannot move outside the confines of everyday experience? That is clearly an empiricist dogma, and is the denial of the possibility of conceptual transcendence. As such, it puts much of contemporary physics at risk. Yet this is not the same problem as the possible existence of a distinct, non-physical reality. It is again an epistemological, rather than a metaphysical issue.

It is not just sceptics who refuse to allow any notion of transcendence. The influence of naturalism as a philosophical position has had the result that even some theologians have felt impelled to give an account of Christianity which rejects any notion of the supernatural, let alone the specific activity of a personal God within the world. The idea of a naturalist theology might appear a contradiction in terms, but there are attempts to make religion and naturalism compatible. For example, one writer, Charley Hardwick, refers to the problems arising in talking about eschatology in a Christian context. He points out that it 'transcends any possible experience or knowledge and conflicts with a scientific picture of the world'.[20] His solution is to accept the apparent strictures of science, and to accommodate religion as best he can within the assumptions, as he sees them, of science. He therefore turns to an existentialist understanding of religion which reinterprets all religious claims in terms of their meaning for us now. Indeed, he wishes to make an even more sweeping claim. He says:

> There is a general consensus among theologians today that no change in all of Christian history is more significant than the relatively recent one in which the traditional otherworldly bias in Christianity has been overcome by an orientation toward life as presently lived in the

world. . . . On the other hand, the traditional eschatological symbols of faith were mainly articulated from within the otherworldly bias. That is one reason why they have become so unbelievable today.[21]

Thus for largely sociological reasons about what people happen at the present time to find acceptable, given the influence of science, he considers it essential to revise all the traditional claims of Christianity. Hardwick is quite open about this. He comments that 'a naturalist theology amounts to a revision of what "God" means in human life'.[22] [It is apparent that he is not just changing the subject from the reality of God to the meaning God has for us. He is actually prescribing the kind of meaning that is now acceptable. He sees a naturalist theology as 'defined ontologically by physicalism'[23] and concludes from this that God cannot be a personal being, that there can be no ultimate purpose in the world, and no way in which this life can be a part of some wider whole.] By definition the whole supernatural underpinning of religion is swept aside, presumably in the name of an unquestioning trust in contemporary science. There can be no Creation, no Resurrection and no personal survival of death. [Theology must instead make itself 'comprehensible within the present importance of human life'.][24] This leaves unanswered the pressing issue of why human life has any importance. The removal of any metaphysical basis for religion does not just make the supernatural claims of religion suspect. It removes all reason for taking any religion seriously, except as a cultural phenomenon. It is certainly not possible to undermine the basis of religion and simultaneously to retain its characteristic ethical claims about humanity. In the end it seems difficult to distinguish theological naturalism from an honest scepticism.

Outside naturalism, there should be no bar to reasoning to the possible existence of something beyond our normal sense-experience, and indeed of something beyond the physical world. Reason does not have to collapse into blind faith merely because of the character of what we are discussing. If reason cannot create a space in which the possibility of divine revelation can be allowed, the ability of humans to recognize any revelation as divine even through 'faith' is put into question. Faith itself must involve a conception of what it is we have faith in. The sceptic will always demand that whatever strange happenings are encountered or strange experiences undergone, they must always be accepted as deviant. A natural explanation, rather than a supernatural one, will always be demanded. Reason must establish the rationality of being willing to go beyond this and allow for the possibility of a revelation of something that is ontologically transcendent.

Within the context of faith in God, our human capacity for reasoning may be seen as rooted in the way that we have been created. It stems from Him, it will be said. However that may be, we certainly have an independent ability to recognize truth and to reason accordingly.[25] The circumstances in which we learn concepts do not tie down their meaning. We can transcend them and reach out to new and even apparently inaccessible realities. Very often, in fact, it is not so much the issue of the limits of our understanding that is in question as the point of reasoning about a God who is totally removed from human concerns and experience. He seems, to adopt an engineering simile, to be like a wheel that is turning without turning any other wheels. An utterly transcendent God, with no contact with us, is not just beyond the horizon of our understanding. He does not seem in any way relevant to our concerns.

A metaphysical 'inertness' is a recipe for the dismissal of metaphysics. The ontological distinctiveness of God must not become transmuted into a view of total unrelatedness between the world and the divine. An inability of God to make any difference means that He will eventually drop out of any reckoning. If God is Creator, He certainly sustains and holds in being that which He has created. Yet if He is simply to be the ultimate ground of everything, it might be very hard to see what more is being claimed than mere acknowledgement of and wonder at the existence of everything. It may be claimed that the character of the physical universe, its order and regularity, can be explained in terms of creation by God. The mere fact of its contingent existence may itself be referred back to the originating power of God. All these claims can begin to flesh out the claim that God is Creator. It could be suggested that any further meddling and tinkering would of itself go against His purposes.

The point in all this is that the character of the physical universe is being traced back to the creative power of God. It is not merely being claimed that He is sustainer of all that happens to exist. That could slide into a form of pantheism. Something more is being asserted, namely that the universe is as it is because of what God has done. A sense is being given to the notion of His ontological separateness in that the explanation depends on that. Yet this may still only produce the God of deism, the originator of the universe who is not subsequently involved in it. Such a God is by definition so distinct that ontological transcendence leads to conceptual transcendence.

It is a recurring temptation to invoke the concept of mystery. It may seem as if the distinction between ontology and epistemology is being retained here, in that it is recognized that there could be a mysterious something beyond our knowledge. For many proponents of negative theology, God becomes the reified Unknown. Yet in fact limitations on our understanding are very often being projected on to the nature of reality. It is too easily assumed that because we apparently do not know the nature of ultimate reality, then it is in its nature mysterious and indeterminate. Once, however, it is conceded that such a reality might have a very definite character, and that our agnosticism need not reflect the intrinsic nature of reality, we must face the possibility that such a reality could be active and not passive. It could approach us on a personal level rather than be totally inert. Such, anyway, is what much religion claims. Revelation of a particular as well as of a general kind, would then become not just possible but even likely. The question returns as to how we can know of an active, even a personal God, except through revelation. The answer must be that we cannot know very much. The existence of human rationality, however, is crucial here. All faith needs a rational basis. Without an ability to reason, we could never even prepare ourselves for the possibility of a God who is revealed. Atheism, itself, as a rational position, allows for the possibility of a God. Otherwise it could not deny what it denies. It is that rational possibility which religion claims is confirmed in revelation.

Notes

1 *Dialogues concerning Natural Religion*, p. 60.
2 *God's World, God's Body*, p. 102.
3 *Ibid.*, p. 103.
4 *Ibid.*, p. 127.
5 *Ibid.*, p. 149.
6 *Ibid.*, p. 143.
7 Levine, *Pantheism*.
8 Pailin, *Probing the Foundations*, p. 80.
9 *Ibid.*
10 *Systematic Theology*, p. 259.

11   *The Essence of Christianity*, p. 13.

12   *Ibid.*, p. 29.

13   *Ibid.*, p. 16.

14   Paden, 'Elements of a new comparativism', p. 6.

15   See my *Reality at Risk*, chapter 6, for a discussion of quantum mechanics.

16   Alston, 'Realism and the Christian faith', p. 51.

17   See my *Reality at Risk*, pp. 13ff.

18   *Religion and Revelation*, p. 340.

19   *The Essence of Christianity*, p. 207.

20   Hardwick, *Events of Grace: Naturalism, Existentialism and Theology*, p. 268.

21   *Ibid.*, p. 266.

22   *Ibid.*, p. 182.

23   *Ibid.*, p. 51.

24   *Ibid.*, p. 193.

25   See *Rationality and Science*, pp. 219ff.

Bibliography

Adriaanse, H. J., 1993, 'After theism', *Traditional Theism and its Modern Alternatives* (ed. S. Andersen). Aarhus: Aarhus University Press.

Alexander, L., 1993, 'Liberalism, religion and the unity of epistemology', *San Diego Law Review*, 30.

Allen, D., 1989, *Christian Belief in a Post-Modern World*. Kentucky: Westminster/John Knox Press.

Alston, W., 1991, *Perceiving God*. Ithaca, NY: Cornell University Press.

Alston, W., 1995, 'Realism and the Christian faith', *International Journal for Philosophy of Religion*, 38.

Alston, W., 1996, *A Realist Conception of Truth*. Ithaca, NY: Cornell University Press.

Audi, R., 1989, 'The separation of Church and State, and the obligations of citizenship', *Philosophy and Public Affairs*, 18.

Audi, R. and Wolterstorff, N., 1997, *Religion in the Public Square*. Lanham, MD: Rowman and Littlefield.

Ayer, A. J., 1946, *Language, Truth and Logic*. 2nd edn, London: Gollancz.

Barbour, I., 1990, *Religion in an Age of Science*. London: SCM Press.

Barth, K., 1962, *Church Dogmatics*. 4 vols. Edinburgh: T. and T. Clark.

Berger, P. and Luckmann, T., 1967, *The Social Construction of Reality*. London: Allen Lane.

Bloor, D., 1976, *Knowledge and Social Imagery*. London: Routledge.

Brink, van den G., Brom, van den L. and Sarot, M., 1992, *Christian Faith and Philosophical Theology*. Kampen: Kok Pharos.

Brooke, J. H., 1991, *Science and Religion: Some Historical Perspectives*. Cambridge: Cambridge University Press.

Buckley, M., 1987, *At the Origins of Modern Atheism*. New Haven, CT: Yale University Press.

Bultmann, R., 1958, *Jesus and the Word*, London: SCM Press.

Bultmann, R., 1960, *Jesus Christ and Mythology*. London: SCM Press.

Burnet, J., 1930, *Early Greek Philosophy*. London: A. and C. Black.

Clarke, P. B. and Byrne, P., 1993, *Religion Defined and Explained*. London: Macmillan.

Churchland, P., 1995, *The Engine of Reason, The Seat of the Soul*. Cambridge, MA: MIT Press.

Coulson, C. A., 1995, *Science and Christian Belief*. London: Oxford University Press.

Cupitt, D., 1990, *Creation out of Nothing*. London: SCM Press.

Cupitt, D., 1991, *What is a Story?* London: SCM Press.

D'Agostino, F., 1993, 'Transcendence and conversation: two conceptions of objectivity', *American Philosophical Quarterly*, 30.

D'Agostino, F., 1996, *Free Public Reason*. New York: Oxford University Press.

Dalferth, I., 1988, *Theology and Philosophy*, Oxford: Basil Blackwell.

Davis, S. T., 1997, ' "Seeing" the Risen Jesus', in *The Resurrection* (ed. S. Davis, D. Kendall and G. Collins). Oxford: Oxford University Press.

Dawkins, R., 1995, *River Out of Eden*. London: Weidenfeld and Nicolson.

D'Costa, G., 1996, 'The impossibility of a pluralist view of religions', *Religious Studies*, 32.

Drees, W., 1995, *Religion, Science and Naturalism*. Cambridge: Cambridge University Press.

Feuerbach, L., 1989, *The Essence of Christianity*, Buffalo, NY: Prometheus Books.

Guthrie, W. K. C., 1962, *History of Greek Philosophy*, vol. 1. Cambridge: Cambridge University Press.

Hampson, D., 1996, *After Christianity*. London: SCM Press.

Hampson, D., 1997, 'On being a non-Christian Realist', in *God and Reality* (ed. C. Crowder). London: Mowbray.

Hardwick, C., 1996, *Events of Grace: Naturalism, Existentialism and Theology*. Cambridge: Cambridge University Press.

Hawking, S., 1988, *A Brief History of Time*. London: Bantam Press.

Helms, R., 1988, *Gospel Fictions*. Buffalo, NY: Prometheus Books.

Herrmann, E., 1994, *Scientific Theory and Religious Belief*. Kampen: Kok Pharos.

Hick, J., 1989, *An Interpretation of Religion*. London: Macmillan.

Hick, J., 1993, *Disputed Questions*. London: Macmillan.

Hick, J., 1997, ' "Religious pluralism": a reply to Gavin D'Costa', *Religious Studies*, 33.

Hume, D., 1993, *Dialogues Concerning Natural Religion* (ed. J. C. A. Gaskin). Oxford: Oxford University Press.

Irigray, L., 1993, *Sexes and Genealogies* (trans. G. C. Gill). New York: Columbia University Press.

James, W., 1890, *Principles of Psychology*. London: Macmillan.

Jantzen, G., 1984, *God's World, God's Body*. London: Darton, Longman and Todd.

Jantzen, G., 1995, *Power, Gender and Christian Mysticism*. Cambridge: Cambridge University Press.

Kaufman, G., 1993, *In Face of Mystery*. Cambridge MA: Harvard University Press.

Kant, I., 1996, *Religion within the Limits of Reason Alone*. New York: Harper and Brothers.

Kierkegaard, S., 1947, *A Kierkegaard Anthology*. London: Oxford University Press.

Kung, H., 1987, *Christianity and the World Religions*. London: Collins.

Levine, M. P., 1994, *Pantheism*. London: Routledge.

Levison, S., 1992, 'Religious language and the public square', *Harvard Law Review*, 105.

Moore, G., 1988, *Believing in God*. Edinburgh: T. and T. Clack.

Murdoch, I., 1992, *Metaphysics as a Guide To Morals*. London: Chatto and Windus.

Nagel, T., 1987, 'Moral conflict and political legitimacy', *Philosophy and Public Affairs*, 16.

Nagel, T., 1991, *Equality and Partiality*. New York: Oxford University Press.

Nakamoto, T., 1990, *Emerging from Meditation* (trans. M. Pye). London: Duckworth.

Ogden, S., 1982, *The Point of Christology*. London: SCM Press.

Paden, W., 1996, 'Elements of a new comparativism', *Methods and Study in the Theory of Religion*, 8.

Pailin, D., 1994, *Probing the Foundations*. Kampen: Kok Pharos.

Peacocke, A., 1993, *Theology for a Scientific Age*. 2nd edn, London: SCM Press.

Phillips, D. Z., 1992, 'Between faith and metaphysics', *Christian Faith and Philosophical Theology* (ed. G. van den Brink *et al.*).

Phillips, D. Z., 1993, *Wittgenstein and Religion*. London: Macmillan.

Phillips, D. Z., 'Introduction', 'Philosophy, theology and the reality of God', 'On really believing', 'Religious beliefs and language-games', 'Authorship and authenticity' and 'Religion in Wittgenstein's mirror', *Wittgenstein and Religion*. London: Macmillan.

Phillips, D. Z., 1995, 'Dislocating the soul', *Religious Studies*, 31.

Phillips, D. Z. 1995, 'At the mercy of method', *Philosophy and the Grammar of Belief* (ed. T. Tessin and M. van den Ruhr).

Placher, W., 1996, *The Domestication of Transcendence*. Kentucky: John Knox Press.

Plantinga, A., 1993, *Warrant and Proper Function*. New York: Oxford University Press.

Plantinga, A. and Wolterstorff, N. (eds), 1983, *Faith and Rationality*. Indiana: Indian University Press.

Polkinghorne, J., 1994, *Quarks, Chaos and Christianity*. London: SPCK.

Polkinghorne, J., 1996a, *Beyond Science*. Cambridge: Cambridge University Press.

Polkinghorne, J., 1996b, *Scientists as Theologians*. London: SPCK.

Putnam, H., 1992, *Renewing Philosophy*. Cambridge MA: Harvard University Press.

Putnam, H., 1996, 'On Wittgenstein's philosophy of mathematics', *Proceedings of the Aristotelian Society, Supplementary Vol.* 70.

Rawls, J., 1993, *Political Liberalism*. New York: Columbia University Press.

Rorty, R., 1989, *Contingency, Irony and Solidarity*. Cambridge: Cambridge University Press.

Rorty, R., 1993, 'Feminism, ideology and deconstruction: a pragmatist view', *Hypatia*, 8.

Rouse, J., 1996, *Engaging Science: How to Understand its Practices Philosophically*. Ithaca, New York: Cornell University Press.

Saler, B., 1993, *Conceptualizing Religion*. Leiden: Brill.

Sherwin-White, A. N., 1963, *Roman Society and Law in the New Testament*. Oxford: Oxford University Press.

Smith, J. Z., 1990, *Drudgery Divine*. London: School of Oriental and African Studies.

Stanton, G., 1995, *Gospel Truth?* London: Harper Collins.

Stroll, A., 1994, *Moore and Wittgenstein on Certainty*. New York: Oxford University Press.

Taliaferro, C., 1994, *Consciousness and the Mind of God*. Cambridge: Cambridge University Press.

Tessin, T. and von der Ruhr, M. (eds), 1995, *Philosophy and the Grammar of Religious Belief*. London: Macmillan.

Tillich, P., 1968, *Systematic Theology*, combined volume. Welwyn: Nisbet.

Trigg, R., 1970, *Pain and Emotion*. Oxford: Oxford University Press.

Trigg, R., 1973, *Reason and Commitment*. Cambridge: Cambridge University Press.

Trigg, R., 1985, *Understanding Social Science*. Oxford: Basil Blackwell.

Trigg, R., 1989, *Reality at Risk: A Defence of* Realism in Philosophy and the Sciences, 2nd edn. London: Harvester Wheatsheaf (Simon and Schuster).

Trigg, R., 1992, 'Reason and faith', in *Religion and Philosophy* (ed. M. Warner). Cambridge: Cambridge University Press.

Trigg, R., 1993, *Rationality and Science: Can Science Explain Everything?* Oxford: Basil Blackwell.

Trigg, R., 1997a, 'Theological realism and antirealism', *A Companion to Philosophy of Religion* (ed. Philip L. Quinn and Charles Taliaferro). Oxford: Basil Blackwell.

Trigg, R., 1997b, 'The grounding of reason', *Proceedings of the Aristotelian Society, Supplementary Vol.* 71.

Vroom, H., 1996, *No Other Gods*. Grand Rapids, MI: W. Eerdmans.

Ward, K., 1991, *A Vision to Pursue*. London: SCM Press.

Ward, K., 1994, *Religion and Revelation*. Oxford: Oxford University Press.

Wiebe, D., 1993, *The Irony of Theology and the Nature of Religious Thought*. Montreal: McGill University Press.

Wiebe, D., 1994, *Beyond Legitimation*. London: Macmillan.

Wilson, E. O., 1978, *On Human Nature*. Cambridge, MA: Harvard University Press.

Wittgenstein, L., 1953, *Philosophical Investigations*. Oxford: Basil Backwell.

Wittgenstein, L., 1966, *Lectures and Conversations on Aesthetics, Psychology and Religious Belief* (ed. Cyril Barrett). Oxford: Basil Blackwell.

Wittgenstein, L., 1969, *On Certainty*. Oxford: Basil Blackwell.

Wittgenstein, L., 1980, *Culture and Value*. Oxford: Basil Blackwell.

Wolterstorff, N., 1995, *Divine Discourse*. Cambridge: Cambridge University Press.

Index